Gangs: Violence, Crime and Antigang Initiatives

GANGS: VIOLENCE, CRIME AND ANTIGANG INITIATIVES

JAY T. SOORDHAS
EDITOR

Nova Science Publishers, Inc.
New York

For permission to use material from this book please contact us:
Telephone 631-231-7269; Fax 631-231-8175
Web Site: http://www.novapublishers.com

LIBRARY OF CONGRESS CATALOGING-IN-PUBLICATION DATA

Available upon request.

ISBN: 978-1-60692-286-6

Published by Nova Science Publishers, Inc. ✢ New York

CONTENTS

Preface		**vii**
Chapter 1	**Best Practices to Address Community Gang Problems** *Michael B. Mukasey, Jeffrey L. Sedgwick and J. Robert Flores*	**1**
Chapter 2	**Violence by Teenage Girls: Trends and Context** *Margaret A. Zahn, Susan Brumbaugh, Darrell Steffensmeier, Barry C. Feld, Merry Morash, Meda Chesney-Lind, Jody Miller, Allison Ann Payne, Denise C. Gottfredson, and Candace Kruttschnitt*	**67**
Chapter 3	**Youth Gangs: Background, Legislation, and Issues** *Celinda Franco*	**99**
Index		**145**

PREFACE

Gang activity and related violence threaten public order in a diverse range of communities in the United States today. Contemporary views of the problem have been formed against the background of a significant adverse secular trend in gang activity during the last four decades. In particular, the rapid growth of gang membership, geographical dispersion, and criminal involvement during the violent crime epidemic — associated with the emergence of the crack cocaine market during the mid-1980s to the early 1990s — have intensified current concerns. The experience of those years continues to mark both patterns of gang activity and public policy responses toward them. This book provides background information on the issue of youth gangs, including data on gangs and gang crime. It reviews existing anti-gang initiatives at the federal, state, and local levels, and describes some of the legislation proposed to address the gang problem, as well as some of the issues raised by those bills.

Chaper 1- Since 2002, the Office of Juvenile Justice and Delinquency Prevention (OJJDP) has attempted to strengthen the reach and breadth of its work on gangs. With the initiation in 2003 of OJJDP's Gang Reduction Program (GRP), millions of dollars have been invested in working in communities with large and growing youth gangs. Experience has shown us that gangs are, in part, a response to community dysfunction. Thus, a primary focus of OJJDP's anti-gang initiatives is to support community efforts to provide their citizens, especially their young people, with a safe and prosocial environment in which to live and grow. Gangs often lure youth with the promise of safety, belonging, economic opportunity, and a sense of identity. OJJDP is dedicated to helping communities replace this false promise with real opportunities for our Nation's youth.

Chapter 2- According to data from the Federal Bureau of Investigation, from 1991 to 2000, arrests of girls increased more (or decreased less) than arrests of boys for most types of offenses. By 2004, girls accounted for 30 percent of all juvenile arrests. However, questions remain about whether these trends reflect an actual increase in girls' delinquency or changes in societal responses to girls' behavior. To find answers to these questions, the Office of Juvenile Justice and Delinquency Prevention (OJJDP) convened the Girls Study Group to establish a theoretical and empirical foundation to guide the development, testing, and dissemination of strategies to reduce or prevent girls' involvement in delinquency and violence.

Chapter 3- Gang activity and related violence threaten public order in a diverse range of communities in the United States today. Congress has long recognized that this problem affects a number of issues of federal concern, and federal legislation has been introduced in the 110th Congress to address some aspects of the issue.

Youth gangs have been an endemic feature of American urban life. They are well attested as early as the 1 8th century and have been a recurrent subject of concern since then. Contemporary views of the problem have been formed against the background of a significant adverse secular trend in gang activity during the last four decades. In particular, the rapid growth of gang membership, geographical dispersion, and criminal involvement during the violent crime epidemic — associated with the emergence of the crack cocaine market during the mid-1980s to the early 1990s — have intensified current concerns. The experience of those years continues to mark both patterns of gang activity and public policy responses toward them. Reports about the increased activity and recent migration of a violent California- based gang, the Mara Salvatrucha (MS-13), have heightened concerns about gangs in certain areas of the country.

Policy development and implementation in this area are bedeviled by discrepant uses of the term "gang" and the absence of uniform standards of statistical reporting. There are reasons for special care in the use of data on gangs and their activity. Without a standardized definition of what is meant by "gang," such as the age group or activities engaged in by its members, or standardized reporting among the state, local, tribal, and federal levels of government, it is difficult to target anti-gang initiatives and evaluate their effectiveness. According to a national gang survey, the most recent estimate indicates that there were about 760,000 gang members in 24,000 gangs in the United States in 2004.

In the 1 10th Congress, several bills have been introduced that would address various aspects of the gang problem. Some of the bills would address the problem through comprehensive gang prevention initiatives, such as H.R. 3846. Other bills address the gang problem through combinations of criminal penalty enhancements, targeted prosecutorial efforts and anti-gang task forces, and gang prevention provisions. These anti-gang proposals include H.R. 880, H.R. 1582, H.R. 3547, H.R. 3922, S. 456, S. 990, and S. 2237.

This chapter provides background information on the issue of youth gangs, including data on gangs and gang crime. It reviews existing anti-gang initiatives at the federal, state, and local levels, and describes some of the legislation proposed during the 110th Congress to address the gang problem, as well as some of the issues raised by those bills.

In: Gangs: Violence, Crime and Antigang Initiatives
Editor: Jay T. Soordhas ISBN 978-1-60692-286-6

Chapter 1

BEST PRACTICES TO ADDRESS COMMUNITY GANG PROBLEMS*

Michael B. Mukasey, Jeffrey L. Sedgwick and J. Robert Flores

FOREWORD

Since 2002, the Office of Juvenile Justice and Delinquency Prevention (OJJDP) has attempted to strengthen the reach and breadth of its work on gangs. With the initiation in 2003 of OJJDP's Gang Reduction Program (GRP), millions of dollars have been invested in working in communities with large and growing youth gangs. Experience has shown us that gangs are, in part, a response to community dysfunction. Thus, a primary focus of OJJDP's anti-gang initiatives is to support community efforts to provide their citizens, especially their young people, with a safe and prosocial environment in which to live and grow. Gangs often lure youth with the promise of safety, belonging, economic opportunity, and a sense of identity. OJJDP is dedicated to helping communities replace this false promise with real opportunities for our Nation's youth.

GRP brings three new ingredients to the classic Comprehensive Gang Model. First, in accord with the President's faith-based and community initiative, GRP prioritizes the recruitment of faith community members and representatives from small community organizations. Clearly, we must always recognize the value large organizations bring to any endeavor; however, it is the local churches and charitable organizations that will continue to live on in these communities long after the Federal Government or large organizations end their work. Indeed, many of the most successful large organizations now partner with small community and faith-based providers for that reason. These small local organizations are often very efficient, raise their own funds, have existing personal relationships with those in need, and understand the culture and language of the local community to a degree that may be difficult for outsiders to emulate. All of that translates into lower cost, faster impact, and longer lasting presence.

---

* This is an edited, excerpted and augmented edition of a National Youth Gang Center Under Cooperative Agreement Number 2007—JV—FX—0008 from The Office Of Juvenile Justice And Delinquency Prevention (OJJDP).

Second, GRP emphasizes multiagency collaboration, not only locally in neighborhoods and communities, but across Federal agencies as well. Work on GRP was substantially easier because funding was extremely flexible. Funds used in this program came from flexible funding streams at OJJDP, as well as the U.S. Departments of Housing and Urban Development, Labor, and Health and Human Services. Grantees were able to fit dollars to need, instead of need to money available.

While agencies continue to work to collaborate and use funds in concert, it is my wish that Congress will see the value in improving grantee ability to blend funds and maximize their use.

Third, GRP stresses the importance of partnering with the private sector. At the outset of this effort, we recognized that success would benefit not only those children who did not become members of gangs, but the community at large, including businesses. When crime and violence are reduced, the business community—especially small businesses that suffer most from theft and vandalism—experience significant benefit. Examples abound, but in Richmond, VA, one can point to large-scale improvements and investments in the physical condition of public housing. Because increased safety meant more stable tenants and better tenant care of property, the private sector operator of those units saw a business reason to contribute to the Richmond GRP effort. Additionally, using OJJDP's planning and resource tool allows communities to see their town or neighborhood as resource rich instead of poor. In many conversations with residents over these past years,

I have heard them express their amazement that their community had strengths, had resources, and had people in their own midst who could help.

When we started GRP with demonstration programs in Richmond, VA; Los Angeles, CA; North Miami Beach, FL; and Milwaukee, WI, more than 5 years ago, the evidence was strong that we would succeed at least at the start. I could not have envisioned the success that these four communities have attained, and where progress was not as sure, we learned important lessons. To the people who gave life to this effort and the communities that now serve as examples to others that it can be done, I wish them continued success and hope that others will follow their lead.

J. Robert Flores
Administrator
Office of Juvenile Justice and Delinquency Prevention.

Purpose And Organization of the Chapter

This Chapter provides guidance for communities that are considering how best to address a youth gang problem that already exists or threatens to become a reality. The guidance is based on the implementation of the Comprehensive Gang Model (Model) developed through the Office of Juvenile Justice and Delinquency Prevention (OJJDP), U.S. Department of Justice (DOJ), and most recently tested in OJJDP's Gang Reduction Program.

The Chapter describes the research that produced the Model, notes essential findings from evaluations of several programs demonstrating the Model in a variety of environments, and outlines "best practices" obtained from practitioners with years of experience in planning, implementing, and overseeing variations of the Model in their communities.

The Model and best practices contain critical elements that distinguish it from typical program approaches to gangs. The Model's key distinguishing feature is a strategic planning process that empowers communities to assess their own gang problems and fashion a complement of anti- gang strategies and program activities. Community leaders considering this Model will be able to call on a strategic planning tool developed by OJJDP and available at no cost. OJJDP's Socioeconomic Mapping and Resource Topography (SMART) system is available online through the OJJDP Web site (go to http://www.ojp.usdoj.gov/ojjdp, and select "Tools").

The main section of the chapter presents best practices for the Comprehensive Gang Model and highlights results of a National Youth Gang Center survey and a meeting of practitioners regarding their experiences in implementing the Model. This section contains specific practices that work best in a step-by-step planning and implementation process for communities using the Comprehensive Gang Model framework and tools.

SECTION 1. DEVELOPMENT OF OJJDP'S COMPREHENSIVE GANG MODEL

Research Foundation of the Comprehensive Gang Model

The Comprehensive Gang Model is the product of a national gang research and development program that OJJDP initiated in the mid-1980s. A national assessment of gang problems and programs provided the research foundation for the Model, and its key components mirror the best features of existing and evaluated programs across the country.

National Assessment of Gang Problems and Programs

In 1987, OJJDP launched a Juvenile Gang Suppression and Intervention Research and Development Program that Dr. Irving Spergel of the University of Chicago directed. In the initial phase, the researchers conducted the first comprehensive national assessment of organized agency and community group responses to gang problems in the United States (Spergel, 1990, 1991; Spergel and Curry, 1993). It remains the only national assessment of efforts to combat gangs. In the second phase, Spergel and his colleagues developed a composite youth gang program based on findings from the national assessment.

In the research phase of the project (phase one), Spergel's research team attempted to identify every promising community gang program in the United States based on a national survey. At the outset, this study focused on 101 cities in which the presence of gangs was suspected. The team found promising gang programs in a broad range of communities across the Nation. Once programs and sites were identified, the team collected information on the magnitude and nature of local gang problems from representatives of each agency or organization that other participants identified as being affiliated with or being a partner in each local program. Spergel and his team of researchers interviewed program developers and reviewed all available program documentation.

The more demanding project goal was to identify the contents of each program and self-reported measures of success. The team made an effort to identify the "most promising" programs. In each of the most promising community programs, the research team identified the agencies that were essential to the success of the program. Finally, Spergel and his team made site visits to selected community programs and agencies.

Spergel and Curry (1993, pp. 371–72) used agency representatives' responses to five survey questions1 to determine the strategies that communities across the country employed in dealing with gang problems. From respondents' answers to these questions, the research team identified five strategies—community mobilization, social intervention, provision of opportunities, organizational change and development, and suppression (see "Five Strategies in OJJDP's Comprehensive Gang Model" on page 2).

Development of the Comprehensive Community-Wide Gang Program Model

Spergel and his colleagues (Spergel, 1995; Spergel et al., 1992; Spergel and Curry, 1993) developed the Comprehensive Community-Wide Gang Program Model as the final product of the gang research and development program that OJJDP funded. From the information gathered through its multimethod study in phase one (Spergel, Curry, et al., 1994), the Spergel team developed technical assistance manuals for each of the 12 types of agencies that should be part of a successful local community response to gangs, including organizations that range from grassroots child-serving agencies to law enforcement, courts, and prosecutors' offices (Spergel, Chance, et al., 1994).

Spergel and his colleagues also offered the general community design of an ideal Comprehensive Community- Wide Gang Program Model. An ideal program should undertake several action steps (Spergel, Chance, et al., 1994, pp. 2–5):

- *Addressing the problem.* A community must recognize the presence of a gang problem before it can do anything meaningful to address the problem.
- *Organization and policy development.* Communities must organize effectively to combat the youth gang problem.
- *Management of the collaborative process.* In a typical community, the mobilization process evolves through several stages before fruition.
- D*evelopment of goals and objectives.* These must include short-term suppression and outreach services for targeted youth, and longer term services, such as remedial education, training, and job placement.
- *Relevant programming.* The community must systematically articulate and implement rationales for services, tactics, or procedures.
- *Coordination and community participation.* A mobilized community is the most promising way to deal with the gang problem.
- *Youth accountability.* While youth gang members must be held accountable for their criminal acts, they must at the same time be provided an opportunity to change or control their behavior.

- *Staffing.* Youth gang intervention and control efforts require a thorough understanding of the complexity of gang activity in the context of local community life.
- *Staff training.* Training should include prevention, intervention, and suppression in gang problem localities.

FIVE STRATEGIES IN OJJDP'S COMPREHENSIVE GANG MODEL

Community Mobilization: Involvement of local citizens, including former gang-involved youth, community groups, agencies, and coordination of programs and staff functions within and across agencies.

Opportunities Provision: Development of a variety of specific education, training, and employment programs targeting gang-involved youth.

Social Intervention: Involving youth-serving agencies, schools, grassroots groups, faith-based organizations, police, and other juvenile/criminal justice organizations in "reaching out" to gang-involved youth and their families, and linking them with the conventional world and needed services.

Suppression: Formal and informal social control procedures, including close supervision and monitoring of gang- involved youth by agencies of the juvenile/criminal justice system and also by community-based agencies, schools, and grassroots groups.

Organizational Change and Development: Development and implementation of policies and procedures that result in the most effective use of available and potential resources, within and across agencies, to better address the gang problem.

- *Research and evaluation. Determining what is most effective, and why, is a daunting challenge.*
- *Establishment of funding priorities. Based on available research, theory, and experience, community mobilization strategies and programs should be accorded the highest funding priority.*

In 1993, Spergel began to implement this model in a neighborhood in Chicago. Soon thereafter, OJJDP renamed the model the Comprehensive Gang Prevention and Intervention Model (Spergel, Chance, et al., 1994, p. iii).

OJJDP'S COMPREHENSIVE GANG MODEL

The 1992 amendments to the Juvenile Justice and Delinquency Prevention Act authorized OJJDP to carry out additional activities to address youth gang problems. An OJJDP Gang Task Force outlined plans for integrated officewide efforts to provide national leadership in the areas of gang-related program development, research, statistics, evaluation, training, technical assistance, and information dissemination (Howell, 1994; Tatem-Kelley, 1994).

This background work led to the establishment of OJJDP's Comprehensive Response to America's Youth Gang Problem. The Comprehensive Response was a five-component initiative that included establishment of the National Youth Gang Center, demonstration and testing of OJJDP's Comprehensive Gang Model, training and technical assistance to communities implementing this Model, evaluation of the demonstration sites implementing the Model, and information dissemination through the Juvenile Justice Clearinghouse. Implementation and testing of the Comprehensive Gang Model were the centerpiece of the initiative. OJJDP prepared two publications specifically to support demonstration and testing of the Model: Gang Suppression and Intervention: Problem and Response (Spergel, Curry, et al., 1994), and Gang Suppression and Intervention: Community Models (Spergel, Chance, et al., 1994).

Communities that use the Comprehensive Gang Model will benefit from the simplified implementation process that OJJDP has created. OJJDP synthesized the elements of the Comprehensive Gang Model into five steps:

1) The community and its leaders acknowledge the youth gang problem.
2) The community conducts an assessment of the nature and scope of the youth gang problem, leading to the identification of a target community or communities and population(s).
3) Through a steering committee, the community and its leaders set goals and objectives to address the identified problem(s).
4) The steering committee makes available relevant programs, strategies, services, tactics, and procedures consistent with the Model's five core strategies.
5) The steering committee evaluates the effectiveness of the response to the gang problem, reassesses the problem, and modifies approaches, as needed.

These steps have been tested in several settings. Information on those initiatives is provided in appendix A.

THE COMPREHENSIVE GANG MODEL IN ACTION—OJJDP'S GANG REDUCTION PROGRAM

Over the years, OJJDP has tested and refined the Comprehensive Gang Model to meet new challenges and address gang problems in new locations. Most recently, OJJDP developed and funded the Gang Reduction Program.

Gangs are often the result of system failures or community dysfunction. So, to address youth gang violence, the OJJDP Administrator decided to test whether the Model could be used to initiate community change in certain cities. In 2003, OJJDP identified four demonstration sites: Los Angeles, CA; Richmond, VA; Milwaukee, WI; and. North Miami Beach, FL. Each test site faced a different gang problem.

Once sites had been identified, OJJDP held meetings with senior political and law enforcement officials and made an offer: OJJDP would provide resources to support a test of the Comprehensive Gang Model if the city agreed to change how they currently addressed youth gang problems. Each city would now focus on balancing gang prevention with enforcement and commit to using community organizations and faith-based groups to ultimately sustain the work. Additionally, each site would have a full-time coordinator, funded by OJJDP, with direct access to senior political and police leadership. This coordinator would be free from substantive program responsibilities and would ensure that each participating agency or organization met its obligations. He or she would also ensure and that the data and information generated by the effort would be collected and shared. Each participating agency remained independent, but was under the oversight of the gang coordinator, who had the ability to obtain support or intervention from OJJDP leadership and local authorities (e.g., mayor, police chief, or governor).

In addition to reducing gang violence, the goal of GRP was to determine the necessary practices to create a community environment that helps reduce youth gang crime and violence in targeted neighborhoods. Because of this, GRP focused on two goals: to learn the key ingredients for success and to reduce youth gang delinquency, crime, and violence. GRP accomplishes these goals by helping communities take an integrated approach when targeting gangs:

- Primary prevention targets the entire population in high-crime and high-risk communities. The key component is a One-Stop Resource Center that makes services accessible and visible to members of the community. Services include prenatal and infant care, afterschool activities, truancy and dropout prevention, and job programs.
- Secondary prevention identifies young children (ages 7–14) at high risk and—drawing on the resources of
- schools, community-based organizations, and faith- based groups—intervenes with appropriate services before early problem behaviors turn into serious delinquency and gang involvement.
- Intervention targets active gang members and close associates, and involves aggressive outreach and recruitment activity. Support services for gang-involved youth and their families help youth make positive choices.
- Suppression focuses on identifying the most dangerous and influential gang members and removing them from the community.
- Reentry targets serious offenders who are returning to the community after confinement and provides appropriate services and monitoring. Of particular interest are displaced gang members who may cause conflict by attempting to reassert their former gang roles.
- The program has several key concepts:
- Identify needs at the individual, family, and community levels, and address those needs in a coordinated and comprehensive response.
- Conduct an inventory of human and financial resources in the community, and create plans to fill gaps and leverage existing resources to support effective gang- reduction strategies.
- Apply the best research-based programs across appropriate age ranges, risk categories, and agency boundaries.
- Encourage coordination and integration in two directions: vertically (local, State, and Federal agencies) and horizontally (across communities and program types).

Highlights of activities from each of the Gang Reduction Program sites—Richmond, VA; Los Angeles, CA; North Miami Beach, FL; and Milwaukee, WI—are presented in the next section.

Section 2: Best Practices for Planning and Implementing the Comprehensive Gang Model

The best practices presented in this chapter are based on years of demonstration and evaluation in many sites across the country. Appendix A provides an overview of these demonstration initiatives, beginning with the initial implementation of the Model in the Little Village neighborhood in Chicago in the early 1990s, through OJJDPsponsored demonstrations of the Model in five sites in the mid-1990s, to OJJDP's current efforts to implement its Gang Reduction Program (GRP).

To determine which practices would be most beneficial to communities intent on implementing the OJJDP Compre hensive Gang Model, the National Youth Gang Center (NYGC) collected data from these sources:

- Comprehensive Gang Model Survey. A Comprehensive Gang Model Survey (see appendix B) was conducted in July 2007. It collected information pertaining to sev eral sites in the original demonstration program (Sper gel Model), the Rural Gang Initiative, the Gang-Free Schools and Communities Initiative, and the Gang Re duction Program, and from selected projects and pro grams in Oklahoma, Utah, Nevada, and North Carolina that used the OJJDP Model, but OJJDP did not fund. The survey included questions about the assessment and implementation processes, program coordination, the lead agency, administrative structure, prevention, intervention and the intervention team, suppression, reentry, organizational change and development, and sustainability.
- Practitioner Meeting. The preliminary survey results were used to develop an agenda for a meeting that OJJDP sponsored in November 2007. Representatives from OJJDP, NYGC, the initial demonstration sites, Gang-Free Schools and Communities programs, Gang Reduction Program projects, and programs in Okla homa, Utah, Nevada, and North Carolina met to dis cuss and record best practices based on their experience with comprehensive anti-gang program ming. The meeting also produced a timeline for use by communities that are considering implementing such efforts.
- Evaluation Reports and Staff Observations. "Best prac tices" of demonstration programs (described in appen dix A) and observations of OJJDP and NYGC staff who have worked with these programs for 15 years were noted in the evaluations.

The best practices identified from these sources are orga nized into seven categories—convening a steering com mittee, administering the program, assessing the gang problem, planning for implementation, implementing the program, selecting program activities, and sustaining the program—and are described below.

CONVENING A STEERING COMMITTEE

How a community begins to address gang problems dif fers depending on the event or events that draw public attention to the issue. In some cases, a high-profile, often tragic event occurs that galvanizes the community and stimulates mobilization to address gangs. In other cases, a groundswell of public support to deal with gangs builds more gradually and lacks only an individual or agency to serve as a catalyst. At some point, key agencies and com munity leaders begin to openly discuss and address gang issues. At that point, a standing task force, committee, or organizational structure (henceforth referred to as the steering committee) should be convened and begin to work on next steps. Ideally, this group oversees an assess ment of the local gang problem and, using data obtained through the assessment, develops strategies to combat it.

In virtually every demonstration of OJJDP's Comprehen sive Gang Model, the effectiveness of its steering commit tee has been crucial in determining the success or failure of the community in implementing a comprehensive approach.

To be effective, the steering committee should:

- Include, at a minimum, representation from the following groups: law enforcement, corrections, probation/parole (juvenile and adult), schools, social services agencies, local units of government, faith- based organizations, religious institutions, employ ment programs, and community residents.
- Make and oversee policy for the project.
- Oversee and provide general direction to the agencies collaborating in conducting an assessment of the gang problem and planning/implementing the project.

The membership of the steering committee is an essential element in determining program success. Steering com mittees with well-respected leaders (chairs or cochairs) who have a reputation for problem-solving and objectiv ity have proven most successful.

Best results have been obtained when the steering com mittee mixes two groups:

- Individuals from upper-level management in key part nering agencies who can effect organizational change within their own agencies

OJJDP COMPREHENSIVE GANG MODEL CORE STRATEGY: COMMUNITY MOBILIZATION CRITICAL ELEMENTS

- Local citizens, including youth, community groups, and agencies, are involved, and programs and functions of staff within and across agencies are coordinated.

- A steering committee is available to initiate the project by involving representatives of key organizations and the community and to guide it over time by responding to barriers to implementation, developing sound policy, lending support to the project where and when appro priate, and taking general ownership of the communi tywide response.
- The steering committee also is charged with creating and maintaining interagency and community relation ships that facilitate program development. For example, the committee could create coordinated outreach and law enforcement policies and practices and facilitate the development of community groups such as block watches, neighbors/mothers against gangs, or other community alliances and coalitions.
- The program is supported and sustained across all levels (top, intermediate, and street/line) of the criminal and juvenile justice systems, schools, community-based and grassroots organizations, and government.
- Individuals with influence within the community, in clud ing residents, and representatives of grassroots community groups, neighborhood associations, reli gious organizations, and advocacy groups.

Steering committees have been most successful when they have established a formal structure, such as adoption of bylaws describing how the committee would function. Using an approach such as Robert's Rules of Or der provides a way to consider opposing opinions and can assist the committee in reaching consensus on dif ficult issues. Execution of memorandums of understand ing (MOUs) among key agencies commits them to assessment tasks and long-term roles in implementing comprehensive strategies to address identified gang problems.

HIGHLIGHTS FROM THE FIELD—CONVENING A STEERING COMMITTEE

Richmond, VA. The organizational structure in Richmond includes an executive committee, leadership committee, and four subcommittees to help with oversight, strategic planning, and implementation. Even though membership remained consistent for the most part, there were some major changes in top leadership during the funded period. These changes included a change in governor, two attorneys general, a mayor, and a new police chief. The strength of the collaborative partnership initially formed allowed for a smooth transition during these changes and allowed staff to remain on task.

Pittsburgh, PA. Pittsburgh's Gang-Free Schools program initiated memorandums of understanding between steering committee members and key agencies that enabled the project to maintain momentum during a citywide financial crisis and sustain participation from agencies that withdrew from other initiatives.

ADMINISTERING THE PROGRAM

Selecting the appropriate lead agency and program direc tor are crucial steps in ensuring program success.

Lead Agency

Unlike other initiatives, the lead agency in these multidis ciplinary programs does not assume control of the initia tive, but instead provides an administrative framework to facilitate the work of the intervention team and the steering committee. A wide variety of agency types have led these initiatives. No matter which agency assumes primary responsibility for this initiative, its credibility and influence within the community are directly correlated to the success of planning and implementation activities. The lead agency has a number of important responsibilities:

- Providing a secure location to house client intake in formation, consent forms, and intervention plans.
- Tracking the activities of the partnering agencies.
- Coordinating the activities and meetings of the inter vention team and the steering committee.
- Providing an administrative framework for hiring staff, if necessary.
- Administering funds and grant contracts as directed by the steering committee.

As set forth in table 1, experience has shown that each type of agency has its advantages and disadvantages. Each community has varying needs based on existing community dynamics (e.g., local politics, existing collabo rations, agencies' management capacities, and the loca tion of the target area), which will inevitably influence the selection of the lead agency for the program.

Lead agencies will incur significant costs when building and administering the multiagency infrastructure of the program. These costs are closely associated with the gang coordinator's position. In OJJDP's GRP demonstra tion, approximately $150,000 was budgeted for the posi tion and necessary support. Although no site used all of those funds in any given year, the value of a full-time employee's ability to focus partners on the message, keep promised work on schedule, and assure that prob lems were quickly brought to the attention of senior po litical or operational leadership far exceeded the cost in dollars. Moreover, in Los Angeles and Richmond, the site coordinators have become part of their employing agen cies, because their leadership does not want to return to their prior way of doing business. In North Miami Beach, the coordinator and others are forming a nonprofit orga nization to raise money and continue the work with sup port from their law enforcement partners.

Table 1. Lead Agency Advantages/Disadvantages: Program Implementation Characteristics

Lead Agency	Advantages	Disadvantages
Law Enforcement	• Law enforcement involved in planning and implementation • Processes in place for crime and gang information sharing • Greater access to daily updates regarding criminal activity • Access to financial and business managementsupport	• Community members may not understand the role of program personnel • It may be difficult to overcome distrust between outreach staff and law enforcement, resulting inobstacles to information sharing
Prosecutors and Other Criminal Justice Entities	• Able to leverage the participation of law enforcement agencies • Access to police incident reports and law enforcement data • Access to financial and business management support	• They may be perceived as interested only in prosecuting/incarcerating gang members • They may not have a strong connection to the target community • There may be historic distrust between criminaljustice entities and service providers
City Government	• Access to key personnel in city departments and elected officials • Access to sensitive data from law enforcement• Credibility and buy-in from city agencies• Access to financial and business management support • Ability to set policy for key agencies	• Shifts in political leadership can destabilize the program • City policies and/or budget constraints may make it difficult to hire personnel
School Districts	• Buy-in from school administrators to ensure local school participation in the intervention team • Access to educational data• Large enough to absorb the program once other funds are spent • Access to financial and business management support	• They may be unwilling to provide services to youth not enrolled in school • Decisionmaking may be bogged down by district policies • Hiring policies may make it difficult for school districts to employ outreach staff
Local Service Providers	• Working knowledge of the target area • Experience with community planning and action	• Agencies may lack experience in working with gang-involved clients • Gang programming may not be given a priority• They lack administrative structure to managefunds/grants
State Agencies	• Resources and credibility • Expertise in grant management and administration • Access to financial and business management support	• The lead agency may be located well away from the actual program activities • State agencies may often be perceived as outsiders without a strong connection to the target community • They have less awareness of local politics and historical issues

The Comprehensive Gang Model in Action—OJJDP's Gang Reduction Program

Richmond, Virginia

The Richmond project (Gang Reduction and Intervention Program [GRIP]) target area consists of two police reporting sectors in south Richmond. The target area is a subur ban-type community of single-family homes and apartments. The area is transitioning from a middle-class to a working-class population, with an increase in Hispanic residents. Traditional "homegrown" African-American gangs also reside in the area. Currently, law enforcement is reporting representation and activity by members of His panic gangs with roots in the western United States and Central America. Law enforcement is concerned about gang crime and delinquency directed against Hispanic workers in the area, who are often reluctant to report crimes. The traditional African-American gangs are the prevalent gang presence in membership and activity.

Prevention activities are aimed at the broad population of families and youth who are at risk of becoming involved in gang and delinquent activity. Prevention activities include:

- One-Stop Resource Center—an information and referral case management entry point to prevention services.
- Prenatal and infancy support.
- English as a Second Language for Hispanic residents.
- Spanish as a Second Language, with an emphasis on providing language skills to those serving the Hispanic population.
- Class Action Summer Camp.
- Richmond school resource officers train the Class Action curriculum in target-area schools under the auspices of the Gang Reduction Program.
- Public awareness programs and community events.
- School-based educational and family wraparound services.
- Sports and life-skill activities and training.
- Theater group to showcase issues involving gang-in volved youth.
- Gang awareness training to community and service providers.
- Hispanic liaison to link the program to local Hispanic residents
- Mentoring/tutoring for youth at risk of gang involvement.
- Immigration services to Hispanic residents.
- Afterschool and summer programs for elementary and middle school youth.
- Arts and recreation for at-risk youth.

Intervention activities are supported by a multidisciplinary intervention team that conducts case-management activi ties, including street outreach to support gang-involved youth, with the goal of providing an alternative to gang membership. Activities with individual youth are targeted toward that goal and tracked via case-management soft ware. Related activities include:

- Job training development and placement through public/private partnerships.
- Entrepreneurial training for at-risk youth.
- Role modeling and mentoring.
- Truancy and drop-out prevention programs.
- Mental health and substance abuse services.
- Educational support and GED services.
- Tattoo removal.
- Community service projects.

Suppression activities include directed police patrols, community policing, community awareness, supporting in creased law enforcement intelligence sharing, establishing a multiagency law enforcement and prosecution response to target gang leaders, increasing the number of school resource officers in target area schools, and expanding neighborhood watch teams in partnership with the Rich mond Police Department and community members. GRIP also supports police department review of crime data for evaluation purposes.

Reentry activities are closely tied to the multidisciplinary intervention team and include self-sufficiency skill training and job training and placement. Support services—such as food, transportation, and other services—are available.

Highlights from the Field—Lead Agency

Richmond, VA. Richmond's GRP demonstration designated the Virginia Attorney General's office as the lead agency, allowing the project to interact with a larger number of partners. The experience and credibility offered through oversight by the attorney general's office allowed the project to leverage greater support.

Los Angeles, CA, and Houston, TX. The lead agency for both the Los Angeles and the Houston demonstrations was the mayor's office. That office was able to influence and coalesce the community around the project.

Miami-Dade, FL. The Miami-Dade County Public Schools served as the lead agency for its community's Gang-Free Schools project. This agency was able to provide consistent and wide-reaching school district support that enabled the project to set up a community-based facility where key partners utilized an existing school district property to co-locate.

Pittsburgh, PA. The Pittsburgh Gang-Free Schools project benefitted from the Pittsburgh Public Schools serving as lead agency because it allowed project staff to access crucial school-level data about clients involved in the program and leverage district-wide services.

Program Director

The gang coordinator or program director is the key to successful implementation of the Comprehensive Gang Model. Selection of a program director with specific skills and abilities is of paramount importance. Best results have been obtained where the steering committee and the lead agency jointly develop a written job description for this position and, in concert, select the program direc tor. This step may be difficult, especially where funding for that position is being raised through joint contribu tions or as a result of a grant. In Los Angeles, the GRP coordinator position was of great interest to the police dePartment and maYOr'S OffiCe. WhIle eaCh agenCY attempted to exercise substantial control on the selection process, OJJDP, by virtue of its funding control, mediated the discussions. The result was that both agen cies have been well served by a talented and committed coordinator who has remained in place during the entire 4-year program.

Program directors with these skills have produced the best results:

- The skills to understand and work within complex sys tems such as criminal justice, education, and social services.
- An understanding of data collection and analysis pro tocols, as well as how to read, interpret, synthesize, and clearly explain data orally and in writing to a wide range of audiences.
- The skills to understand and develop short- and longterm plans for implementation.
- The skills to move flexibly among a variety of complex tasks—from public speaking and writing grants to managing program funds and effectively supervising personnel.
- The skills to work well with personnel at different lev els of responsibility, from agency heads to grassroots personnel, and from a variety of disciplines: law en forcement, education, social services, justice systems, and outreach.
- Meeting facilitation, conflict resolution, and consen sus-building skills that enable the program director to serve as an intermediary between agencies, resolve differences of opinion during meetings, and effectively address potentially inflammatory and emotional topics.
- The skills to understand the risk factors leading to gang involvement, local gang activities and gang research, community dynamics and history, and pre vention/intervention/suppression strategies; and to explain these concepts to others from a variety of educational and cultural backgrounds.
- The skills to supervise, engage, and motivate staff from a variety of agencies and racial/cultural/economic backgrounds, including staff over whom the director may not have direct supervisory authority. This is especially important when working with outreach staff who may have prior offending histories, prior gang affiliation, and unstable work histories.

Program directors who generate passion and enthusiasm, and who inspire others, achieve solid results. The impor tance of the program director's role cannot be overstated.

Assessing the Gang Problem

Conducting a comprehensive assessment of the community's gang problem is the foundation for planning and implementing the Comprehensive Gang Model.

Where aSSeSSmentS Were dOne methOdICallY and comprehensively, efficient and effective targeting resulted. The assessment process helped projects determine types and levels of gang activity, gang crime patterns, community perceptions, and service gaps. The assessment also assisted steering committees in identifying target populations to be served, understanding why those populations merited attention, and making the best use of available resources.

Members of the steering committee must share power and influence during the assessment phase. Real power- sharing among key agencies at this juncture has not only been shown to have an influence on data collection, but has been particularly beneficial in forming and maintain ing the partnerships needed for success over the life of the project.

Communities should make sure that each participating agency benefits from collaboration. Clear communication is critical. Simply assuming that overall goals will be meaningful to all partners may result in some partners feeling discouraged or that they are being asked to do work that only benefits other groups or interests. Since partners interested in addressing gangs share many inter ests in helping the at-risk population, and almost all work that improves the community or situation of at-risk kids adds to anti-gang efforts, finding shared goals need not be difficult. Once each partner identifies their interest and goals, they should keep a record of how well those interests are met. Meeting goals may involve raising funds to help a service provider, increasing the number of volunteers who provide specific aid, or increasing local or national media exposure. Finally, collecting base line data will help demonstrate the value of each partner's work and the collaboration's ability to leverage resources.

Selecting representatives from a cross-section of agencies to work on each assessment task will produce stronger coalitions. The steering committee should designate an agency to coordinate the assessment process.

Prior to beginning work on the assessment, the steering committee should identify the scope and extent Of the aSSeSSment. WIll the aSSeSSment be COndUCted communitywide? If a smaller area of the community is to be assessed, some preassessment work should be done, including a scan of overall violent crime statistics, to iden tify an appropriate target area.

OJJDP'S reCentlY deVelOPed the Web-baSed SOCIOeCOnOm ic Mapping and Resource Topography (SMART) system, which provides a substantial amount of community-level data, from the U.S. Census to Uniform Crime Report (UCR) data, and a Community Disadvantage Index (a re search and data derived index that provides a way to compare the strength of one community against anoth er). The SMART system is free of charge and available on lIne (gO tO the OJJDP Web SIte, httP://WWW.OJP.USdOJ.gOV/ ojjdp, and select "Tools").

Because of the importance of the assessment, it is critical that the steering committee allots sufficient time to con duct data collection and analysis. The more extensive the assessment, the more time-consuming and expensive this process will be. Because most communities do not have unlimited funds, best results were produced when the steering committee identified and prioritized critical data to be collected and set a reasonable timeline for these activities. This timeline may range from 3 months to more than a year, depending on the scope of the assessment.

Data collection was initiated more quickly and proceeded more smoothly when the steering committee established written agreements with the key agencies. These written agreements identified the types of data to be collected, specified whether an archival record review was needed, and indicated the time frame within which the review should be conducted. If analysis and explanation of the data are required, the written agreement should also set forth these responsibilities. Furthermore, based on expe riences at multiple sites, the written agreement ensures that the data, once collected, are available to all parties and cannot be hidden or removed from the assessment. Progress is enhanced when the steering committee agen cies agree to underwrite or conduct pieces of the assess ment and to create contracts for specific tasks that the assessment requires. Ideally, these written agreements will also commit key agencies to ongoing data collection.

To ensure that data are collected consistently and with out discrepancies, and where State law does not define these terms, the steering committee must establish defi nitions of "gang," "gang member," and "gang crime."

In many cases, it may be necessary to conduct a manual archival record review of law enforcement data during the initial assessment. Most sites found these manual ar chival record reviews to be a necessary, but expensive and time-consuming, process. They also found it best to iden tify protocols that, when key agencies and the steering committee put them into place, would make it easier to collect data in the future. Some sites ultimately amended computerized police incident reports to include a "gang related" check box. Other sites established protocols to channel specific types of reports to the gang unit for regular review.

Assistance from a local research partner trained in statisti cal analysis can benefit an assessment greatly. Some data, such as gang crime data, community demographic data, and school statistics, can almost certainly be collected without a research partner. But sites planning to inter view gang members; conduct focus groups with parents, community residents, or school staff members; or use in- depth survey instruments should consider engaging a re search partner with some expertise in data analysis. That partner can work through processes such as obtaining consent and ensuring and protecting confidentiality. The research partner also should perform more complex data analyses, as required. As with other service providers, staff should establish a detailed scope of work or a job description for the research partner. The scope of work may include a summary of the data reports to be devel oped and a timeline for completion. The scope of work also should include a process for addressing issues that may arise with the research partner's quality of work and timeliness.

In addition to collecting the data mentioned above, sites that conducted comprehensive assessments found that they were better equipped during the planning and im plementation process to design appropriate responses, target appropriate populations to serve, and implement program activities if they did the following:

- Investigated underlying demographic factors that affect local gang problems.
- Measured the extent of gang activity in schools.
- Included qualitative educational factors affecting local youth.
- Surveyed residents and youth about perceptions of gangs.
- Inventoried community resources to address gangs.

OJJDP Comprehensive Gang Model
Core Strategy: Organizational Change and Development
Critical Elements

- Policies and procedures that result in the most use of available and potential resources within and across agencies are developed and implemented.
- The policies and practices of organizations, particularly of agencies providing intervention team staff, are adapted to conform to the goals and objectives of the project as identified through the strategic planning exercises.
- Each program, agency, or community representative on the steering committee ensures that its internal units are cooperating with and supporting the work of the intervention team.
- Various agencies learn not only to understand the com plex nature of the gang problem and cooperate closely with each other in the development and implementation of the program, but also to assist other organizations, particularly agencies involved with the intervention team, to achieve their respective mission objectives.
- In the process of collaboration, a team approach means a maximum sharing of information about targeted youth such that activities of team members are modified in a generalist direction (e.g., police take some responsibility for social intervention and outreach workers assist with the suppression of serious crime and violence).
- A case management system and associated data system are established so that contacts and services by all mem bers of the intervention team can be monitored for purposes of effective targeting, tracking youth entry into and exit from the program, and measuring out comes at individual and program area levels.
- Staff development and training for the intervention team are conducted for the different types of team participants separately and collectively, especially regarding data sharing, joint planning, and implementation activities.
- Special training, close supervision, and administrative arrangements are established, particularly for youth outreach workers and law enforcement, to carry out their collaborative roles in a mutually trustworthy fashion.
- Organizational policies and practices become inclusive and community oriented with special reference to the interests, needs, and cultural background of local resi dents, including the targeted youth.

The Comprehensive Gang Model in Action—
OJJDP's Gang Reduction Program
Los Angeles, California

The Los Angeles Gang Reduction Program site is located in the Boyle Heights area, 3 miles east of downtown Los An geles. It is home to a large immigrant population made up mostly of residents from Mexico and Central America. Five maJOr gangS InhabIt the target area, InClUdIng WhIte Fence (established in the 1930s), Varrio Nuevo Estrada "VNE" (established in the 1970s and inhabiting the Estrada Courts Public Housing Development),

Indiana Dukes, Opal Street, and EIghth Street (InhabItIng WYVernWOOd APart ments). A number of street-front, grassroots community organizations, health providers, churches, and youth cen ters are located in the neighborhood and have a history of involvement in gang prevention and intervention activi ties. Five public elementary and middle schools are located in the target area, with more than 5,000 students enrolled. The Los Angeles Police Department's Community Law En forcement and Recovery (CLEAR) Program is a targeted gang suppression program and operates as a partner in the Boyle Heights community.

Prevention activities focused on providing youth with al ternatives and support to prevent or resist gang involve ment include:

- Early College Awareness and Literacy Program for fifth grade students and their parents.
- Afterschool programs for elementary and middle school youth at high risk of gang membership.
- The Story Project"—an afterschool multimedia com munication program to encourage school attendance and increase students' grade point average.
- Prenatal and infancy support for high-risk mothers to reduce risk factors related to gang involvement.
- Intensive case management for youth and families residing in the target area, including mentoring for high-risk males ages 10–14.
- Gang awareness training for schools, residents, local businesses, and parents.

Intervention and reentry activities are primarily case man aged by a multidisciplinary team. Other intervention ser vices for gang members in the Los Angeles plan include:

- Individual and group counseling for behavior, substance abuse, and other needs.
- Educational and vocational training.
- Tattoo removal.
- Anger management and conflict resolution.

Suppression activities are conducted in the target area by the CLEAR program. CLEAR involves targeted gang en forcement, prosecution, and community awareness.

HIGHLIGHTS FROM THE FIELD—ASSESSING THE GANG PROBLEM

Los Angeles, CA. The Los Angeles GRP project identified gaps in services by conducting a community resource assessment and holding focus groups in the community. This information helped the project in the development of the strategic plan and mapping out funding levels for each of the program's components—primary prevention, secondary prevention, intervention, re-entry, and suppression.

Richmond, VA. An assessment of police incident reports for gang-affiliated offenses led to a change in the way that the police department captured gang-related incidents. Reports now require officers to input any information that assists with identifying gang affiliation.

Pittsburgh, PA. In Pittsburgh, the assessment process used in the Gang-Free Schools project led to extensive changes in the Pittsburgh Bureau of Police's methods of capturing gang crime data and the creation of a new gang intelligence collection system. Pittsburgh Public Schools surveyed all students in three grades (5, 7, and 9) across the entire school district. These student surveys helped the community address widespread denial.

Houston, TX. In Houston, the GFS demonstration conducted an archival review of police incident reports that revealed that more than 80 percent of police incidents involving gangs were missed in the existing data collection system, and has led to routine record reviews by the gang enforcement squad in the target community.

Planning for Implementation

The steering committee serves as the primary decision- making body for implementation planning. It should use the assessment as a guide in formulating a strategic plan to mitigate the community's gang problem.

The steering committee should synthesize data collected from the assessment into a usable form for planning pur poses. Specifically, the steering committee needs to know the following information:

- Types of gang-related crime.
- Patterns of change in gang incident rates.
- Locations of gang crime.
- Increases/decreases in numbers of gangs and gang members.
- Level of citizen concern about gang activity.
- Community perceptions of gang activity.
- Gang-related activity in schools.
- Changes in community demographics. Planning objectives are used to:
- Determine the criteria for targeting clients that this multidisciplinary approach will serve (age, race, gen der, gang affiliation, etc.).
- Determine a geographic area of the community to be served (if necessary).
- Determine the goals of the program; intervention, prevention, and suppression strategies; and types of services to be provided. Activities, goals, and objectives also are identified based on the problems described during the gang assessment.
- Determine the targets for intervention by the multidis ciplinary team and the composition of the team itself.
- Assign staff members to an intervention team to coor dinate provision of services to clients and manage cli ent cases.
- Practices that have proved helpful to the planning pro cess include:
- Providing steering committee members with a copy of the assessment report and thoroughly discussing the data and the problems identified as a result of the data review.
- Conducting training on the program model with each of the partnering agencies prior to the planning process.

- Introducing the model in a formal manner with multimedia materials, such as OJJDP's online Strategic Planning Tool (http://www.iir.com/nygc/tool/), which helps identify programs and compare existing commu nity resources with existing needs.
- • Engaging representatives from other communities that have successfully implemented comprehensive models to provide training and guidance on program plan ning and implementation.
- Attending neighborhood association, chamber of com merce, and other community meetings on a regular basis to hear their ideas on gang programming.

The Comprehensive Gang Model in Action— OJJDP's Gang Reduction Program North Miami Beach, Florida

The North Miami Beach Gang Reduction Program, known as PanZou (reclaiming the community), target area com prises the city of North Miami Beach, which is located in northeast Miami-Dade County, FL. The area was originally a middle-class retirement area with few services for youth and families. The community has changed over the last 20 years to a working-class area populated by a largely Hai tian population, and residents have to rely on services pro vided in other areas of Miami-Dade County. Transportation is an issue, as is the lack of service providers who are famil iar with the primary Haitian language, Creole. Local law enforcement reports indicate that the city population is approximately 50 percent Haitian, with undocumented Haitians representing an estimated additional 10 to 15 percent. The city economy is primarily service-oriented without the presence of any major industries.

Prevention activities are aimed at the broad at-risk popu lation, with several appropriate activities also available to gang youth being served at the intervention level. The project also is involved in various community awareness activities. A One-Stop Resource Center is operating in the target area. Prevention activities include:

- Mentoring for youth at risk of gang involvement.
- Early literacy for Haitian youth.
- Youth empowerment (life skill classes) and midnight basketball.
- Strengthening Families Program, focused on parenting skills and reducing substance abuse and behavioral problems in youth ages 10–14.
- Intensive case management.
- Alternatives to suspension for middle and high school youth.
- Truancy interdiction.
- Developing Intelligent Voices of America (DIVAs) for young women (ages 8–18) to develop social, emotional, and behavioral competence.
- Man-Up! For young men between the ages of 12–18 to develop social, emotional, and behavioral competence.
- Increased recreational opportunities for elementary and middle school youth.
- Self-sufficiency training.

Intervention activities are centered on a multidisciplinary team providing intensive case management and street out reach to gang members and their families. Activities include:

- Substance abuse counseling.
- On-the-job training.
- Referrals to community agencies, including counseling and tattoo removal.
- Six Rounds to Success Boxing Program (mentoring and physical and boxing skills).
- Community service opportunities.

Suppression activities involve additional directed foot and bike patrols in "hot spot" gang-crime areas, identification of gang leaders, and coordination with juvenile probation on gang activity. In partnership with the Gang Reduction Program, the North Miami Beach Police Department cre ated a specialized gang unit, increased gang intelligence gathering, and increased participation with the local Mul tiagency Gang Task Force.

HIGHLIGHTS FROM THE FIELD—PLANNING FOR IMPLEMENTATION

Gang Reduction Program. All GRP projects found that involving individuals from experienced sites was effective in training on implementation activities such as the operation of the multidisciplinary intervention team.

Richmond, VA. Richmond invited approximately 100 people to participate on their four working subcommittees broken down into the following groups: prevention, intervention, suppression, and reentry. The subcommittees consisted of State and local government, nonprofit, for-profit, faith-based, and community organizations. They determined gaps in community services and made recommendations. Participation by these large groups allowed for greater input from the community and a commitment to seeing the program succeed.

Los Angeles, CA. The Los Angeles GRP used the community resource assessment and focus groups to help develop their strategic plan and map out funding levels for each programmatic area of the project.

Riverside, CA. Riverside, one of OJJDP's initial demonstration sites, placed emphasis on training steering committee members on the Model and the importance of their roles as decisionmakers and in oversight of the project. An orientation on the project was also implemented for each new steering committee member.

IMPLEMENTING THE PROGRAM

The implementation process is accelerated when the steering committee agencies, the lead agency, and the program director conduct startup and capacity-building activities prior to beginning services. These activities include:

- Developing contracting protocols and/or requests for proposals.
- Developing program policies and procedures.

- Selecting intervention team members.
- Determining what training is needed for key agencies to serve gang-involved youth and how and by whom this training will be conducted.
- Determining sources of clients and referral processes.
- Creating a consent and intake process for clients.
- Determining how outcome data from clients will be collected, stored, and analyzed.
- Developing job descriptions for key personnel.
- Training intervention team members on their roles and responsibilities.

Maintaining the Steering Committee

- The role of the steering committee during program im plementation may include:
- Making decisions regarding program changes or expansion.
- Ensuring that the program is responsive to the needs of program clients and the community.
- Ensuring that key agencies continue to participate in and support the program.
- Conducting training and activities to increase commu nity awareness of the program.
- Identifying ways to ensure long-term sustainability.

The members of the steering committee should be cham pions of the program as a vehicle for change within the community. The chair and/or cochair should be passionate and committed to the program and should work to en sure that the steering committee maintains its momentum.

As the steering committee's role shifts from planning to implementing gang strategies, it may be difficult to keep committee members engaged. Strategies used to main tain effective steering committees have included:

- Holding meetings consistently at a regular time/date.
- Developing a newsletter for program partners.
- Engaging steering committee members in gang aware ness education and community mobilization activities.
- Identifying an active and committed chairperson with positive visibility in the community.
- Providing a formal orientation process for new members.
- Holding annual retreats to identify future activities and reinvigorate the group.
- Making personal contact with all members periodically (program director).
- Acknowledging members' key contributions.
- Providing members with written materials and reports on program activities in advance of meetings.
- Using meeting time productively—not to report on activities, but for decisionmaking.
- It is also the role of the steering committee to plan for sustaining the program. Sustainability planning should begin during the assessment and planning phase and continue throughout the life of collaboration. Ideally, the implementation plan

developed during the initial planning stage should include goals related to sustainability, such as ensuring ongoing data collection and analysis for the purpose of self-evaluation.

- In FY 2008, OJJDP pilot tested two faith-based and com munity organization sustainability training events. (Infor mation from these trainings is available on the OJJDP Web SIte.) AnY PrOgram targetIng ChIldren, YOUth, Or families must be able to sustain efforts over time. Failure to sustain a program may do harm—it might inhibit per sonal action or reaffirm the notion that no one is willing to make a long term commitment to the child or the community.

As partners come on board, they should be asked what they plan on doing to sustain their involvement for the long term and whether they can help other partners do the same. In Richmond, VA, OJJDP partnered with the Virginia Attorney General and the Mayor of Richmond to hold a public education campaign for local organizations that support local programming and social services. The event brought partners together with funders and indi VIdUalS WIth aCCeSS tO a WIde VarIetY Of reSOUrCeS. WhIle OJJDP did not play any role in matching partners' needs to resources, this sort of public education often has that effect. Partners should consider how they will keep their communities aware of their work and of their needs.

New members should be trained prior to attending steer ing committee meetings. Providing orientation to new members is vital to ensuring that the multidisciplinary gang program remains true to identified problems and long-term goals. This orientation should include provid ing new members with copies of the assessment, the im plementation plan, and an overview of current activities.

Other ways to keep stakeholders engaged in the steering committee include:

- Holding periodic elections for chair and/or cochair.
- Conducting refresher training on program goals and the program model.
- Ensuring that regular steering committee attendance is addressed in MOUs between the key agencies.
- Directing contacts by the chair and/or cochair(s) with key agencies that are not regularly participating.

Elections and subsequent turnover in political offices can affect the steering committee. Agency responsibilities may shift under new administrations. Changes in political leadership may also mean shifts in programmatic and funding priorities. OJJDP encountered this situation in both Los Angeles and Richmond. From the outset, the OJJDP administrator supported addressing as early as pos sible the leadership issue, both on the community and political level. Both Los Angeles and Richmond leadership were told that they had to agree up front to do business differently in the pilot areas and to recognize and accept

that by focusing on a particular area the project would probably have some impact on surrounding areas. This is because gangs will respond to increased attention in the pilot area by moving away. Leaders must also accept that funding was limited to filling gaps in existing programs and not creating new "mouths" to feed. Leaders also committed to develop ways to sustain what they built during the program with their own funds or private com munity resources.

These discussions took substantial time and required high-level involvement. In Los Angeles, the police and mayor had significant input about whether to accept the funding under the conditions offered, and the city coun cil weighed in and considered the issue for nearly 4 months.

Having existing MOUs or written agreements can help these multidisciplinary programs remain a priority despite changes in administration. Other activities that have been shown to be helpful in maintaining momentum include:

- Ongoing data collection.
- Self-evaluation to show program success.
- Regular reporting on outcomes to steering committee members and elected officials.
- Recognition of the achievements of individual clients.
- Regular awards ceremonies to highlight the contribu tions of key individuals and agencies and the accom plishments of program clients.
- Regular briefings by program staff to key agencies and elected officials.

Planning for personnel and leadership changes must be part of any long-term endeavor. One of the most impor tant reasons for continuing any program or effort is if it saves money or effectively leverages limited resources. No one will end programs that can document that they are saving taxpayer dollars and increasing public safety.

OJJDP Comprehensive Gang Model Core Strategy: Provision of Opportunities Critical Elements

- The community, through an appointed steering com mittee, develops a variety of educational, training, and employment programs or services targeted to gang youth and those at high risk of gang involvement.
- Special access to social and economic opportunities in the community is provided for gang-involved youth and youth at high risk of gang involvement.
- Opportunities and services are provided in such a way that they do not encapsulate, segregate, or alienate gang youth or those at high risk from mainstream institutions.
- Mechanisms for identifying and addressing youth at risk of gang involvement are in place in the elementary, middle, and high schools within the targeted area(s).
- Education, training, and job opportunity strategies are integrated with those of social services, particularly youth outreach work, along with close supervision and social control, as necessary.
- Local residents and businesses are supportive and involved in the provision of educational and training opportunities and job contacts for targeted gang youth and those at high risk.

- Access to social opportunities also is provided to other gang members and associates of targeted youth.

Highlights from the Field—Maintaining the Steering Committee

Riverside, CA. During implementation, many steering committee members stopped attending meetings because they did not feel they were needed at the table after the planning stage. The project director held face-to-face meetings with former and current members to provide current information about the project and their role.

Pittsburgh, PA. Steering committee members were provided a packet of meeting materials prior to meetings to ensure that time was not wasted during the meeting. The steering committee chair ensured that the meeting time was reserved for substantive issues impacting the project.

Richmond, VA. Staff are extremely dedicated to maintaining and growing partnerships. In addition, staff receive requests from organizations and persons who wish to become involved in the collaborative partnership.

The Intervention Team

The intervention team is a primary component of the comprehensive approach. The steering committee should determine the composition of this team and assign repre sentatives to serve on it. Because the intervention team brings together individuals from disparate disciplines and experiences, building a functional team is probably the most complex aspect of the model.

The intervention team:

- Identifies appropriate youth/clients/individuals for this program.
- Engages these people to work with the team.
- Assesses them on an individual basis to determine their needs, goals, and issues.
- Develops an individualized intervention plan for each client.
- Ensures that multiple services in the individualized in tervention plan are integrated.
- The team should work together to determine whether referred individuals are appropriate for their services and then work as a team to serve these clients.
- Key agencies should quantify and clarify their participa tion on the intervention team through MOUs (previously discussed under steering committee). These memoran dums should address information sharing/confidentiality issues, the role each member will play in the team, the member's participation level on the team, and other re sponsibilities the member's agency may have in interven tion team activities.

At a minimum, the following key agencies that are crucial to an effective intervention team should be represented on the team:

- Law enforcement representatives involved in gang in vestigation and enforcement.
- Juvenile and adult probation/parole officers who will have frequent contact with program clients.
- School officials who can access student educational data for program clients and leverage educational services.
- Appropriate social service and/or mental health pro viders who can leverage services and provide outcome information to the team.
- A representative who can assist in preparing program clients for employment and find them jobs.
- Outreach workers who can directly connect to pro gram clients on the street, in their homes, or at school.

Other agencies may be asked to participate on an as- needed basis, including faith-based organizations, recreational programs, community development organi zations, and grassroots organizations.

Based on data collected during the assessment process, screening criteria for clients should be regulated by the steering committee. The screening criteria are designed to help the team narrow down possible referrals to en sure that they serve the most appropriate clients for gang intervention. Items to consider when developing target criteria include a demographic profile from police inci dent reports, an aggregate demographic profile of known gang members from gang intelligence files, and information collected from student surveys and school data. The screening criteria should be strictly adhered to; otherwise, the program risks losing its desired focus and effect.

The intervention team should develop protocols for client intake assessments, obtaining consent/releases to serve clients, and sharing information across agency boundaries.

Sharing data across service areas and with law enforce ment raises many issues. Successful efforts are character ized by solid relationships, clear protocols, and a commitment that information sharing is done to help individuals and not law enforcement. Other data and in formation sharing protocols already exist for law enforce ment purposes, and judicial warrants are always available in the appropriate case.

Outreach Staff

The outreach component of this model is critical to pro gram success. An outreach worker's primary role is to build relationships with program clients and with other gang-involved youth in the community. Outreach workers typically work in the community, connecting with hard to-serve youth. These workers often constitute the pri mary recruitment tool for the program and serve an important role in delivering services. Outreach workers are the intervention team's eyes and ears on the street, giving the team perspective on the personal aspects of gang conflicts and violence and how these affect the team's clients. In addition to relationship building, out reach workers' responsibilities include:

- Identifying appropriate clients and recruiting them for the program.

- Identifying youths' needs and goals to help the team develop a more comprehensive intervention plan.
- Coaching and providing role models for each youth.
- Coordinating appropriate crisis responses to program clients following violent episodes in the community.
- Providing assistance to families in distress, ranging from accessing basic needs to helping resolve family conflicts.
- Visiting clients who are incarcerated and helping to reconnect them to services when they are released from custody.
- Resolving conflicts and/or mediating between clients, their families, other youth, and/or agencies.
- Acting as a liaison between program clients and ser vice providers/schools to facilitate client access to services.
- WOrKIng WIth ClIentS WhO are SeeKIng emPlOYment, from helping these youth develop résumés, to identifying their skills and qualifications, to helping them apply for jobs or work with workforce services programs.
- Conducting gang awareness presentations in schools.

Developing written job descriptions for outreach staff helps ensure that all parties are aware of the role of out reach workers within the team and the community. Some programs have hired former gang members. The ratio nale behind hiring individuals with previous gang con nections is their perceived ability to gain street credibility. However, these previous ties may cause strained relation ships between the outreach workers and other partners such as schools, law enforcement agencies, and other criminal justice entities. One option to ensure that out reach workers have street credibility is to hire individuals from the target community who do not have gang ties.

If programs hire former gang members, it is extremely important that local law enforcement vet these hires to ensure that the prospective outreach workers' gang ties are indeed broken. Further, outreach workers need to understand that their conduct in the community must be above reproach, or else the entire program's integrity can be compromised. Agencies that hire former gang mem bers need to monitor these employees' behavior on and off the job to ensure that they stay true to their mission in the program.

Outreach workers may be employed by the lead agency, or the steering committee may contract outreach services from an existing program. Table 2 illustrates the pros and cons to both of these approaches.

Almost all communities that have implemented compre hensive initiatives have found that intensive professional development will likely be needed. Most skilled outreach workers have excellent relationship-building skills with youth, as well as indepth knowledge of the community and the youth who live there. However, outreach workers may have difficulty interacting with partners from other disciplines and navigating the educational and/or criminal justice systems. Outreach workers will likely need training on administrative requirements of the job, such as man aging a caseload, maintaining appropriate professional boundaries with clients, communicating effectively, and documenting client contacts.

Building trust between street outreach workers and law enforcement officers must begin with the first meeting of the team. Outreach workers must understand that they are not police officers and should be discouraged from riding in police vehicles, attending meetings in police sta tIOnS, Or CarrYIng POlICe radIOS. Whether he Or She haS had prior law enforcement experience or has a concealed carry permit, an outreach worker cannot carry weapons on his person or in his or her vehicle. Similarly, law en forcement officers need to understand that the outreach WOrKer IS nOt a POlICe InfOrmant. WIth the exCePtIOn Of information that could prevent bodily harm, law enforce ment should not expect street outreach workers to pro vide police officers with gang intelligence.

Outreach worker turnover can affect the program's pro cess. Program staff should develop a contingency plan when an outreach worker position is vacant to ensure that client services are not disrupted and that client refer rals are processed according to program policies. Projects that do not have a contingency plan will experience dif ficulty maintaining contact with active intervention cli ents and will have a waiting list for referrals.

OJJDP Comprehensive Gang Model Core Strategy: Social Intervention Critical Elements

- Youth-serving agencies, schools, grassroots groups, faith-based and other organizations provide social services to gang youth and youth at high risk of gang involvement as identified through street outreach and driven by the problem assessment findings.
- Social intervention is directed to the target youth indi-vidually and not primarily to the gang as a unit, al though understanding and sensitivity to gang structure and "system" are essential to influencing individual gang youth and providing effective intervention.
- All key organizations located in the target area are encouraged to make needed services and facilities available to gang youth and youth at high risk of gang involvement.
- Targeted youth (and their families) are provided with a variety of services that assist them to adopt prosocial values and to access services that will meet their social, educational, and vocational needs. Mental health ser vices are a critical ingredient.
- Street outreach is established to focus on core gang youth and later on high-risk youth, with special capacity to reach both nonadjudicated and adjudicated youth.
- The primary focus of street outreach services is ensuring safety while remaining aware of and linking youth and families to educational preparation, prevocational or vocational training, job development, job referral, parent training, mentoring, family counseling, drug treatment, tattoo removal, and other services in appropriate ways.
- Outreach activities such as recreation and arts are carefully arranged so as not to become a primary focus but a means to establish interpersonal relationships, develop trust, and provide access to opportunities and other essential resources or services.
- In-school and afterschool prevention and education programs such as Gang Resistance Education and Training (G.R.E.A.T.), anti-bullying, peer mediation, tutoring, and others are offered within the target area(s), as are community programs to educate parents, businesses, and service providers.

HIGHLIGHTS FROM THE FIELD—INTERVENTION TEAM

Richmond, VA. At the beginning of the GRP project, the project coordinator recognized that many organizations had come together on the team that were not used to sharing information or strategizing together. Professional bonds and the ability to communicate across agencies have been strengthened through the collaborative process, which resulted in the free exchange of information between organizations. The project has recognized and responded to the growing Hispanic population of the target area by providing culturally appropriate activities to that population. The Richmond intervention team has recommended funding for more than 50 programs, many of which can be used as referral sources to the intervention team.

Los Angeles, CA. Establishing policies and procedures, such as an information sharing protocol, helped to clearly define members' roles and boundaries, which facilitated the team's functioning. Establishing individual relationships among team members by participating in team trainings and team retreats helps build rapport and trust among members, which in turn helps the functioning of the entire team.

Riverside, CA. Information shared by outreach workers and probation during intervention team meetings helped provide missing links in investigations or follow-up with cases. The team also worked together to identify gaps in services and participated in joint staff training that focused on how to work effectively with gang-involved youth.

Pittsburgh, PA. The team was able to bring together representatives from law enforcement, probation, and outreach, along with school representatives, from agencies that had a long history of distrust and hostility. The relationships of mutual respect established by the intervention team led to widespread support among participating agencies.

Table 2. Comparison of Advantages and Disadvantages of Internal Versus Contract Outreach

Lead Agency	Advantages	Disadvantages
Outreach Staff Employed by Lead Agency	Greater COntrOl and aCCOUntabIlItY OVer the JOb performance of outreach workers OPPOrtUnItIeS fOr IntenSIVe PrOfeSSIOnal development	ManY lead agenCIeS maY reSISt hIrIng IndIVIdUalS who have a criminal history OUtreaCh WOrKerS mUSt maIntaIn bOUndarIeS tO avoid being considered police informants OUtreaCh WOrKerS maY nOt haVe a StrOng COnneC tion to the community, and it may take time to develop these connections
Outreach Staff Employed by Contracted Entity	Often haVe a lOng-StandIng hIStOrY WOrKIng WIth high-risk populations in the community MaY have an existing client base that can be lever- aged for this program	SteerIng COmmIttee and/Or lead agenCY maY haVe less control over the job performance of outreach workers

HIGHLIGHTS FROM THE FIELD—OUTREACH STAFF

Los Angeles, CA. The Los Angeles GRP outreach provider provided a "one-stop shop" for job training and preparation, job placement, counseling, and case management. The outreach provider also partnered with the mentoring program working with prevention clients to complete a mural project. Successful intervention clients spoke to prevention clients about their experiences and ways to avoid similar pitfalls.

Richmond, VA. Richmond partnered with the high school located in the target area that was experiencing behavioral challenges with at-risk and gang- involved youth. The school allowed Richmond staff to conduct meetings and bring resources directly to the school. These resources included the outreach workers and mentors. Richmond staff's involvement in the school has led to ongoing conversations with State and private organizations to bring a free health clinic directly into the high school.

North Miami Beach, FL. Outreach staff in North Miami Beach were selected based on their professional experience and their ability to work with the Haitian population, the program's primary target population. In addition to staff being bilingual and having experience working with the Haitian population, they also provide support and education to program clients by facilitating participant self-help groups.

Pittsburgh, PA, and Houston, TX. Outreach workers for the Gang-Free Schools programs in Pittsburgh and Houston worked with law enforcement and school representatives to identify potentially volatile situations following violent incidents in the community, and to keep the peace on school campuses in the target area. Outreach workers routinely were involved in mediations between rival gangs in the target area and counseling with program clients.

Miami-Dade, FL. Outreach staff from the Miami- Dade Gang-Free Schools project identified families of program clients that were in need of food and basic assistance and built relationships with these families by providing gift baskets at the holidays and ongoing food delivery.

Law Enforcement Personnel

The selection of law enforcement personnel is crucial to the success of the program. Law enforcement officers se lected to work with the program should have:

- A strong connection with the community and the abil ity to build trusting relationships with community members, outreach workers, and other intervention team members.
- A clear understanding of the gang culture.
- The ability to communicate effectively with gang members.
- An understanding of the need for a comprehensive approach to address the gang problem.
- The respect of their peers, which may have a positive impact on the entire agency's perception of the program.

Program staff may face significant challenges initially en gaging law enforcement in the program. There may be historical distrust between law enforcement and other program partners. Staff may have to use unconventional strategies to initially engage law enforcement, such as providing overtime pay to conduct gang-crime analysis and to target and expand suppression strategies, recog nizing their participation, and bestowing awards.

Consistent representation from law enforcement agen cies is crucial to program success. This ensures that offi cers understand their roles, are familiar with program clients, and have established relationships with program partners. Some programs found that establishing a peri odic rotation for law enforcement representatives gave the program greater exposure within law enforcement agencies, resulting in an improvement in the agency's understanding and attitudes toward the program.

HIGHLIGHTS FROM THE FIELD—LAW ENFORCEMENT PERSONNEL

Los Angeles, CA. The Los Angeles GRP partnered with the Los Angeles Police Department CLEAR suppression program to participate on the intervention team. The project developed a simplified referral system using a "ticket book" for street patrol officers to make referrals to the project for youth and their families.

Richmond, VA. The Richmond GRP intervention team included sector patrol officers and gang unit representatives. The project partnered with the police department as they initiated a new gang unit by providing equipment, gang member tracking software, and arranging technical assistance from existing gang units in other communities to provide feedback and consultation. They supported overtime for directed patrol in high-risk areas of the target community.

Miami-Dade, FL. Using information provided by the intervention team, gang enforcement officers in the Miami-Dade Gang-Free Schools project adjusted schedules and officer coverage to address immediate gang-related issues in the community. As a result, gang incidents dropped substantially on and around school campuses in the target area.

THE COMPREHENSIVE GANG MODEL IN ACTION—OJJDP'S GANG REDUCTION PROGRAM MILWAUKEE, WISCONSIN

In 2004, the Milwaukee Gang Reduction Program was launched in the target area comprising three neighbor hoods located in the central area of the city: Metcalfe Park, Midtown, and Amani. The area is economically de pressed, with high unemployment and school dropout rates, and has a history of gang crime and violence, includ ing Chicago-influenced gangs. Several middle and elemen tary schools, including two charter schools, are located in the communities; however, many of the area students do not attend public school in the target area.

Prevention activities were a priority for the Milwaukee program, given the population and nature of the target area. Activities included:

- "Finding Paths to Prosperity"—a primary prevention program that included financial literacy.
- Truancy intervention.

- "Positive Alternatives to Violence"—afterschool career development program.
- Vocational life skills for youth ages 12–17 at risk of gang involvement.
- Parental support (first-time single mothers).
- Subsidized youth employment.
- Family empowerment program to help families with high-risk youth access health care.
- Behavioral health program targeted at youth with signs of early delinquency.
- Community mobilization to direct residents to programs.

Intervention and reentry activities were centered on a multidisciplinary team approach to case management for gang members. Street outreach was provided to recruit and SUPPOrt YOUth aSSIgned tO the team. The "WraP around Milwaukee" model, an identified best practice, was used to establish a service-vouchering system to support the multidisciplinary intervention team's services to clients. Service vouchers were available for training, counseling, skills training, or other identified needs that promote and including jsupport self-sufficiency, ncluding ob training and place ment and related concerns—such as tattoo removal and work attire—for gang members and those returning to the community from confinement.

Suppression activities were coordinated and tracked through a community prosecutor with the Milwaukee County District Attorney's Office and the Milwaukee Police Department officers assigned to the project. The community prosecutor coordinated prosecution decisions regarding gang-related and other crime and abatement procedures aimed at reducing crime. The community pros ecutor also coordinated a suppression team that targets gang leaders and habitually violent offenders for suppres sion activities. The Milwaukee Gang Reduction Program supported an information system with assistance from the local High Intensity Drug Trafficking Area to assist community prosecution in compiling and sharing gang intelligence among the local police district, the police department's gang intelligence unit, and other levels of local law enforcement. operations in spring 2007.

Selecting Program Activities

Selecting the appropriate program activities is an impor tant step to ensure program goals are achieved. Activities fall into four general categories—intervention, preven tion, suppression, and reentry.

Intervention Activities

The intervention team, especially the outreach workers, is a primary service-delivery mechanism in this comprehen sive approach. Some best practices include the following:

- Intervention team members should review each client at referral; obtain consents to serve the client; perform an intake evaluation (one or more members can be assigned to this task); and then, as a team, discuss the client's needs and issues and brainstorm together to create an appropriate intervention plan for each client.

- If referrals to services at specific agencies will be made by the team, the agency receiving the referral needs to follow up with the team to provide updated informa tion on the client's behavior and participation. Service providers need to be readily accessible and culturally competent and should regularly participate in inter vention team meetings to ensure that they can pro vide client status updates and are aware of client service needs.
- Types of services that most teams will need to provide include employment assistance, vocational training, remedial/alternative education assistance, group coun seling, individual counseling, substance abuse services, mentoring, and services for families (such as support groups and/or parenting classes).
- It is important to clearly outline the roles and responsibilities of each member of the team, as well as rulesabout information sharing prior to accepting clients.
- Setting a consistent meeting place, time, and day of the week will help to ensure regular participation by key agencies. Another strategy to ensure that the meeting does not go past the scheduled end time is to establish a client rotation schedule.

Highlights From The Field—Intervention Activities

Richmond, VA. The most successful programs were those that were either offered directly in the target area or where transportation was provided. Even though Richmond has public transportation, the community readily engaged with groups that brought services to them. An example is the One- Stop Resource Center, which is located in the middle of an apartment complex with more than 4,000 residents. Many of Richmond's programs are housed in the center, including a free health clinic and computer lab for area youth.

Los Angeles, CA. The GRP program's outreach provider is a well-respected and established service provider within the target community. The provider offers the majority of the project's intervention services, including job readiness, job placement, counseling, and case management services.

Riverside, CA. The intervention team created services that did not exist previously. They established a job training program for clients that covered topics such as how to fill out job applications, how to conduct an interview, and appropriate interpersonal skills on the job site.

Houston, TX. Good communication and trust building with clients and their families were the biggest factors to successfully targeting gang members and at-risk youth. Providing the services directly and

through referrals to other agencies showed the clients that the project staff were serious about offering help.

Miami-Dade, FL. Miami-Dade created an on-the-job training program by partnering with a local home- builder. With the assistance of school personnel and outreach staff, this program provided an incentive to engage youth from the target area in gaining needed job skills, improving social interactions, and boosting school attendance.

PREVENTION ACTIVITIES

Even if their initial strategies did not include prevention, most comprehensive gang programs have eventually in corporated prevention programming. These prevention strategies should have a direct connection to the prob lems identified in the assessment process (and through ongoing data collection) and also should be specific to gang issues to accomplish the desired effect of reducing gang violence. Primary prevention strategies focus on the entire population in communities. Secondary prevention strategies are activities and services targeted to youth ages 7–14 who are at high risk of joining gangs.

Primary prevention activities undertaken by these initia tives have included conducting workshops and trainings to increase community awareness about gangs, hosting communitywide events, and working to change conditions contributing to gang involvement within the tar geted community. Targeted prevention activities successfully utilized by these types of initiatives have in cluded tutoring, mentoring, and afterschool care.

Secondary prevention programming is often focused on the families, siblings, or associates of intervention clients. The steering committee may also identify the need to increase access to secondary prevention programming or to expand the types of services available after program implementation begins as a result of gaps in services, ex tended service waiting periods, and changes in commu nity dynamics. To avoid duplication, a survey of existing resources should be undertaken to identify available pre vention activities and services.

Just as with intervention programming, both primary and secondary prevention service providers must understand the gang culture and possess experience working with at- risk youth and their families.

OJJDP COMPREHENSIVE GANG MODEL CORE STRATEGY: SUPPRESSION CRITICAL ELEMENTS

- There are formal and informal social control procedures and accountability measures, including close supervision or monitoring of gang youth by agencies of the crimi nal and juvenile justice systems, and also by community- based agencies, schools, and grassroots groups.
- Gang suppression or control is structurally related to community- and problem-oriented policing and to gang enforcement and tactical units.
- Police administration and police officers on the inter vention team assume key roles in the development and implementation of important aspects of the program, not only through suppression but through gang preven tion, social intervention, and community mobilization.
- Gang crime data collection and analysis (i.e., crime anal ysis) are established to accurately and reliably assess the gang problem and its changes over time. Definitions of gang-related incidents, gangs, and gang members are maintained. Gang intelligence is routinely collected and analyzed. It is also highly desirable to have gang crime data geo-coded and analyzed, preferably using auto mated "hotspot" mapping techniques.

- Police contact with targeted youth is regularly and ap propriately quantified, shared, and discussed with other members of the intervention team for purposes of team planning and collaboration. Contacts should be gener ally consistent with the philosophy of community and problem-oriented policing.
- Aggregate-level data bearing on the gang problem are regularly shared with all components of the project, particularly the steering committee.
- Professional respect and appropriate collaboration be tween police and outreach workers and other team members are essential.
- Tactical, patrol, drug/vice, community policing, and youth division units that have contact with targeted youth and gang members provide support to the inter vention team through information sharing and mutual collaboration and support.
- Targeted enforcement operations, when and where necessary, are consistent with program goals and are coordinated with the intervention team to have the maximum impact.

Highlights from the Field—Prevention Activities

Richmond, VA. Through meetings with community representatives, project staff learned that there was a need for a number of programs that ultimately led to the funding of more than 50 programs. For example, community members identified the need for longer afterschool hours and options for summer activities. The project expanded their partnership with Boys and Girls Clubs, and also entered into a partnership with the faith-based Richmond Outreach Center to provide additional activities and longer hours. A viable One-Stop Office has been a key part of integrating services to clients. The ability of the Office of the Attorney General to reach out to all partners and successfully communicate the overall goals of the project has contributed to successfully integrating services for clients.

Miami-Dade, FL. The main prevention efforts were a direct response to a student survey that asked students what would keep them from getting involved in gang activities. The response was "something to do or a job." The project designed an on-the-job training program that has been a main draw for students. The greatest success of the on-the-job training component of the project was the resulting level of pride and commitment that the youth showed while participating in the program. This component provides long-term effects and knowledge that the youth can use for career advancement and entrepreneurship.

Houston, TX. Gang awareness presentations resulted in more calls from residents to report suspected gang-related crime according to reports from police.

Suppression/Social Control Activities

Suppression in these comprehensive programs goes beyond law enforcement activities. Ideally, all program partners work together to hold the targeted youth ac countable when necessary. Law enforcement's role in these programs includes:

- Ongoing crime data analysis.

- A high level of information sharing between agencies and across disciplines.
- Participation in the intervention team and steering committee.
- Suppression activities tailored to address specific gang- related problems.
- Apprising other intervention team members of unsafe situations.

Gang crime data should drive gang suppression strategies used in the target community and should also be respon sive to the local community, the intervention team, and the steering committee. These strategies should be viewed as part of a larger whole, rather than as singular, one-time-only activities.

Some examples of successful suppression strategies include:

- Participating in joint police/probation activities, includ ing conducting probation searches of the homes and vehicles of gang-involved probationers.
- Targeting enforcement to the times, places, and events where data analysis and historic gang enforcement patterns indicate gangs are active.
- Designing investigative strategies to address specific gang-related crimes.
- Executing directed patrols of locations where gang members congregate.
- Conducting community forums to address incidents.
- Establishing community prosecution and/or vertical prosecution strategies to prosecute gang crime more effectively.
- Making informal contacts with targeted youth and their families.

Program partners should work together with law en forcement to enforce community norms for youth behav ior. These activities may be used in concert with suppression strategies to address less serious antisocial, gang-related behavior. Examples of ways that other part ner agencies can assist with suppressing gang activity include:

- Use of in- and out-of-school suspensions, when needed.
- Tracking and reporting of attendance/grades.
- Tracking of program participation.
- Being aware of and supporting conditions of probation/parole.
- Reinforcing program requirements and supporting other programs' rules.

In the best programs, suppression is integrated with services. Even outreach workers play a significant role in addressing negative behaviors with program clients and requiring accountability.

Reentry Activities

Reentry within these comprehensive programs is often handled as an overlapping function with intervention. Because gang-involved individuals are almost constantly entering or leaving one system or another, and because many of them are frequently incarcerated for brief periods of time, intervention clients are generally served during incarceration through regular contacts and pre release planning.

Program staff should develop a policy for serving clients who become incarcerated during the program. The length and location of incarceration may affect the pro gram's ability to maintain contact and services to a client. In general, clients serving sentences of less than 6 months to 1 year should receive at least monthly contacts from outreach workers or other team members—face-to-face or by e-mail or telephone. The intervention team may consider closing the cases of clients serving long-term sentences, but it should remember that any contact with a client during incarceration may have a positive impact.

Beyond maintaining intervention clients, it is recom mended that the program be aware of the influence of incarcerated gang members returning to the community and develop policies to address these individuals. For in stance, the program may want to establish a relationship with probation/parole authorities, and also with correc tions personnel, to identify gang members who are due to be released. Outreach staff can visit these inmates pri or to release to help develop a supportive plan for their return to the community and to recruit them. into the program.

Common needs for clients reentering the community in clude housing, drug and alcohol treatment, and job train ing and placement. Especially critical are job training and placement opportunities for convicted offenders, and programs should consider ways to make these opportuni ties economically feasible for both intervention and reen try clients. Transportation assistance that addresses safety issues for these clients is also important.

Probation/parole representatives who serve on the inter vention team can also ensure that clients receive needed services and supervision. Probation and parole officers are familiar with reentry services within the community and can educate the team members on available services. Programs may want to augment existing services in com munities where reentry programs are inadequate for the target population or are scarce.

HIGHLIGHTS FROM THE FIELD—SUPPRESSION/SOCIAL CONTROL ACTIVITIES

Richmond, VA. The directed patrol program used crime statistics and crime data logs to determine high crime days and times in the target area. Additional foot, bicycle, motorcycle, and walking officers were added during those times. This resulted in a significant decrease in crime during those periods. During the funded periods, Richmond dropped from being the 5th most dangerous city to the 15th. More recently, it has dropped to 29th.

Riverside, CA. Any proposed suppression strategies were discussed at the intervention team meeting and brought to the attention of the steering committee for their guidance and approval.

North Miami Beach, FL. North Miami Beach partnered with the local police department to implement directed patrols and the continuation of a truancy interdiction program.

Houston, TX. The law enforcement and criminal justice partnership assisted in providing more visibility and presence of gang unit officers to deter youth on probation from committing more crimes. The police improved their gang intelligence process through getting to know youth and families on a personal level and interaction with other criminal justice agencies. This strategy also helped prevent gang shootings or fights around schools and parks. Police initially started out with a "suppression only" mentality, but soon understood the benefits of establishing a relationship with gang members that would then lead to information that could help solve or prevent crimes.

Miami-Dade, FL. Changes were made to the field interview cards officers used to more effectively capture gang information and gang crime data. This change was a result of the direction of the steering committee's leadership and their commitment to communicate with law enforcement

HIGHLIGHTS FROM THE FIELD—REENTRY ACTIVITIES

Houston, TX. Outreach workers in Houston maintained regular contact with incarcerated clients, and developed prerelease case management plans to help individuals transition back into the community.

Richmond, VA. Richmond funds two programs with two agencies to provide offender reentry programs to inmates prior to release back into the community. These programs help incarcerated youth deal with issues such as completion of high school education, drug and alcohol abuse, and family and parenting issues. In addition, Richmond has partnered with faith-based programs that offer residential programs for reentering offenders.

SUSTAINING THE PROGRAM

Programs should begin planning for long-term sustain- ability during the initial stages of implementation. Pro grams that were sustained long-term had two key practices. First, they standardized and institutionalized data collection to show program outcomes. Access to these data was invaluable for leveraging funds and resources. Second, these programs utilized strong and engaged steering committees that shared ownership and responsibility for the programs among the key agencies. The importance of these two factors in sustaining multi-agency programs cannot be overstated.

Other successful strategies included:

- Participating in statewide efforts to further develop anti-gang strategies backed by Federal and State funds. Programs that can demonstrate positive out comes and that have a good reputation in the target community are more likely to be funded as a part of larger efforts.
- Seeking the local business community's support for specific elements of the program such as the interven tion team, outreach staff, or specific prevention programs.
- Pursuing commitments from key agencies to dedicate staff time to the project prior to implementation through the use of MOUs or letters of commitment.
- Leveraging funds from other agencies or planning for the program to be absorbed within an established agency.

- Requiring sustainability planning from contracted agencies. This may enable program partners to iden tify resources to sustain that element of the program after the original funding expires.

Table 4. Timeline for Implementing a Comprehensive Gang Program

This timeline provides a general idea of the activities in each phase and, based on experiences of other comprehensive projects, the approximate length of time it takes to complete the activities in each phase. Each community's administrative structure and practices, community politics, and community readiness will dictate the actual length of each phase.

Assessment and Planning (6–12 months) • Identify key stake holders. • Form a steering committee. • Establish gang definitions. • Hire a project coordinator. • Solicit a research partner. • Conduct a comprehensive community assessment (including the community resource inventory).	• Provide gang awareness training to project service providers. • Develop a community resource referral and feedback process. • Develop a program referral process. • Train project partners on the project referral process. • Develop a data collection and analysis system.
Capacity Building (3–6 months) • Complete the contract procurement process for program services. • Develop program policies and procedures. • Advertise, hire, and train new staff to provide services. • Develop a client referral and recruitment process. • Select intervention team members. • Conduct intervention team training.	Full Implementation (12–18 months) • Initiate program services. • Initiate client referral process. • Begin client intake process for prevention and intervention clients. • Begin conducting client reviews during intervention team meetings. • Begin providing focused suppression efforts. • Begin conducting community prevention activities. • Reach program caseload capacity.

See table 4 for a timeline that provides a general idea of the activities in each phase and, based on experiences of other comprehensive projects, the approximate length of time it takes to complete the activities in each phase. Each community's administrative structure and practices, community politics, and community readiness will dictate the actual length of each phase.

See "Implementation Tools" for a list of publications,tools, and other resources to help communities assess their gang problems, develop implementation plans for addressing gang problems and establish intervention teams, plan strategies for reaching out to and interven ing to change the risky behaviors of gang-involved youth, and develop management information systems for cap turing program referral and individual client and contact data. Many of these resources can be customized for indi vidual communities.

HIGHLIGHTS FROM THE FIELD—SUSTAINING THE PROGRAM

Los Angeles, CA. The mayor has identified six additional zones to implement the comprehensive anti-gang model. The mayor's Office of Gang Reduction and Youth Development was created and a deputy mayor was chosen to oversee the city's gang prevention, intervention, and reentry efforts.

Richmond, VA. Richmond has hosted meetings on sustainability for its service providers in partnership with the Department of Justice. Most of the organizations providing services through funding have agreed to sustain their programs beyond the funded period. Richmond's staff is committed to seeking out private and foundation funding to continue to sustain other programs as needed. Richmond has also been asked to share the OJJDP Model with other jurisdictions across the Virginia Commonwealth.

North Miami Beach, FL. North Miami Beach incorporated as a nonprofit entity after Federal funds were exhausted. Incorporating as a nonprofit allows the project to apply for grants they would not have been eligible for under a state agency.

Miami-Dade, FL. The strong level of support for the project from agencies on the steering committee led to the project being sustained by existing agencies once Federal funding was exhausted.

IMPLEMENTATION TOOLS

A Guide to Assessing Your Community's Youth Gang Problem contains a blueprint for conducting an indepth assessment of the gang problem in the community and tools for the assessment process. It describes the data vari ables, sources of data, and data-collection instruments. It also provides suggestions on how to organize and analyze the data and guidelines for preparation of an assessment report that will present the results of the data-collection effort. For users' convenience, individual chapters or the entire document can be downloaded at http://www.iir. com/nygc/acgp/assessment.htm.

Planning for Implementation provides a guide to develop ment of an implementation plan for comprehensive gang programs. It also describes the work of an intervention team, including street outreach workers' roles. For users' convenience, individual chapters or the entire document can be downloaded at http://www.iir.com/nygc/acgp/ implementation.htm.

Strategic Planning Tool—This electronic tool was devel oped to assist in assessing a community's gang problem and planning strategies to deal with it and can be found at www.iir.com/nygc/tool. The tool has four nterrelated components. The "Planning and Implementation,"

"Risk Factors," and "Program Matrix" components provide information for all communities, but the "Community Resource Inventory" component can be customized for any community.

Helping America's Youth Community Guide—This Commu nity Guide steers community representatives through key steps in forming partnerships and in providing customized strategic planning tools and informational resources to

enhance youth serving efforts. It provides information about programs that successfully deal with risky behaviors and can be found at http://guide.helpingamericasyouth.gov/programtool.cfm. Programs can replicate these strate gies to meet their local needs. The Program Tool database contains risk factors, protective factors, and programs that have been evaluated and found to work.

Client Track—This free management information system was developed by the National Youth Gang Center to assist comprehensive programs with capturing client and referral data. The Access-based database captures program referral information, individual client data (including a detailed intake assessment), program service data, contacts with clients by length and agency, and intervention plans. It is available on compact disc upon request from the National Youth Gang Center.

NOTES

1 The five survey questions were: (1) What are your units' or organizations' goals and objectives in regard to the gang problem? (2) What has your department (or unit) done that you feel has been particularly successful in dealing with gangs? (3) What has your department (or unit) done that you feel has been least effective in dealing with gangs? (4) What do you think are the five best ways of dealing with the gang problem that are employed by your department or organization? and, (5) What activities do gang or special personnel perform in dealing with the problem?

2 Individuals and collective factors were identified as having community mobilization as a strategy based on their use of one or more goals and/or activities from a list of options in Spergel's research that led to formulation of the Comprehensive Gang Model. For example, any strategy that attempted to create community solidarity, education, and involvement was viewed as using community mobilization strategies. Prevention efforts involving multiple agencies were treated as community mobilization. All references to meetings with community leaders and attending meetings of community associations were regarded as reflecting a community organization strategy. Networking was considered the most basic community mobilization strategy as long as networks were not restricted exclusively to justice system agencies. Creating networks of law enforcement agencies only was classified as another strategy: suppression. Advocacy for victims was subsumed under the community mobilization strategy when the programs attempted to integrate offenders back into the community or to repair relations between victims and offenders. Victim advocacy was labeled suppression when the program was clearly a strategy of crime control.

ACKNOWLEDGMENTS

In 2002, President George W. Bush directed Federal Executive branch agencies to undertake a review of programs and resources available to disadvantaged youth and families. The final report of the White House Task Force for Disadvantaged Youth included several recommendations to increase support to needy children and families and to reduce duplication and waste so that more resources would become available. The Task Force also recommended expanding collaborative efforts among Federal agencies to improve service delivery and increase efficiency. Under the Department's leadership, the Office of Juvenile Justice and Delinquency Prevention (OJJDP) began an aggressive and intensive pilot program in 2003 to test the effectiveness of the Comprehensive Gang Model developed by Dr. Irving Spergel and his colleagues at the University of Chicago.

OJJDP's Gang Reduction Program (GRP) is the work of many people and colleagues at OJJDP, the National Youth Gang Center, and prosecutors, police, and community leaders at every level of government. Moving from theory to practice, however, cannot be done without the assistance of key individuals. OJJDP wishes to thank William B. Woodruff, former OJJDP Deputy Administrator, for his early leadership on the GRP; Phelan Wyrick, Ph.D., OJJDP's first Gang Program Coordinator; Bobby Kipper, Esther Welch, and Mark Fero, who, as part of the GRP leadership team under Virginia Attorneys General Jerry Kilgore and Bob McDonnell, took a vision and brought it to life in Richmond, VA; Los Angeles Gang Coordinator Mildred Martinez, who has helped lead changes under Mayors Hahn and Villaraigosa; and Governors Jeb Bush of Florida and of Jim Doyle of Wisconsin, whose willingness to support this program made it possible to see progress and learn important lessons in North Miami Beach and Milwaukee.

REFERENCES

Howell, J.C. (1994). Recent gang research: Program and policy implications. Crime and Delinquency 40(4):495–515.

Spergel, I.A. (1990). Strategies and perceived agency effectiveness in dealing with the youth gang problem. In C.R. Huff (ed.), Gangs in America (pp. 288–309). Newbury Park, CA: Sage Publications, Inc.

Spergel, I.A. (1991). Youth Gangs: Problem and Response. Washington, DC: U.S. Department of Justice, Office of Justice Programs, Office of Juvenile Justice and Delinquency Prevention.

Spergel, I.A. (1995). The Youth Gang Problem. New York, NY: Oxford University Press.

Spergel, I.A., Chance, R., Ehrensaft, C., Regulus, T., Kane, C., and Laseter, R. (1992). Technical Assistance Manuals: National Gang Suppression and Intervention Program. Chicago, IL: University of Chicago, School of Social Service Administration.

Spergel, I.A., Chance, R., Ehrensaft, C., Regulus, T., Kane, C., Laseter, R., Alexander, A., and Oh, S. (1994). Gang Suppression and Intervention: Community Models. Washington, DC: U.S. Department of Justice, Office of Justice Programs, Office of Juvenile Justice and Delinquency Prevention.

Spergel, I.A., and Curry, G.D. (1993). The national youth gang survey: A research and development process. In A. Goldstein and C.R. Huff (eds.), The Gang Intervention Handbook (pp. 359–400). Champaign, IL: Research Press.

Spergel, I.A., Curry, G.D., Chance, R., Kane, C., Ross, R., Alexander, A., Simmons, E., and Oh, S. (1994). Gang Suppression and Intervention: Problem and Response, Washington, DC: U.S. Department of Justice, Office of Justice Programs, Office of Juvenile Justice and Delinquency Prevention.

Tatem-Kelley, B. (1994). A Comprehensive Response to America's Gang Problem. Washington, DC: U.S. Department of Justice, Office of Justice Programs, Office of Juvenile Justice and Delinquency Prevention.

APPENDIX A: DEMONSTRATION AND TESTING OF THE COMPREHENSIVE GANG MODE

Throughout the development and implementation of the Comprehensive Gang Model, OJJDP has attempted to evaluate the effectiveness of the Model through a variety of demonstration initiatives. Evaluation findings from these initiatives are presented here.

LITTLE VILLAGE IMPLEMENTATION OF THE COMPREHENSIVE GANG MODEL

With funding that the U.S. Department of Justice (Violence in Urban Areas Program) provided in March 1993, Spergel began implementing the initial version of the Comprehensive Gang Model in the Little Village neighborhood of Chicago, a low-income and working-class community that is approximately 90 percent Mexican- American (Spergel, 2007). Called the Gang Violence Reduction Program, the project lasted 5 years. The program targeted and provided services to individual gang members (rather than to the gangs as groups). It targeted mainly older members (ages 17–24) of two of the area's most violent Hispanic gangs, the Latin Kings and the Two Six. Specifically, the Little Village program targeted more than 200 of the "shooters" (i.e., the influential members or leaders of the two gangs). As a whole, these two gangs accounted for about 75 percent of felony gang violence in the Little Village community—including 12 homicides in each of the 2 years before the start of project operations (Spergel, Wa, and Sosa, 2006).

The primary goal of the project was to reduce the extremely high level of gang violence among youth who were already involved in the two gangs. Outreach youth workers—virtually all of whom were former members of the two target gangs—attempted to prevent and control gang conflicts in specific situations and to persuade gang youth to leave the gang as soon as possible. Drug-related activity was not specifically targeted. Instead, outreach activities included a balance of services, such as crisis intervention, brief family and individual counseling and referrals for services, and surveillance and suppression activities. (Spergel, Wa, and Sosa, 2006).

As seen in table A1 (page 43), the process evaluation of the Gang Violence Reduction Program (Spergel, Wa, and Sosa, 2006) revealed that it was implemented very well.

Altogether it achieved an "excellent" rating on the following 8 (of 18) program implementation characteristics: interagency/street (intervention) team coordination, criminal justice participation, lead agency project management and commitment to the model, social and crisis intervention and outreach work, suppression, targeting (especially gang members), balance of services, and intensity of services.

Spergel (2006) examined the effects of the Little Village project on the approximately 200 hardcore gang youth targeted for services during the period in which they were served by the program. The following are some of his findings:

- •Self-reports of criminal involvement showed that the program reduced serious violent and property crimes, and the frequency of various types of offenses including robbery, gang intimidation, and drive-by shootings.
- The program was more effective with older, more violent gang offenders than with younger, less violent offenders.
- Active gang involvement was reduced among project youth, mostly for older members, and this change was associated with less criminal activity.
- Most youth in both targeted gangs improved their educational and employment status during the program period.
- Employment was associated with a general reduction in youth's criminal activity, especially in regard to reductions in drug dealing.
- Spergel (2006) next compared arrests among project youth versus two control groups, one that received minimal services, and the other that received no services from project workers. This comparison revealed the following:
- Program youth had significantly fewer total violent- crime and drug arrests.
- The project had no significant effect on total arrests, property arrests, or other minor crime arrests.

Because the Little Village project specifically targeted the most violent gangsters and the common presumption is that such youth are typically drug involved, Spergel examined program effects on subgroups of offenders with violence and drug involvement and with violence and no drug involvement, using the comparison groups. Program effects were strong for both of these groups, but slightly stronger for the violence and no-drug subsample.

Spergel (2006) also compared communitywide effects of the project on arrests in Little Village versus other nearby communities with high rates of gang crime. His analysis compared arrests in the periods before and during which the program was implemented and revealed the following:

- The project was less effective in its overall impact on the behavior of the target gangs as a whole, that is, changing the entrenched pattern of gangbanging and gang crime among the target gangs than in reducing crime among targeted members. Gang violence was on the upswing during the project period (1992–1 997) in this general area of Chicago—one of the deadliest gang-violence areas of the city—but the increase in homicides and other serious violent gang crimes was lower among the Latin Kings and Two Six compared with the other Latino and African-American gangs in the area.

- Similarly, the increase in serious violent gang crimes was lower in Little Village than in all other comparable communities. Residents and representatives of various organizations perceived a significant reduction in overall gang crime and violence in Little Village during the program period.

In summary, although the outcomes for the Little Village project are mixed, the results are consistent for violent crimes across analyses at all three impact levels: (1) individual, (2) group (gang), and (3) community (especially in the views of residents). A similar impact was not seen on gang drug activity, although drug selling was reduced among older gang members when the project helped them get jobs. Given that the project targeted gang violence, not drug activity, this result was not completely unexpected.

The evaluation suggested that a youth outreach (or social intervention) strategy may be more effective in reducing the violent behavior of younger, less violent, gang youth. A combined youth outreach and police suppression strategy might be more effective with older, more criminally active and violent gang youth, particularly with respect to drug-related crimes. The best indicators of reduced total offenses were older age, association with probation officers, and spending more time with a wife or steady girlfriend. The best predictors of reduced violent offenses were a youth's avoidance of gang situations, satisfaction with the community, and more exposure to treatment for personal problems.

Interactive and collaborative project outreach worker efforts, combining suppression, social support, and provision of social services, were shown to be most effective in changing criminal involvement of gang members. Larger program dosages (multiple providers and greater frequency and duration of services) proved to be important and were associated with reduced levels of arrests for violent crimes. Four types of services or sanctions predicted successful outcomes among program youth: suppression (particularly by police), job referrals by youth outreach workers, school referrals (mainly by outreach youth workers), and program dosage (contacts by all workers together).

Initial Demonstration Sites

In the first of its initiatives, OJJDP competitively selected five sites that demonstrated the capacity to implement the Comprehensive Gang Model: Mesa, AZ; Riverside, CA; Bloomington-Normal, IL; San Antonio, TX; and Tucson, AZ. Each of these projects was funded in 1995, and OJJDP anticipated that these sites would be funded for 4 or 5 years and would adopt the two main goals of the Model:

- To reduce youth gang crime, especially violent crime, in targeted communities.
- To improve the capacity of the community, including its institutions and organizations, to prevent, intervene against, and suppress the youth gang problem through the targeted application of interrelated strategies of community mobilization, social intervention, provision of opportunities, organizational change and development, and suppression.

OJJDP emphasized the five strategies in the implementation process described above. Brief descriptions of each of the projects follow.

The target area for the Mesa Gang Intervention Project, coordinated by the City of Mesa Police Department, was defined by the service areas of two junior high schools that were home to approximately 18 gangs with an estimated 650 members. The project intervention team comprised the project director, a case management coordinator, two gang detectives, one adult and three juvenile probation officers, two outreach workers, and a youth intervention specialist—all of whom were housed in a central location in the target area. The project team used a case-management approach to ensure that progress was made with each youth in accordance with an intervention plan. Gang detectives and probation officers held program youth accountable through surveillance and routine monitoring and support, while outreach workers and staff from community-based agencies ensured delivery of services such as counseling, job referrals, drug and alcohol treatment, and other social services.

In general, both program and comparison youth reduced their average levels of arrests (and self-reported offenses). However, program youth had an 18-percent greater reduction in total arrests than comparison youth (Spergel, Wa, and Sosa, 2005a). The reduction in total arrests was greater for the oldest age group (18-year-olds and older) and the youngest age group (12- to 14-year-olds) than it was for 15- to 17-year-olds. Females in the program showed a significantly greater reduction in arrests than did males.

Project success was also evident at the program area level. Total incidents of crime that youth typically committed (including violent, property, and drug-related crimes and status offenses) declined 10 percent more in the program area than in the average of the three comparison areas. Furthermore, the program was more effective with gang youth who frequented the target area as compared with program gang youth who associated with gangs in the comparison areas.

The evaluators observed that the Mesa Gang Intervention Project did not incorporate all of the elements of the Comprehensive Gang Model in program development, particularly the use of outreach workers in the neighborhood and collaboration with grassroots organizations (Spergel, Wa, and Sosa, 2005a).

The program evaluators identified the major factor that contributed to the project's success as highly skilled community and lead agency staff who were committed to a balanced social intervention and control approach, particularly the provision of social intervention services to moderately delinquent, nonviolent, and at-risk youth (Spergel, Wa, and Sosa, 2005a). However, the evaluators noted that the program should have included more seriously delinquent youth in the target group.

Riverside Building Resources for the Intervention and Deterrence of Gang Engagement

Officials changed the original name of the Riverside (California) Comprehensive Gang Model to Building Resources for the Intervention and Deterrence of Gang Engagement (BRIDGE) in 1999 and focused its 5-year (1995–2000) operation on two areas of the city with high rates of gang crime—Eastside and Arlanza (Burch and Kane, 1999; Spergel, Wa, and Sosa, 2005b). A steering committee that consisted of public, private, grassroots, and faith-based organizations guided the project. The project director and the steering committee shifted the project focus to the development of an intervention team to deal directly with gang youth referred by the Riverside County Juvenile Probation Department. Reducing incidents of youth gang violence became the main program goal. Gang-involved youth ages 12–22 years old in the two communities were targeted for intervention.

Formation of an intervention team was a key factor in the success of the program (Spergel, Wa, and Sosa, 2005b). The intervention team consisted of several core members, including the project coordinator, police officers, probation and parole officers, the outreach worker, the social service provider, and others. In daily meetings, the team shared information that provided opportunities for intervention with project youth. Case management involved the development and implementation of a treatment plan by the intervention team. Eligible clients had to meet several criteria: being a known gang member, residing in or engaging in gang activity within the target area, having a history of violence, and warranting intensive supervision by police and probation working as a team. Police and probation officers made home visits, performed area surveillance, made arrests, and maintained other controls on project youth.

The project effectively reduced arrests for both serious and nonserious violent crimes after program participation and in comparison with a control group (Spergel, Wa, and Sosa, 2005b). Program youth also had fewer repeat drug arrests. The largest reduction in total violent crime arrests occurred when probation officers, police officers, outreach workers, and job and school personnel integ rated their services for youth. Total services—that is, a combination of individual counseling, job services, school-related services, suppression activities, family counseling, group services, and material services—accounted for much of the reduction in arrests. Youth who received services for 2 years or more showed the greatest reductions in number of arrests. However, there was no evidence that the project reduced either program youth's involvement in gangs or the size of gang membership in the project area.

Bloomington-Normal Comprehensive Gang Program

This project included all of Bloomington and Normal, IL, in its target area, where eight gangs with 640 members were located. These twin cities are centrally located within the State in McLean County, midway between Chicago and St. Louis. (Burch and Kane, 1999; Spergel, Wa, and Sosa, 2005c). The lead agency was Project Oz, a youth-serving organization with many years of experience meeting the social service needs of youth and families. The Community Youth Liaison Council (formerly the Bloomington Mayor's 1990 Task Force to Study Gangs) served as the project's steering committee. Key day-to-day management staff and personnel included the

project director, the project coordinator, the crime analyst and, to some extent at the beginning, the local evaluator. These central figures operated largely within the framework of perspectives, intentions, and interests of the Community Youth Liaison Council and its principal constituent organizations. Gang-suppression tactics were given the highest priority by the Bloomington-Normal gang program.

The program evaluation concluded that the Bloomington-Normal gang program did not follow the Comprehensive Gang Model. The evaluators found that the program focused extensively on suppression and failed to implement several key components of the Model:

It emphasized a suppression approach. It did not include grassroots groups, and did not develop an adequate outreach worker approach. Little attention was paid to an appropriate mix of strategies for different youth, to the modification of the roles of the different types of workers, and to how different agency workers were to function together to create an improved, interorganizational, street-level-worker structure and process to meet the interests and needs of gang youth, and the needs of the community, within the framework of the Model. (Spergel, Wa, and Sosa, 2005c, pp. 14–15, 17)

In summary, the evaluators found that, when appropriate statistical controls were used, the program had no effect in steering individual youth away from gangs and delinquency, as compared with similar youth in the comparison site (Spergel, Wa, and Sosa, 2005c). Rather, the program was associated with an increase in arrests for program youth, particularly those without prior arrest records. However, there was evidence (based on self-reports) that parts of the program were useful in reducing subsequent offenses for certain youth.

San Antonio Gang Rehabilitation, Assessment, and Support Program

The target community of the San Antonio (Texas) Gang Rehabilitation, Assessment, and Services Program (GRAASP), located on the outer limits of the southwest side of the city, was home to 15 gangs with an estimated 1,664 members. The program area initially included three small neighborhoods (Burch and Kane, 1999; Spergel, Wa, and Sosa, 2005d). The San Antonio Police Department was the lead agency. The project coordinator, outreach staff, and job developer operated out of a project office near the target area. Street-based outreach workers assisted other social service agency employees, probation officers, a job developer, Texas Youth Commission staff, city police assigned to community policing and tactical units, and others to provide services, opportunities, and support to youth in the program, while also instituting sanctions, including arrest, for criminal or delinquent acts. Outreach workers met monthly to discuss coordination and case management.

A lack of management attention and oversight hindered efforts to establish an intervention team and provide outreach services (Spergel, Wa, and Sosa, 2005d). GRAASP focused on individual program youth (and to some extent their families) using a case-method approach. There was no structural or systematic means for providing services to, and establishing interrelated controls for, program youth. Coordination of services, if it occurred, was on an ad hoc basis, at the request of GRAASP outreach workers. It is likely that the absence of a significant GRAASP effect was because the police department, local agencies, and grassroots groups did not adequately support the Model.

The evaluators observed that the leadership may never have come to understand the nature of the Comprehensive Gang Model initiative and the structure required to develop and implement it in San Antonio (Spergel, Wa, and Sosa, 2005d). Unfortunately, the dimensions of San Antonio's gang problem were never specifically defined. Gang suppression strategies lacked a targeted focus.

GRAASP essentially became an outreach, social-service support program to gang-involved youth who were referred mainly by juvenile probation and parole officers. An integrated interagency approach to the gang problem that focused on provision of opportunities to gang members was needed but never developed. In the end, the limited efforts to meet the social-development and social- control needs of program youth were inadequate. Although arrest levels for program youth were generally lower than for comparison youth (except for drug arrests), none of the differences in arrest levels was statistically significant. The evaluators observed an increase in the total number of arrests was for both program and comparison youth.

Tucson Comprehensive Gang Program

The Tucson (Arizona) project focused on four neighborhoods where four main gangs with an estimated 350 members were located. The project operated from offices in a Boys & Girls Club in the target area. Street outreach workers, probation officers, a police gang unit officer, and others worked daily to provide youth with services and opportunities, to encourage youth to pursue constructive and positive activities, and to hold youth accountable for negative or criminal acts. Weekly meetings of the entire project team to review progress and reevaluate community needs supplemented weekly outreach staff meetings. The Our Town Family Center was designated as the lead agency, although its interest was limited largely to service delivery, and it had little experience in dealing with gang youth who were juvenile offenders (Spergel, Wa, and Sosa, 2005e).b

Key findings from the evaluation that compared outcomes for youth in the program with outcomes for a comparable group of unserved youth (and also compared outcomes among program youth) include the following:

- Although program youth showed a decrease in yearly total arrests versus nonprogram youth, the difference was not statistically significant.
- There was less of an increase in arrests for serious violent crime for program youth than for comparisonyouth, but the difference was not statistically significant.
- The program may have decreased more yearly arrests among 15- and 16-year-olds than with the youngest age group (10- to 14-year-olds).
- Behavioral improvements among females involved in the program were marginally better than among program males. The researchers speculated that the greater number of contacts that outreach youth workers and case managers had with program females may have made this marginal difference.

In summary, a comprehensive communitywide approach to the youth gang problem did not develop in Tucson (Spergel, Wa, and Sosa, 2005e). Existing organizational, interorganizational, and community interests and structures prevented the program from adopting the Comprehensive Gang Model. The focus of the lead agency was on an early intervention program, particularly addressed to younger youth, using mainly its own social services. The Tucson Police Department became only peripherally involved in support of the program, and key community agencies and grassroots organizations were not integrally involved in program development. Lastly, and most significant, the project had few discernable positive impacts on the delinquent behavior of youth who were served.

Process and Impact Evaluation Findings

To develop a composite picture of the process and impact outcomes of the initial Comprehensive Gang Model implementations, the evaluators combined the Chicago Little Village evaluation with the studies of the five demonstration sites (Spergel, Wa, and Sosa, 2006). The evaluations across the five sites—Mesa, Tucson, Riverside, San Antonio, and Bloomington-Normal—were simultaneous and interrelated, but not interdependent, requiring extensive collaboration among local projects.

Spergel and his colleagues assessed (a) program elements, (b) strategies, and (c) operating principles in terms of their importance to successful implementation of theComprehensive Gang Model. This assessment was based on interviews with program staff and youth, service tracking records, and field observations (see table A1). Although none of the sites fully implemented these three critical program implementation requirements, the three sites (Chicago, Mesa, and Riverside) that showed the largest reductions in violence and drug-related crimes implemented more of them.

Three of the communities (Tucson, San Antonio, andBloomington-Normal) either made fatal planning mistakes (such as selecting a lead agency that failed to perform) or involved key agencies in the community that were unwilling to work together. But when it was well-implemented in three of the sites, the Comprehensive Gang Model effectively guided these communities (in Chicago, Mesa, and Riverside) in developing services and strategies that contributed to reductions in both gang violence (Chicago, Mesa, and Riverside) and drug-related offenses (Chicago and Mesa) (Spergel et al., 2006). At the successful sites, a key factor was length of time in the program. When youth were in the program for 2 or more years, there were fewer arrests for all types of offenses. In general, arrest reductions were greater among older youth and females than among younger youth and males. General deterrence effects (across the project area) were not as strong as the program effects for individual youth. Nevertheless, these three sites were somewhat successful in integrating police suppression with service-oriented strategies. In summary, the evaluation indicates that, when properly implemented, a combination of prevention, intervention, and suppression strategies was successful in reducing the gang problem (Spergel, Wa, and Sosa, 2006).

Rural Gang Initiative

In 1999, OJJDP launched the Rural Gang Initiative in response to feedback from the field that a gang violence reduction approach was needed for rural communities and findings from the 1997 National Youth Gang Survey that the number of gangs and gang members in rural areas was growing. This initiative was the first attempt to adopt the Comprehensive Gang Model in a nonmetropolitan area and served as a test case to determine whether rural communities can successfully implement (or need to implement) such a resource-intensive approach.

TABLE A1. Program Implementation Characteristics: Degree of Importance and Levels of Implementation

Program Implementation Characteristics	Degree of Importance to Program Success†	Levels of Implementation by Project Site‡					
		Chicago	Mesa	Riverside	Bloomington-Normal	San Antonio	Tucson
City/County Leadership	***	2	4	4	1	1	1
Steering Committee	**	1	4	3	1	1	0
Interagency Street Team/Coordination	***	4	4	3	0	0	0
Grassroots Involvement	*	3	1	1	0	1	0
Social Services: Youth Work, Individual Counseling, Family Treatment, and Recreation	**	3	3	3	2	3	3
Criminal Justice Participation	***	4	4	4	1	1	0
School Participation	**	1	3	3	3	2	0
Employment and Training	**	3	1	4	3	1	0
Lead Agency/Management/Commit	***	4	4	4	0	0	0
Social Intervention: Outreach and Crisis Intervention	**	4	3	3	1	1	0
Community Mobilization: Interagency and Grassroots	**	1	3	2	1	0	0
Provision of Social Opportunities: Education, Job, and Culture	**	3	2	2	2	1	0
Suppression	***	4	4	3	0	0	0
Organizational Change and Development	***	2	4	4	0	0	0
Targeting Gang Members/ At-Risk Gang Youth	***	4	2	3	1	3	3
Balance of Service	***	4	3	3	0	0	0
Intensity of Service	*	4	3	3	1	0	0
Continuity of Service	**	2	1	2	2	0	2

Source: Spergel, Wa, and Sosa, 2006, pp. 216–217

†Importance of characteristic to success: ***=extremely, **moderately, *=somewhat ‡Levels of implementation: 4=excellent, 3=good, 2=fair, 1=poor, 0=none.

Through a competitive process, OJJDP selected four communities to participate in the Rural Gang Initiative: Glenn County, CA; Mt. Vernon, IL; Elk City, OK; and Cowlitz County, WA. Each of the four sites completed the first-year assessment and implementation plan, both activities required by the OJJDP grant.

OJJDP determined that the assessment in two sites (Cowlitz County and Elk City) did not indicate an ongoing gang problem serious enough to merit an intensive approach such as the

Model. However, OJJDP did agree that the communities needed to address various risk factors through prevention strategies and create interventions for use when gang behavior did occur. OJJDP made suggestions to guide these sites in writing a new proposal to obtain reduced funding to address their particular gang problems. In one site, data from the assessment served as a basis for successful grant applications to support services and activities identified in the assessment.

Mt. Vernon and Glenn County received approval for an additional year's funding to implement the Model. Both communities operated an intervention team and provided services to clients for an additional 2 years. Steering committees were also active in both sites. However, turnover in the project coordinator position in both sites hampered a consistent understanding and application of the Model strategies over time. In 2002, grant funds had expired and neither site could sustain the project with local funding or new grants.

The national evaluation of the Rural Gang Initiative was not completed because of staffing issues with the national evaluators, and OJJDP elected not to continue the evaluation. Nonetheless, the evaluation team had prepared an interim process evaluation report and cross-site analysis for the first year of the program. The interim report examined three activities—community mobilization, assessment, and implementation planning—and revealed the following (National Council on Crime and Delinquency, 2000, pp. 54–56):

- Each of the four sites had a catalyst who envisioned the community as a viable candidate for the process, essentially initiating the process.
- The significant role that the project coordinator played cannot be overstated. This role is pivotal to the orchestration of the project.
- The support of law enforcement in the project had a positive effect in each site.
- There appears to be a direct correlation between the intensity of efforts expended to ensure appropriate agency representation on the steering committee and resultant gains in inclusiveness.
- Lack of automated gang crime data can hamper data collection for the assessment.
- Mobilizing and educating agency representatives who will collect the information facilitates the assessment process.
- The movement from assessment data to development of an implementation plan proved challenging to the steering committees.
- Steering committees struggled with prioritizing problems and determining appropriate target populations using the assessment data.

Gang-Free Communities and Schools Initiative

In 2000, OJJDP began the Gang-Free Communities and Schools Initiative, comprising two programs—the Gang- Free Communities Program and the Gang-Free Schools Program.

Gang-Free Communities Program

The Gang-Free Communities Program was funded in six sites in 2001: Broward County, FL; Lakewood, WA; East Los Angeles, CA; Louisville, KY; San Francisco, CA; and Washington, DC; although the Louisville and Washington, DC, sites soon dropped out of the program.c The Federal funds were seed money for Model implementation startup, and communities were to leverage local resources in addition to Federal funds to continue demonstrating the Model.

The remaining four sites were successful in conducting assessments and developing implementation plans for the chosen target areas. Each site began implementation of the Model, some more successfully than others. Lakewood, WA, and Broward County, FL, began implementation immediately, including serving clients through an intervention team. The remaining two sites were unsuccessful in fully coalescing their communities and key agencies to fully participate in the steering committees, to develop viable intervention teams, and to enroll clients. In late 2003, OJJDP announced that it would not invite the sites to apply for continued funding, and by early 2004, all sites had expended Federal funding and could not continue the projects with local funding or other grants.

Although there was no evaluation of the Gang-Free Communities Program, OJJDP did request the National Youth Gang Center to develop a "process description" of the four active sites during the assessment and planning phases. This process description provided a limited number of lessons learned (National Youth Gang Center, 2003, pp, 46–48):

- Key project personnel—such as the project coordinator, staff from the lead agency, and key steering committee members—should be on board before plans for conducting the assessment are completed.
- Complicated hiring processes and layers of bureaucracy in large cities complicate a timely selection of staff and disbursal of funds.
- Having a capable, full-time project coordinator is critical to the successful operation of the project.
- The project coordinator must have frequent contact with the lead agency for the effective and timely execution of the tasks associated with the Gang-Free Communities process.

Gang–Free Schools Program

In 2000, as part of the Gang–Free Communities and Schools initiative, OJJDP provided funding to fully develop a school component to the Comprehensive GangModel. The distinctive features of the Gang-Free Schools Program is the planning and implementation of special or enhanced programs within the school setting and the linking of the school component to community-based gang prevention, intervention, and suppression activities. Four sites—Houston, TX; Pittsburgh, PA; Miami-Dade County, FL; and East Cleveland, OH—participated in this program.d

Several best practices and/or lessons learned were identified in the evaluation report on the Gang-Free Schools projects. The following excerpts from the report address key factors that influence the success (or failure) of a project.

Community Capacity

If communities do not have services in place and prior existing relationships (with memorandums of understanding [MOUs]) in place, [then they] will not be able to provide the necessary interventions to their clients. A community capacity assessment should be part [of this effort]. When . . . cities . . . are beleaguered with financial problems, . . . the financial issues tend to impede the level of services, programming, and activities that are available to youth and their families. [These programs] need the support of surrounding community organizations and police departments in order to be completely successful. . . . Additionally, local budget constraints may hamper the institutionalization and sustainability of the program in the future.

(COSMOS Corporation, 2007, p. xiv)

Role of the Project Coordinator

The role of the project coordinator is one of the most critical elements contributing to the success of the project. The title "project director" would perhaps be more reflective of the duties and responsibilities of this individual. . . . Traits of successful project coordinators include having an ability to network and effectively communicate the issues; being integrated within the city's existing organizational infrastructure (e.g., within the school system, mayor's office, etc.); having in-depth information about key project issues; maintaining a deep long-term commitment to the project; and an understanding of basic research principles. Because this role requires the project coordinator to serve as the liaison to various oversight entities (the steering committee, the intervention team), the project coordinator should have outstanding interpersonal skills and an energetic and outgoing personality.

(COSMOS Corporation, 2007, pp. xiv–xv)

Project Location

Intervention programs of this nature may be more productive when situated and managed within school systems (e.g., board of education), as opposed to law enforcement agencies. Law enforcement agencies naturally tend to focus on suppression components rather than embracing a more broad-based approach, leading to uneven pursuit of activities.

(COSMOS Corporation, 2007, p. xv)

Range of Intervention Activities Offered and Age Span of Clients Eligible to Participate

Programs like the [Gang-Free Schools] project may have long-term success with juveniles and young adults if intervention strategies are intermingled with prevention strategies and are offered to both younger and older clients. More and more youth are getting actively involved in gang-related and juvenile delinquent activities at a younger age, especially in elementary school. Thus, a model that incorporates both prevention and intervention strategies that are age appropriate (e.g., 8 to 24 years old) may yield greater benefits over time for society generally and the youth population specifically.

(COSMOS Corporation, 2007, p. xv)

In addition to the more common and obvious youth interventions, such as employment and educational opportunities, . . . [communities] should be urged to customize intervention programs according to the cultural issues and needs of the individuals in each city. Some young people . . . needed extra help with learning and understanding the English language, and others needed major assistance with drug, alcohol, and mental [health] problems. Furthermore, some of the youth lacked positive role models, so they may benefit from a strong mentoring component in an intervention program.

(COSMOS Corporation, 2007, p. xvi)

Parental and Community Member Involvement

Parents' and community members' involvement in the steering committee and intervention team may be key to learning the true tone and inner workings of a community and to getting young people to actively participate in the intervention programs.

(COSMOS Corporation, 2007, p. xvi).

Role of Outreach

It may be imperative to have community members who have been active in the project neighborhood to serve as outreach workers because young people seem to relate to, respond to, and respect these individuals more. Outreach workers from the participating neighborhoods have a strong record and seem to be better predictors of referring youth who will benefit from the intervention programs and who will stay active in the program.

(COSMOS Corporation, 2007, p. xvi)

Project Title

Two cities involved in GFS created different project names that did not include the word "gang." . . . The term "gang" being used in the project name or during school or community discussion seemed to be a hindrance when seeking youth involvement in the program . . . A project name that does not use . . . "gang," but reflects that the purpose is to diminish juvenile delinquency through intervention and/or prevention may increase youth enrollment in the project.

(COSMOS Corporation, 2007, p. xvii)

The four sites enrolled more than 400 clients in their programs during the more than 4-year project period. The majority of youth remained enrolled in the program for more than 2 years. During their time in the program, outreach workers made frequent contact with the youth, with the average length of each contact ranging from 33 to 41 minutes. Analysis shows that the more time the outreach workers spent per contract, the more likely the youth would remain in the program. It was also noted that greater length of time per contact was positively related to less alcohol use and fewer arrests at the Houston site.

Evaluation data show that youth currently attending school were less likely than their peers who were not attending school to be rearrested and to use drugs and alcohol over the duration of the study. Also, youth who were more involved in their gangs were more likely to be expelled more often from school, to receive disciplinary infractions at school, and to be jailed more often.

(COSMOS Corporation, 2007, p. xx)

GANG REDUCTION PROGRAM

As part of U.S. Department of Justice's Anti-Gang Initiative, OJJDP's Gang Reduction Program is designed to reduce gang activity in targeted neighborhoods by incorporating a broad spectrum of research-based interventions to address the range of personal, family, and community factors that contribute to juvenile delinquency and gang activity. The program integrates local, state, and Federal resources to incorporate state-of-the-art practices in prevention, intervention, and suppression. The program was implemented in four demonstration sites—Richmond, VA; Los Angeles, CA; North Miami Beach, FL; and Milwaukee, WI—beginning in 2003.

As part of the initiative, the Urban Institute (UI) is conducting a 3-year evaluation to assess program implementation, examine outcomes related to reductions in crime and gang activity, and identify improvements in prosocial activities and protective factors in the lives of high-risk.

The brief strategic planning process was the first major challenge faced by all sites. The short time allowed for Phase I planning permitted the implementation of some activities, but these were generally extensions of programs already in place. In all sites, much or most of Phase I was actually devoted to further problem identification and information gathering in an effort to understand the nature of local problems, resources, and relevant evidence-based practices.

Much of the progress achieved to date at each of the sites is attributable to the leadership of each site's coordinator. Coordinators, however, would have benefited from more direction and technical assistance on organizing local efforts. Sites independently developed similar organizational designs: steering committees (termed 'advisory' in Los Angeles) representing broad community interests. Coordinators relied on steering committees for management and decision-making support. The inclusive committees were a mixed blessing: while they represented diverse interests related to gang reduction, some participating organizations expected to secure substantial funding from GRP, and disrupted planning and implementation because of individual agency priorities rather than participating to fulfill the mission of GRP. Early in the process, competition for funds, political infighting, and unrealistic expectations had occasional negative effects on collaboration, communication, and committee functioning. These effects diminished over time.

Substantial variation in the levels of collaboration and communication existed. Stakeholders focused on suppression efforts, especially in Los Angeles and Richmond, seemed to function more collaboratively and effectively because of prior experience working together. Where functioning was more problematic, member attrition and turnover was more prevalent.

Conforming to strict procurement rules had negative effects on implementation. The time required to get programs up and running in target communities was longer than anyone anticipated. Also, some capable providers with little experience in the competitive bidding process were disqualified due to missed deadlines or submission of incomplete applications. In other cases, complicated application procedures discouraged providers from applying.

Significant implementation successes were observed in all sites. Sites developed strategic plans approved by OJJDP and consistent with target area needs and problems; local governance and communication have steadily improved and partnerships among members have developed; coordinator outreach resulted in a broad participation in GRP planning and implementation; a significant number of specific programmatic activities across all GRP components were operational by late 2007; and GRP has improved communication about gang issues within the target areas and among participating organizations.

The findings on the effects of GRP in each site were mixed. The results revealed that only one site, Los Angeles, showed a significant reduction in crime rates, with levels of serious violence, gang related incidents, gang-related serious violence, and citizen reports of shots fired all decreasing significantly after the implementation of GRP there. Smaller drops in those measures were found in the comparison area, and no evidence of displacement was identified. In Milwaukee and North Miami Beach, no significant changes in the measures were found after GRP implementation, and in Richmond, the period after implementation actually saw a modest increase in serious violence and gang-related measures. While the comparison area in Richmond also saw increases in two of the measures, those increases were to a smaller degree than in the target area. Increased crime awareness and reporting of gang crimes among target area residents may help to explain the unexpected increases in some crime measures that were found in Richmond.

While very little strategic planning for sustainability had taken place at any of the four sites at the time of the previous report in 2006, by late 2007, three of the four sites had undertaken significant steps towards sustaining at least portions of the initiative beyond the federal funding period. In Los Angeles, the GRP model was implemented city-wide with local funding and termed 'Gang Reduction Zone Program.' In North Miami Beach, after struggling to find a government- based fiscal agent to sustain the partnership, the initiative was incorporated as a non-profit organization in late 2007. In Richmond, the close relationship that developed between the Virginia Office of the Attorney General (OAG) and the Richmond Police Department (RPD) through the GRP effort had ensured that a significant portion of the efforts undertaken by the RPD would be sustained, and the OAG was also planning an expansion of the model into other parts of the city.

The UI evaluation is continuing, and final evaluation findings will be made available by OJJDP as soon as they are released.

NOTES

a) These project descriptions are adapted from the OJJDP Fact Sheet, "Implementing the OJJDP Comprehensive Gang Model" (Burch and Kane, 1999), and also refer to information provided in the more comprehensive project and evaluation reports.

b) It is noteworthy that the Tucson Police Department had previously organized a community policing effort in the Las Vistas/Pueblo area—the original program area. In 1995, a separate citywide coalition of agencies was formed, known as TASK 1 (Taking a Stand for Kids)—a consortium of many organizations with an interest in reducing violence and addressing the gang problem. Our Town attempted to use this group as the project's steering committee, but this did not materialize. At the same time, the Mayor's Task Force on Youth Violence—comprising criminal-justice and other agencies and community leaders—seemed to be taking a different, more suppression-oriented approach to the gang problem than either the TASK 1 or Our Town leadership.

c) The Louisville site dropped out of the program shortly after an assessment was completed in 2001, stating that the data collected were not conclusive enough to support implementing such a comprehensive program. They were also concerned that the impending merger of city and county governments posed significant issues that affected the viability of the project. After September 11, 2001, homeland security and related activities took precedence in Washington, DC, for several months. The grantee was the Metropolitan Police Department, which was focusing all its attention on more immediate problems. Further, the grantee and the lead agency could not find compatible ground on which to launch this initiative. Consequently, the Washington, DC, site was unable to complete an assessment.

d) The lead agency for the Gang-Free Schools project in Houston was the Mayor's Anti-Gang Office, a division of the Mayor's Office of Public Safety and Drug Policy. The lead agency convened a steering committee composed of members from several key agencies, including the Houston Police Department, Houston Mayor's Office, Houston Independent School District, and Harris County Juvenile Probation (COSMOS Corporation, 2007, pp. 3.14–1 6). The steering committee, in conjunction with the Mayor's Anti- Gang Office, selected Houston's target area for the Gang-Free Schools initiative (COSMOS Corporation, 2007, pp. 3.14, 18). This area—directly east of downtown—originally included five police beats commonly referred to as the Greater East End, populated primarily by residents of Mexican origin. This target area included five distinct neighborhoods: Magnolia, the Second Ward, Lawndale, Eastwood, and Idylwood. Between 2003 and 2007, 128 youth were enrolled as clients by and received services from the project.

The School District of Pittsburgh served as the lead agency for the Pittsburgh project (COSMOS Corporation, 2007). The steering committee and the assessment team initially assessed the entire city of Pittsburgh because crime was so widely dispersed over many areas of the city. The steering committee considered 23 areas from four regions of the city (north, south, east, and central), ultimately selecting the east region as the target area. From 2003 to 2007, 93 youth were enrolled as clients by and received services from the project.

The Miami-Dade County Public Schools served as lead agency for the Miami project, with the Miami-Dade County School Police Department performing most of the administrative functions (COSMOS Corporation, 2007, p. 6.11). The steering committee was composed of key agencies that provided services throughout metropolitan Miami-Dade County. It selected a project coordinator who would work directly with the school police but not within the local law enforcement agency. Northwest Miami-Dade County was selected as the target area for implementation (COSMOS Corporation, 2007, pp. 6.18–19, 22). From the period 2003–2006, 150 youth were enrolled in and received services from the project.

The Cuyahoga County (Cleveland) Prosecutor's Office served as the East Cleveland Gang-Free Schools project's lead agency. A steering committee composed of key agencies that pledged their support to the initiative was convened, and the steering committee selected the entire city of East Cleveland as the target area rather than attempting to target particular neighborhoods. (COSMOS Corporation, 2007, p. 5.9, 5.12). The project encountered numerous difficulties during the assessment process, including the failure of research partners to attend steering committee meetings, turnover in the project coordinator role, and an assessment report that was judged inadequate (COSMOS Corporation, 2007, p. 5.11, 5.15). However, despite staffing problems and external issues, the project completed the assessment phase with a core group of participants who were willing to contribute time and resources to implementing the Gang-Free Schools project (COSMOS Corporation, 2007, p. 5.15). During the period 2003–2006, 98 youth were enrolled in and served by the project.

REFERENCES

Burch, J., and Kane, C. (1999). Implementing the OJJDP Comprehensive Gang Model. Fact Sheet #112. Washington, DC: U.S. Department of Justice, Office of Justice Programs, Office of Juvenile Justice and Delinquency Prevention.

Cahill, M., Coggeshall, M., Hayeslip, D., Wolff, A., Lager- son, E., Scott, M., Davies, E., Roland, K., and Decker, S. (2008). Community Collaboratives Addressing Youth Gangs: Interim Findings from the Gang Reduction Program. Washington, DC: Urban Institute Justice Policy Center.

COSMOS Corporation (2007). National Evaluation of the Gang-Free Schools Initiative. Unpublished draft report submitted to the Office of Juvenile Justice and Delinquency Prevention. Bethesda, MD: COSMOS Corporation.

National Council on Crime and Delinquency (2000). National Evaluation of the First Year of the OJJDP Rural Gang Initiative: Cross-Site Analysis. Unpublished draft report submitted to the Office of Juvenile Justice and Delinquency Prevention. Oakland, California: National Council on Crime and Delinquency.

National Youth Gang Center (2003). Gang-Free Communities Process Description. Unpublished draft report submitted to the Office of Juvenile Justice and Delinquency Prevention. Tallahassee, Florida: National Youth Gang Center.

Spergel, I.A. (2007). Reducing Youth Gang Violence: The Little Village Gang Project in Chicago. Lanham, MD: AltaMira Press.

Spergel, I.A., Wa, K.M., and Sosa, R.V. (2005a). Evaluation of the Mesa Gang Intervention Program (MGIP). Washington, DC: Unpublished report submitted to the Office of Juvenile Justice and Delinquency Prevention. Accessible at the National Criminal Justice Reference Service.

Spergel, I.A., Wa, K.M., and Sosa, R,V. (2005b). Evaluation of the Riverside Comprehensive Community-Wide Approach to Gang Prevention, Intervention and Suppression. Report submitted to the Office of Juvenile Justice and Delinquency Prevention. Washington, DC: Unpublished report. Accessible at the National Criminal Justice Reference Service.

Spergel, I.A., Wa, K.M., and Sosa, R.V. (2005c). Evaluation of the Bloomington-Normal Comprehensive Gang Program. Report submitted to the Office of Juvenile Justice and Delinquency Prevention. Washington, DC: Unpublished report. Accessible at the National Criminal Justice Reference Service.

Spergel, I.A., Wa, K.M., and Sosa, R.V. (2005d). Evaluation of the San Antonio Comprehensive Community-Wide Approach to Gang Prevention, Intervention and Suppression. Report submitted to the Office of Juvenile Justice and Delinquency Prevention. Washington, DC: Unpublished report. Accessible at the National Criminal Justice Reference Service.

Spergel, I.A., Wa, K M., and Sosa, R.V. (2005e). Evaluation of the Tucson Comprehensive Community-Wide Approach to Gang Prevention, Intervention and Suppression. Report submitted to the Office of Juvenile Justice and Delinquency Prevention. Washington, DC: Unpublished report. Accessible at the National Criminal Justice Reference Service.

Spergel, I.A., Wa, K.M., and Sosa, R.V. (2006). The comprehensive, community-wide, gang program model: Success and failure. In J. F. Short and L. A. Hughes (eds.), Studying Youth Gangs (pp. 203–224). Lanham, MD: AltaMira Press.

APPENDIX B: MULTISTRATEGY GANG INITIATIVE SURVEY

The purpose of the survey is to gather information regarding multistrategy gang initiatives in your community and to solicit observations pertaining to several types of anti-gang initiatives funded by the Office of Juvenile Justice and Delinquency Prevention. Not all topics and questions apply to every project. Follow-up interviews will be conducted with some respondents to help gather further information on trends identified through the survey. If you have any questions, please contact Ms. Kimberly Hale at 800–446–0912, extension 248.

Site you represent:

Please provide a written response to each question:

Assessment/Implementation Planning

1. Did your project conduct a communitywide assessment of your gang or youth violence problem? Yes No

2. What data were most useful in developing the implementation plan?

3. Describe the process your project used to select a target area of the community.

4. Describe how the project identified service gaps in the target community and how those service gaps were addressed.

5. What suggestions do you have for strengthening the data collection process to assist in program planning and implementation?

6. If applicable, describe the roles and responsibilities of your project's research partner during the assessment and implementation process.

Project Coordinator Role

7. Describe the critical skills and characteristics project coordinators should possess to successfully direct a multistrategy gang initiative.

8. What significant obstacles did the project coordinator encounter during assessment and/or implementation? How did the project coordinator overcome the obstacles?

Lead Agency

9. Describe your project's administrative structure, including the type of lead agency, if any (e.g., city government, law enforcement, school district).

10. What were the advantages and disadvantages of your project's administrative structure and lead agency?

Steering Committee/Advisory Board

11. Did your site use a committee made up of partner agencies, such as a steering committee/advisory board? If not, skip to the Prevention Services section.
    Yes No

12. Describe the steering committee/advisory board's formal and informal roles in the project (e.g., leadership, types of decision making, resource development).

13. Describe the process used to select representatives for this group.

14. Describe the process used to establish and update formal agreements regarding this body's functioning (e.g., bylaws, memorandums of understanding).

15. What major challenges did your project encounter in developing and maintaining your site's steering committee, and what strategies did your project use to address them?
16. What strategies should be used to create and maintain a successful steering committee or advisory board?

Prevention Services

17. Describe the main prevention efforts your project engaged in for youth at high risk of gang involvement and their families.

18. How did your project identify prevention strategies that were used?

19. Describe successes and challenges that your project experienced in implementing prevention strategies.

Intervention Team

20. What main agencies participated on your intervention team?

21. Which agencies were most critical to the effective functioning of an intervention team? Describe their roles in ensuring that clients receive optimum case management and services.

22. In what ways was the intervention team able to create a positive impact, beyond providing case management and services to clients (e.g., institutional change, resource development)?

23. What agencies were most difficult to engage in the intervention team and why?

24. Describe challenges that your intervention team encountered in becoming organized and operational, and discuss the strategies used to address the challenges.

Suppression

25. What types of suppression strategies were utilized in conjunction with this project?

26. What role did law enforcement/criminal justice agencies play on the intervention team?

27. Describe how new or existing suppression strategies were implemented by the project.

28. What other social control mechanisms were utilized by agencies participating in the project to address clients' negative behaviors?

Reentry

29. Describe program services that were provided to previously incarcerated clients returning to the community.

30. What challenges did your project face in providing services to this population?

Organizational Development

31. Describe policy and procedural changes that participating agencies made as a result of their participation.

32. Describe the strategies that your project used to engage nonfunded partners in activities. How effective were those strategies?

Resources

33. List and describe the resources your project used for guidance in planning and implementing the project.
34. What additional resources and support would have been helpful to your project for planning and implementing the project?

Sustainability

35. Is your project working to sustain the multistrategy gang initiative model long-term? If no, skip to the Lessons Learned section. Yes No

36. Describe the plans your project is exploring or has in place to sustain the project.

37. Describe the funding or collaboration challenges your project has encountered in sustaining your multistrategy gang program.

Lessons Learned

38. How successful was your project in targeting gang members and at-risk youths?

39. What factors contributed most to successfully targeting these groups in your project?

40. How successful was your project in integrating services for clients or "wrapping" them around youth and their families?

41. What factors contributed most to successfully integrating services for clients?

42. How successful was your project in providing a balance of prevention, intervention, and suppression strategies?

43. What factors contributed most to successfully providing a balance of prevention, intervention, and suppression strategies?

If you are interested in participating in a follow-up interview, please include your name, e-mail address, and phone number below.

Name:

E-mail Address:

Phone Number:

In: Gangs: Violence, Crime and Antigang Initiatives
Editor: Jay T. Soordhas
ISBN 978-1-60692-286-6

Chapter 2

VIOLENCE BY TEENAGE GIRLS: TRENDS AND CONTEXT*

Margaret A. Zahn, Susan Brumbaugh, Darrell Steffensmeier, Barry C. Feld, Merry Morash, Meda Chesney-Lind, Jody Miller, Allison Ann Payne, Denise C. Gottfredson, and Candace Kruttschnitt

According to data from the Federal Bureau of Investigation, from 1991 to 2000, arrests of girls increased more (or decreased less) than arrests of boys for most types of offenses. By 2004, girls accounted for 30 percent of all juvenile arrests. However, questions remain about whether these trends reflect an actual increase in girls' delinquency or changes in societal responses to girls' behavior. To find answers to these questions, the Office of Juvenile Justice and Delinquency Prevention (OJJDP) convened the Girls Study Group to establish a theoretical and empirical foundation to guide the development, testing, and dissemination of strategies to reduce or prevent girls' involvement in delinquency and violence.

The Girls Study Group Series, of which this Bulletin is a part, presents the Group's findings. The series examines issues such as patterns of offending among adolescents and how they differ for girls and boys; risk and protective factors associated with delinquency, including gender differences; and the causes and correlates of girls' delinquency.

STUDY GROUP MEMBERS

Dr. Margaret Zahn, Senior Research Scientist, RTI International; Professor, North Carolina State University

Dr. Robert Agnew, Professor, Department of Sociology, Emory University

Dr. Elizabeth Cauffman, Assistant Professor, Department of Psychology and Social Behavior, University of California, Irvine

---

* This is an edited, excerpted and augmented edition of a National Youth Gang Center Under Cooperative Agreement Number 2007—JV—FX—0008 From The Office Of Juvenile Justice And Delinquency Prevention (OJJDP).

Dr. Meda Chesney-Lind, Professor, Women's Studies Program, University of Hawaii at Manoa
Dr. Gayle Dakof, Associate Research Professor, Department of Epidemiology and Public Health, University of Miami
Dr. Del Elliott, Director, Center for the Study and Prevention of Violence, University of Colorado
Dr. Barry Feld, Professor, School of Law, University of Minnesota
Dr. Diana Fishbein, Director, Transdisciplinary Behavioral Science Program, RTI International
Dr. Peggy Giordano, Professor of Sociology, Center for Family and Demographic Research, Bowling Green State University
Dr. Candace Kruttschnitt, Professor, Department of Sociology, University of Minnesota
Dr. Jody Miller, Associate Professor, Department of Criminology and Criminal Justice, University of Missouri–St. Louis
Dr. Merry Morash, Professor, School of Criminal Justice, Michigan State University
Dr. Darrell Steffensmeier, Professor, Department of Sociology, Pennsylvania State University
Ms. Giovanna Taormina, Executive Director, Girls Circle Association
Dr. Donna-Marie Winn, Senior Research Scientist, Center for Child and Family Policy, Duke University

In June 2005, Newsweek ran a story media accounts. This chapter assesses titled "Bad Girls Go Wild," which the accuracy of these assertions using described "the significant rise in violent the best available data. Drawing on behavior among girls" as a "burgeoning national crisis" (Scelfo, 2005)—a - depiction that echoes other recent information from official arrest sources, nationally based self-report and victimization surveys, and studies reported -in the social science literature, the Bulletin examines the involvement of girls in violent activity (including whether such activity has increased relative to the increase for boys) and the contexts in which girls engage in violent behavior.

One of the most consistent and robust findings in criminology is that, for nearly every offense, females engage in much less crime and juvenile delin quency than males. In recent years, however, the extent and character of this gender difference in offending are increasingly being called into question by statistics and media reports suggesting the increasing involvement of girls in the juvenile and criminal justice systems. During the past two and-a-half decades, official statistics suggest that female delinquency has undergone substantial changes compared with male delinquency. Between 1980 and 2005, arrests of girls increased nationwide, while arrests of boys decreased (Federal Bureau of Investigation, 2006). These arrest trends, along with high-profile cases of female delinquency, have become the main support for media headlines.

However, because arrest counts are a product of both delinquent behavior and official responses to it, researchers and policymakers face a dilemma about how to interpret the arrest statistics. Do the increases in arrests indicate real changes in girls' behaviors, or are the increases a product of recent changes in public sentiment and enforcement policies that have elevated the visibility and reporting of girls' delinquency and violence? This chapter attempts to answer this question.

TRENDS IN GIRLS' VIOLENCE

This Bulletin relies on three data sources—official arrest data, self- report data, and victimization data— to examine trends in girls' violence from 1980 through 2005. Each source has strengths and weaknesses and provides a somewhat different picture of crime.

Data Sources

Official sources of data on delin quency include information col lected and disseminated by local agencies such as police, as well as State and national organizations that disseminate information col lected at the local level. The primary source of official data on delinquency comes from the Federal Bureau oflnvestigation's (FBI's) Uniform Crime Report (UCR), published annually. Each UCR reflects thousands of local police reports on crimes known to police and on arrests, from which the FBI compiles statistics on the type of crime (roughly 30 broad categories), the location of the arrest (urban, sub urban, or rural), and the demograph ic characteristics of the offender (e.g., age, gender).

Self-report surveys on juvenile crime and its correlates are another major source of information. In addition to the detailed information on respon dent characteristics, the main benefit of self-report data is the information obtained on crimes that were com mitted by youth but not known to the police. Most self-report delinquency surveys are cross-sectional (i.e., cover only one point in time) and localized (i.e., limited to a particular commu nity or region). Among the surveys that provide longitudinal or trend data on youth delinquency for the Nation as a whole, the authors use Monitoring the Future (MTF).[1] MTF is an ongoing study of the behaviors, attitudes, and values of American secondary school students. Each year, a total of approximately 50,000 8th, 10th, and 12th grade students are surveyed (12th graders since 1975, and 8th and 10th graders since 1991).

Victimization surveys provide a third important source of information on delinquent behavior. These types of data provide a different perspective. Whereas information on self-reported delinquent activity is collected from the offender, the source of infor mation for victimization surveys is the victim of criminal activity. The Census Bureau has conducted the National Crime Victimization Survey (NCVS) for the Bureau of Justice Statistics annually since 1973. Each year, NCVS interviews individuals age 12 and older in a nationally rep resentative sample of approximately 50,000 households. Victims of various types of crimes (including violent and property crimes) report detailed characteristics of criminal events, including time and location, level of physical and property damage, and— in the case of violent crime—the perceived characteristics (e.g., age, gender, race) of the offender(s).

VIOLENCE DEFINED

Many different sources of data examine violence and girls' involvement in it. However, these sources often rely on different definitions and measures of violence. Official criminal justice system data sources (e.g., Uniform Crime Reports) use legal definitions focusing on homicide, rape, robbery, aggravated assault (which usually involves assault with a weapon or assault producing injury), and simple assault (a behavior defined differently in various jurisdictions). Self-report studies and those involving interviews with adolescents focus on a variety of behaviors including, for example, fighting and weapon-carrying. Some studies include relational aggression in their definitions of violent behavior (see p. 11 for a discussion of relational aggression).

In general, this Bulletin defines violence as behaviors that inflict or threaten to inflict bodily injury on other persons.

Primary Data Sources

- Uniform Crime Reports (UCR) arrest data.
- Monitoring the Future (MTF).
- National Crime Victimization Survey (NCVS).

Trends in Arrests for Violent Offenses: UCR Data

In 2005, out of 14 million arrests, 2.1 million involved juveniles (Snyder, forthcoming).[2] Juveniles comprised about 15 percent of arrests for all offenses, about 16 percent of arrests for Violent Crime Index[3] offenses, and about 26 percent of arrests for Property Crime Index [4] offenses. Girls comprised nearly one-third (29 per cent) of all juvenile arrests, about one-third (34 percent) of arrests for Property Crime Index offenses, and less than one-fifth (18 percent) of arrests for Violent Crime Index offenses. Although serious and vio lent crimes capture media and public attention, the vast majority of juve nile arrests are for less serious offens es—nonindex and status offenses[5 accounted for three-quarters (76 per cent) of all juvenile arrests.

Only 4 percent of juvenile arrests in 2005 were for Violent Crime Index offenses; aggravated assaults accounted for two-thirds (64 per cent) of Violent Crime Index juve nile arrests (3 percent of all juvenile arrests). Girls comprised about one- quarter (24 percent) of all juvenile arrests for aggravated assault. By contrast, simple assaults accounted for 12 percent of all juvenile arrests; other than larceny-theft and “all other offenses,” simple assault was the offense for which police made the largest number of juvenile arrests (247,900). Significantly, girls account ed for one-third (33 percent) of juve nile arrests for simple assault, the largest female proportion of arrests for any type of violent crime.

Although girls comprise a smaller overall portion of juvenile arrests than boys, the two groups’ arrest pat terns have diverged somewhat over the past decade. As the percentage changes in table 1 indicate, juvenile arrests generally decreased between 1996 and 2005, but the decrease was greater for boys than for girls; the exception to the general trend was arrests for simple assault, which increased for girls while decreasing for boys.[6]

Arrests for aggravated assault com prise the single largest component of the Violent Crime Index, and arrests for simple assault are the largest component of nonindex violent arrests. As shown in table 1, boys' arrests for aggravated assault decreased nearly one-quarter (–23 percent) between 1996 and 2005, while girls' arrests decreased far less (–5 percent). In contrast, girls' arrests for simple assault increased nearly one-quarter (24 percent), while boys' arrests decreased slightly (–4 percent). For Violent Crime Index offenses, arrests of males decreased more substantially (–28 percent) than did arrests of females (–10 percent). Between 1996 and 2005, the over all total of juvenile arrests dropped about 22 percent, primarily because arrests of males decreased 29 per cent, whereas arrests of females decreased 14 percent.

LIMITATIONS

All three data sources have limitations. The official or arrest data capture only detected offenses—those that are known to the police or that result in an arrest. Reporting police agencies also vary widely in their reporting coverage. Some jurisdictions have 100-percent reporting, while other jurisdictions are underrepresented. Moreover, because offense categories are very broad, conclusions may be misleading.* For example, the increase in girls' arrests for "serious crimes" (i.e., UCR Index Crimes, as discussed and defined later in this Bulletin) is largely attributable to the inclusion of larceny-theft in that category. Furthermore, arrest data may be affected by changes in enforcement policy that may affect one gender more than the other. Given the gender difference in the character and context of delinquency (i.e., that girls generally engage in less serious forms of crime), changes in laws and enforcement toward targeting less serious forms of lawbreaking may disproportionately impact the risk of arrest for females.

Limitations of self-report and victimization data are that they typically cover only a few forms of lawbreaking and have sampling deficiencies (e.g., MTF is administered in schools and so would underreport crimes committed by youth who have dropped out of school or are frequently truant, and NCVS only interviews victims who are age 12 and older). These data are, however, particularly useful for thinking about whether girls' delinquency trends reflect changes in underlying behavior or changes in enforcement and arrest policies—at least when data sources overlap for the forms of law-violating behavior being measured. For example, longitudinal arrest data on assault can be compared with information on assaults collected in self-report and victimization surveys over time. Confidence in recent assertions regarding levels of violence among girls is enhanced if all of these sources agree on the nature of the trends, whereas confidence is diminished if the sources disagree.

*Reporting agencies classify each arrest by the most serious offense charged in that arrest. If a juvenile is arrested for an aggravated assault and a simple assault, only the aggravated assault is counted in the report—the accompanying simple assault would not be represented in the data. This means that UCR data may be underrepresenting certain offenses when they are committed at the same time as more serious offenses.

Table 1. Percent Change in Male and Female Juvenile Arrests for Violent Crimes, 1996–2005

Type	Girls	Boys
Aggravated assault	–5.4%	–23.4%
Simple assault	24.0	–4.1
Violent Crime Index	–10.2	–27.9
All crimes	–14.3	–28.7

Source: Crime in the United States, 2005—Table 33 (FBI, 2006).

Steffensmeier and colleagues (2005) assess statistically whether the gen der difference in arrest trends over the past two decades has been nar rowing, widening, or has remained essentially stable. Based on UCR arrest data from 1980 through 2003, their analysis found that the gender difference in arrest rates is essentially stable for homicide, rape, and rob bery but has narrowed considerably for aggravated assault and simple assault (Steffensmeier et al., 2005).

The gender difference for the Vio lent Crime Index has also narrowed significantly, but this narrowing is largely attributable to the rise in female juvenile arrest rates for aggra vated assault during the 1990s (see figure 1). If arrests for aggravated assault are omitted from the Index, the trend is essentially stable.

To better show what a narrowing or widening gender difference in vio lence means, figure 1 plots juvenile female and male arrest rate trends for aggravated assault, simple assault, and the Violent Crime Index (sum of arrests for homicide, robbery, rape, and aggravated assault), along with the female percentage of arrests, according to the UCR.

Over the past two decades, clear changes have occurred in girls' arrests and between boys' and girls' patterns of arrests in aggravated and simple assault. As figure 1 indicates, boys' and girls' arrests for aggravated assault diverged conspicuously—the female arrest rate in 2003 (88.3 girls per 100,000) was nearly double the arrest rate in 1980 (45 girls per 100,000). Although males' arrest rate for aggravated assault was five times higher than that of females, males' proportional increase from 1980 to 2003 (12.5 percent, from 239.4 to 269.5 boys per 100,000) was much more modest than that of girls.

The juvenile arrest rate for simple assaults is more than three times greater than the rate for aggravated assaults. Again, changes in the arrest rates of females for simple assault over the past two decades have greatly outpaced those of males. The arrest rate of girls for simple assault in 2003 was more than triple (3.5 times) the rate in 1980 (478.3 versus 129.7 per 100,000). Although male arrests for simple assaults started from a higher base rate, that rate barely doubled over the same period(934.4 versus 462.7 per 100,000). Arrest rates for both groups peaked in the mid-1990s, and then male rates exhibited a much sharper dropoff than female rates. Moreover, while the male juvenile arrest rate for Violent Crime Index offenses was lower in 2003 than in 1980, the rate for girls was much higher—the girls' arrest rate for Violent Crime Index offenses rose from 70.4 to 103.1 per 100,000 between 1980 and 2003, a 46-percent increase. Thus, the juvenile "crime drop" of the past decade reflects primarily changes in arrest rates for boys.

In general, the gender difference in arrests has narrowed considerably for aggravated assault and simple assault and has also narrowed for the Violent Crime Index—the female percentage of juvenile arrests held steady during the 1980s, followed by a fairly steep rise in the female share of juvenile arrests during the 1990s. The Index trend essentially matches the pattern for aggravated assault, primarily because the large arrest volumes for aggravated assault (two-thirds of all Violent Index offenses) swamped the effects of arrest trends in the other Index violent crimes during the 1990s.

Figure 1 helps clarify whether the movement in arrest rates is similar for both genders and whether substantial gender differences in juvenile arrests for violent offenses still exist.

Data indicate that trends in arrest rates are roughly similar for both genders across all violent crime cat egories, but with some divergence since the mid-1990s. For example, arrest rates rose for both boys and girls over much of the past two decades, particularly during 1986–94. Then rates leveled off or declined in the late 1990s for boys, while rates for girls merely stabilized or contin ued to inch upward. Therefore, the narrowing difference in trends (par ticularly for both types of assault) is at least partly a function of the recent downward movement in boys arrest rates for violence.

Figure 2 compares the simple/ aggravated assault arrest rate ratios (arrest rate for simple assault divided by the arrest rate for aggravated assault) over two decades for boys and girls. These ratios and changes in the ratios indicate the relative seriousness of offenses for which police have arrested juveniles. In 1980, the ratio for girls was 2.9, which means that police arrested girls for simple assault about three times as often as they arrested girls for aggra vated assault. They arrested boys for simple assault about twice (1.9 times) as often as they arrested boys for aggravated assault. By 2003, police arrested girls more than five times (5.4) as often for simple assault as for aggravated assault. By contrast, the ratio of boys' arrests for simple to aggravated assault was just over threefold (3.5). These ratios show that (1) arrests for simple assault are more common than for aggravated assault (i.e., the ratios for both boys and girls are greater than 1.0) and (2) simple assaults comprise a larger percentage of arrests for girls than for boys (i.e., the simple/aggravated assault ratios are consistently higher for girls than for boys), particularly in recent years.

These differences in ratios are partly explained by gender differences in the underlying trends for aggravated and simple assaults. The large decline in boys' arrests for aggra vated assaults over the past decade raised their ratio of simple to aggra vated assault. By contrast, the larger increase in the girls' ratio of simple to aggravated assault is attributable to their large increase in arrests for simple assault over the same period.

The statistics on juvenile arrests for assault point to certain con clusions about the seriousness of girls' violence, especially relative to the seriousness of boys' vio lence. Although juvenile arrests for assault—regardless of gender—are far more likely to involve simple assault than aggravated assault, the fact that the ratio of simple to aggra vated assault arrests is much higher for girls than boys suggests that most girls' violence is of a less serious nature than boys' violence. More ver, one of the reasons that boys are more likely than girls to be charged with aggravated assault is that boys use weapons more frequently and physically inflict more injury on their victims—both indicators of the relative seriousness of boys' versus girls' violence. Finally, although girls' rate of arrest for simple assault has increased over the decades, their arrest rate for aggravated assault has not.

Despite dramatic changes in the number and rate of arrests and in simple/aggravated assault ratios, the question remains whether these trends signify a real change in girls' underlying violent behavior or reflect other factors.

Researchers have examined the changing nature of assaults over the past decades by comparing ratios of aggravated assaults to homicides (e.g., Zimring, 1998) or ratios of assaults to robberies (e.g., Zimring and Hawkins, 1997; Snyder and Sickmund, 2000). Because arrests for assault increased without cor responding increases in arrests for homicide or robbery, these analysts attribute the increases in assault arrests to changes in law enforce ment policies, such as responses to domestic violence, rather than to actual increases in assaults.

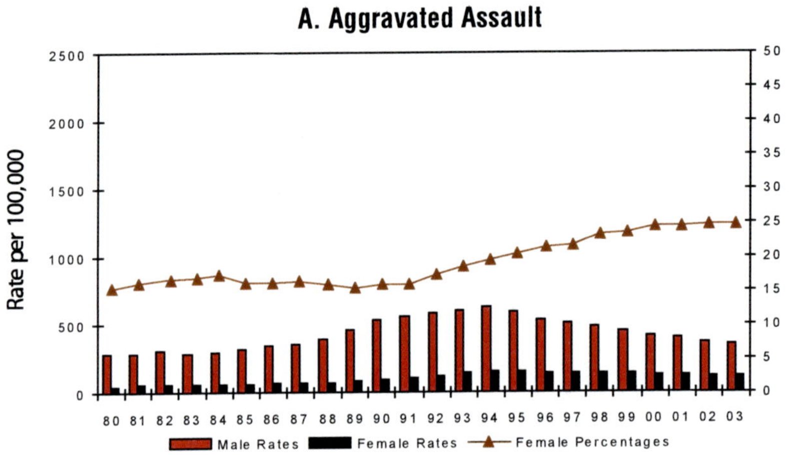

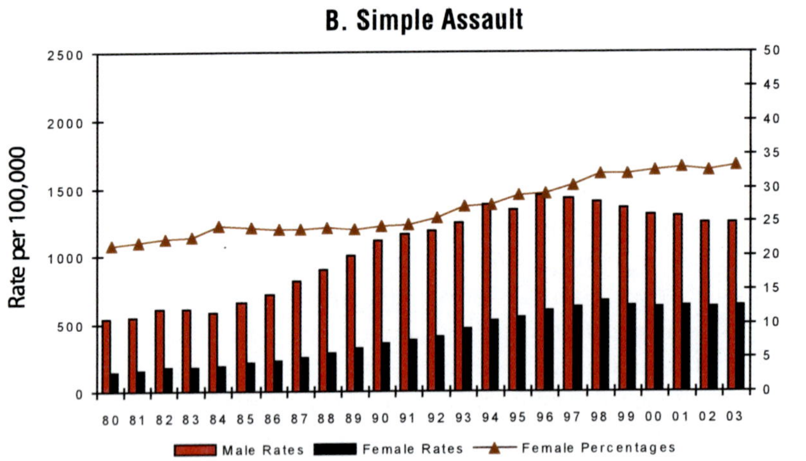

Figure 1 (Continued)

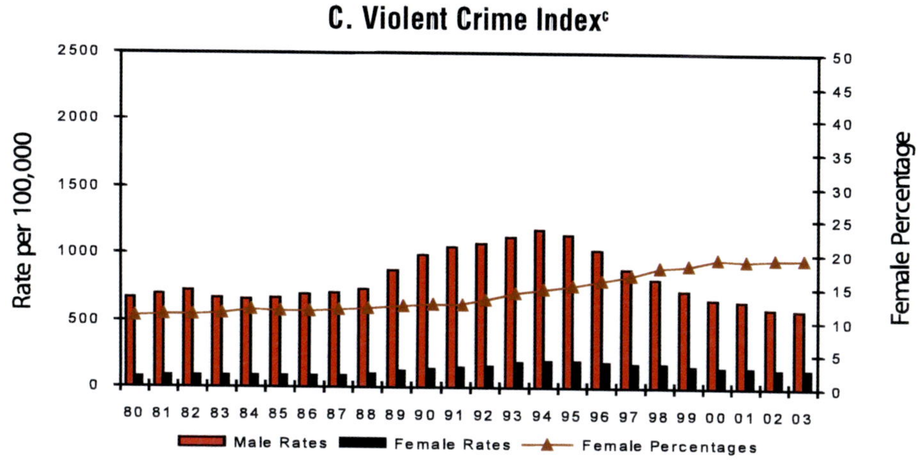

[a] Rates are adjusted for the gender composition of the population and for changes in UCR coverage over time. The population base includes ages 12–17.

[b] Female Percentage = Female Rate / (Female Rate + Male Rate) x 100%

[c] The Violent Crime Index includes homicide, aggravated assault, rape, and robbery

Source: Steffensmeier et al., 2005. Permission was given by the American Society of Criminology to reprint this figure, which was originally published in *Criminology* (Vol. 43, No. 2).

Figure 1. Trends in Juvenile Female and Male Arrest Ratesa (per 100,000) and Juvenile Female Percentage of Arrestsb for Violent Offending: Uniform Crime Reports, 1980–2003.

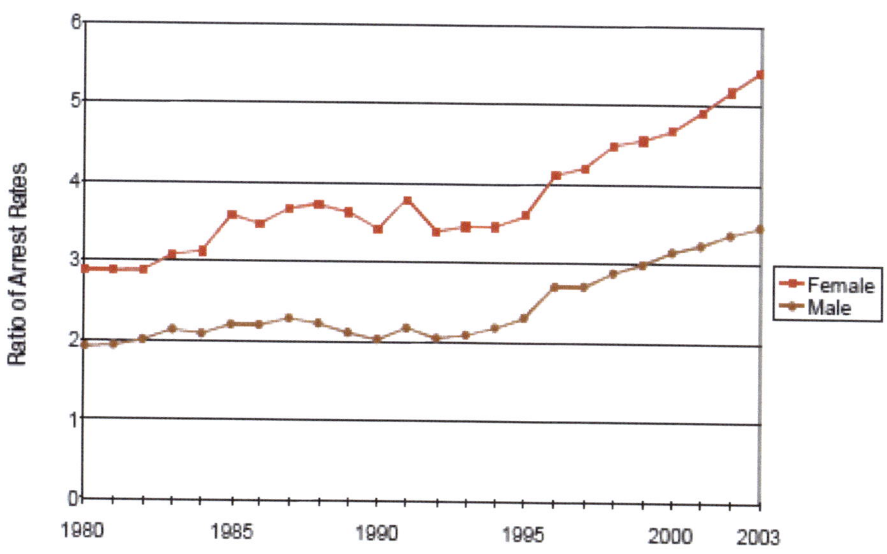

Source: National Center for Juvenile Justice (February 28, 2005), available at www.ojjdp.ncjrs.org/ojstatbb/ crime/excel/jar_20050228.xls.

Figure 2. Ratio of Simple/Aggravated Assault Rates for Juvenile Males and Females, 1980–2003.

Several factors relevant to interpreting statis tics on girls' arrests for assault must be considered:

- Law enforcement policies that lower the threshold for reporting an assault or for classifying an assault as ag gravated may create the appearance of a "crime wave" when the underlying behavior remains relatively stable.
- Heightened sensitivity to domestic violence has led many States and localities to implement "manda tory arrest" policies in response to domestic disturbances. Behaviors once considered "ungovernable" (a status offense) may, in a domes tic situation, result instead in an arrest for simple assault—possibly in response to the Juvenile Justice and Delinquency Prevention Act of 2002, which requires States to decriminalize and deinstitution alize status offenses (Schneider, 1984; Mahoney and Fenster, 1982; Chesney-Lind and Sheldon, 2004; Girls Inc., 1996).
- Family dynamics may also con tribute to gender differences in juvenile arrests for assault. Par ents have different expectations about their sons' and daughters' obedience to parental authority (Chesney-Lind, 1988), and these expectations may affect how the justice system responds to a girl's behavior when she "acts out" with in the home (Krause and McShane, 1994). Research indicates that girls fight with family members or siblings more frequently than boys, who more often fight with friends or strangers (Bloom et al., 2002). Some research suggests that girls are three times as likely as boys to assault a family member (Franke, Huynh-Hohnbaum, and Chung, 2002).
- Policies of mandatory arrest for domestic violence, initially adopt ed to protect victims from further attacks, also provide parents with another method for attempting to control their "unruly" daugh ters. Regardless of who initiates a violent domestic incident, law enforcement first responders may consider it more practical and efficient to identify the youth as the offender, especially when the parent is the caretaker for other children in the home (Gaarder, Rodriguez, and Zatz, 2004).
- It is possible that school officials' adoption of zero-tolerance poli cies toward youth violence may increase the number of youth referred to police for schoolyard tussles that schools previously handled internally.

One way of assessing the "policy change hypothesis" is to compare girls' arrest trends for violent offenses to trends reflected in self-report and victimization data, using MTF and NCVS. Unlike the UCR, these data are not limited to cases that come to the attention of the police or result in arrests. If higher female arrest rates for violent crime are a byproduct of policy changes, then one would expect to find disagreement between official and unofficial data sources, with arrest data showing noticeably larger gains in female violence than found in self-report or victimization data. In contrast, if higher female rates reflect true changes in the aggressive tendencies of girls, then data sources should generally be in agreement.

Trends in Self-Reported Assaults: Monitoring the Future Data

As with the UCR arrest data, Steffensmeier and colleagues (2005) used MTF data from 1980 through 2003 to explore female- versus-male trends with tests to determine any statistical differences. Focusing on self-reported assaults, the research ers calculated prevalence (one or more incidents) and high frequency (five or more incidents) estimates for an assault index comprising three assault items[7] for 12th graders (ages 17–18). Data indicate marked stabil ity in the separate trends for both boys and girls for the assault index over the 1980–2003 period, regard less of whether prevalence or high- frequency measures are used.

These statistical patterns are illus trated in figure 3 (p. 8), where the trends over the past two decades show overall stability (i.e., random fluctuations rather than any consis tent upward or downward trend). Assault rates among both girls and boys are relatively unchanged over this period, although female assault levels are consistently lower than male levels for both prevalence and high- frequency measures. Also, the gender difference in high-frequency violent assaults is quite large: Girls account for an average of about 15 percent of high-frequency assaults, compared with about 35 percent for less frequent or minor involvement in violence.

What Do We Learn from Self-Report Data?

In contrast to official arrest statistics, self-report data from the Monitoring the Future surveys show that levels of assault for juvenile females and males have been fairly constant over the past two decades and that female involvement in violence has not increased relative to male violence.

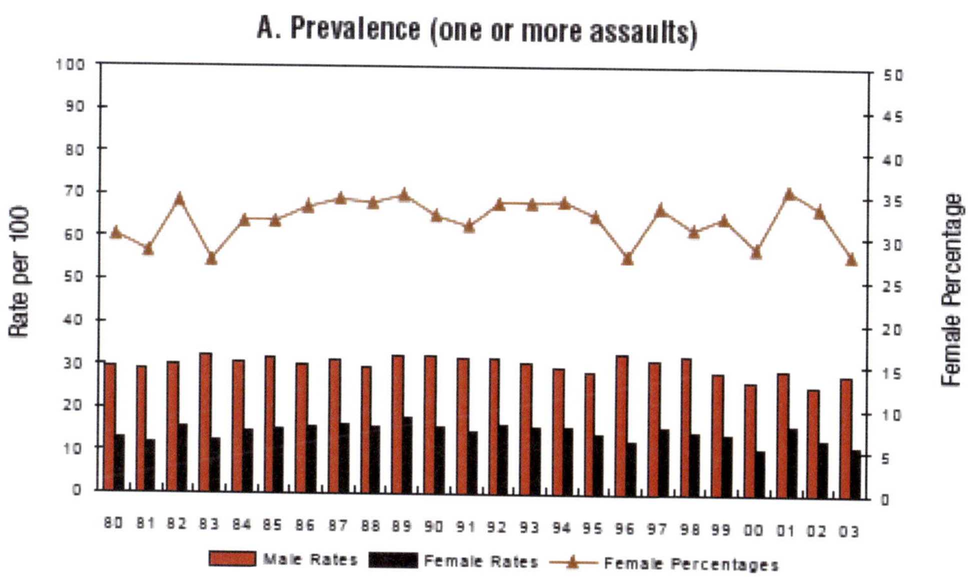

Figure 3 (Continued)

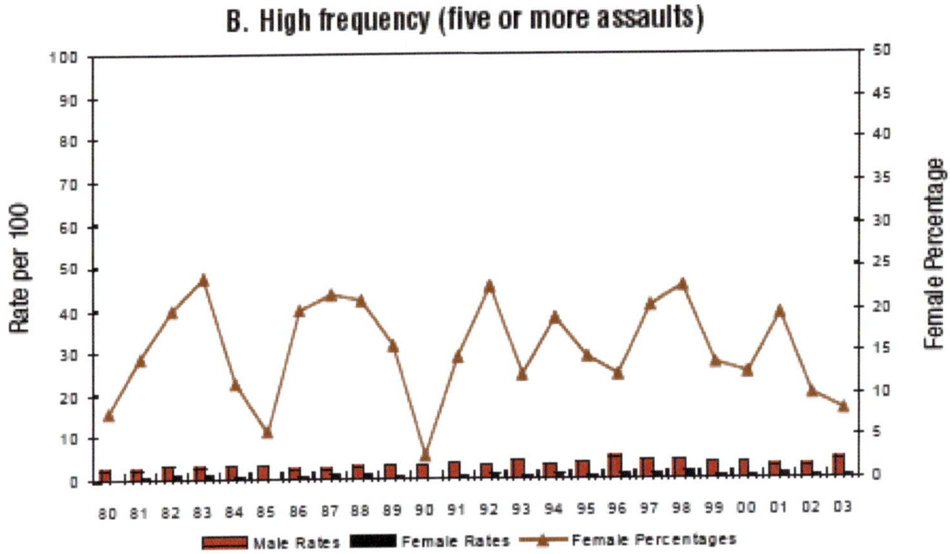

* Items in the assault index include (1) hit instructor/supervisor, (2) fight at school/work, and (3) hurt someone badly in a fight. Source: Steffensmeier et al., 2005. Permission was given by the American Society of Criminology to reprint this figure, which was originally published in *Criminology* (Vol. 43, No. 2).

Figure 3. Trends in Female and Male Self-Reported Assault* and Female Percentage of Violent Offending: Monitoring the Future, 1980–2003 (17- and 18-year-olds).

TRENDS IN VICTIMS' REPORTS OF ASSAULTS: NATIONAL CRIME VICTIMIZATION SURVEY DATA

Steffensmeier and colleagues (2005) also analyzed NCVS data to explore trends in assault and violence as reported by victims. Again, their analy sis relies on statistical tests and illustra tive plots of female- versus-male trends during 1980–2003. The results indicate that the rates of violence among ado lescent females relative to rates among adolescent males have changed very little during this period (i.e., year-to-year changes in female versus-male rates are not statistically significant). This is true for violent offenses in general and assault in par ticular. The trends for both aggravated

The gender difference in violence is fairly comparable between NCVS and assault and simple assault are stable, a pattern contrary to UCR arrest trends, which show a narrowing gen der gap. The gender difference in NCVS trends is also stable for the Vio lent Crime Index, also contrary to the UCR trends.

Figure 4 (p. 9) illustrates these findings by showing NCVS rates of violence for juvenile males and females (per 100,000), along with the relevant female percentages. Based on NCVS reports, girls' violence levels are much lower than boys' levels. Girls' rates typically rise when boys' rates rise and decline when boys' rates decline (i.e., male and female rates move in tandem), yielding a stable gender gap in overall violence. Similar to UCR data, girls' and boys' 1980s through the early 1990s and then tapered off, but the rise is smaller and the decline is greater in the NCVS series than in the UCR series.

The NCVS data show both girls' and boys' rates of assault dropping con siderably in recent years, whereas the UCR data show that assault arrest rates declined only for boys. This tell ing difference between the two data sources supports the conclusion that policy shifts and changes in enforce ment may have had a greater impact on arrest rates than have actual changes in the behavior of girls.

UCR figures in earlier years, but the two sources diverge in more recent years, as would be expected based on the policy change hypothesis. For example, the female percentage for the assault index (defined the same in the NCVS as in the UCR as aggravated assaults, simple assaults, and other offenses against persons) in the early 1980s was about 18–20 percent in both the NCVS and the UCR—essentially no difference; by the late 1990s, however, the percent age holds steady at about 20 percent in the NCVS but jumps to about 30 percent in the UCR. Sizable declines have considerably outpaced the much smaller declines in UCR assault arrest rates, particularly among adolescent girls.

Several conclusions can be drawn from the NCVS data:

- First, gender differences in juvenile violent offending, including assault, have not changed mean ingfully or systematically in the NCVS data since 1980. The NCVS assault finding stands in sharp contrast to UCR arrest statistics, where the gender difference has narrowed significantly for both simple and aggravated assault.
- Second, the NCVS series reveals sharp declines in assault crimes among both girls and boys since about the mid-1990s, but girls' declines are not seen in the UCR arrest data. This discrepancy in the two data sources may be caused in part by changes in policies and practices.
- Third, these possible changes in policy are particularly salient for girls, whose arrest figures havegain insight into female offending patterns, the Girls Study Group has explored the context in which girls exhibit violence. In a nationally representative sample, research has found that for both girls and boys, physical aggression is most common among same-sex peers, accounting for about 50 percent of incidents in which adolescents are violent (Franke et al., 2002). For girls who are physi cally assaultive, a family member is the second most common target (20.2 percent of girls' compared with continued to rise or barely level off compared with victim reports that show sizable declines in girls' assaults since at least the mid-1990s.

What Do We Learn From Victimization Data?

In contrast to official arrest statistics, victimization data from the National Crime Victimization Survey show very little change in the gender gap for assault crimes and the Violent Crime Index over the past two decades and since the 1994 peak in violent crimes.

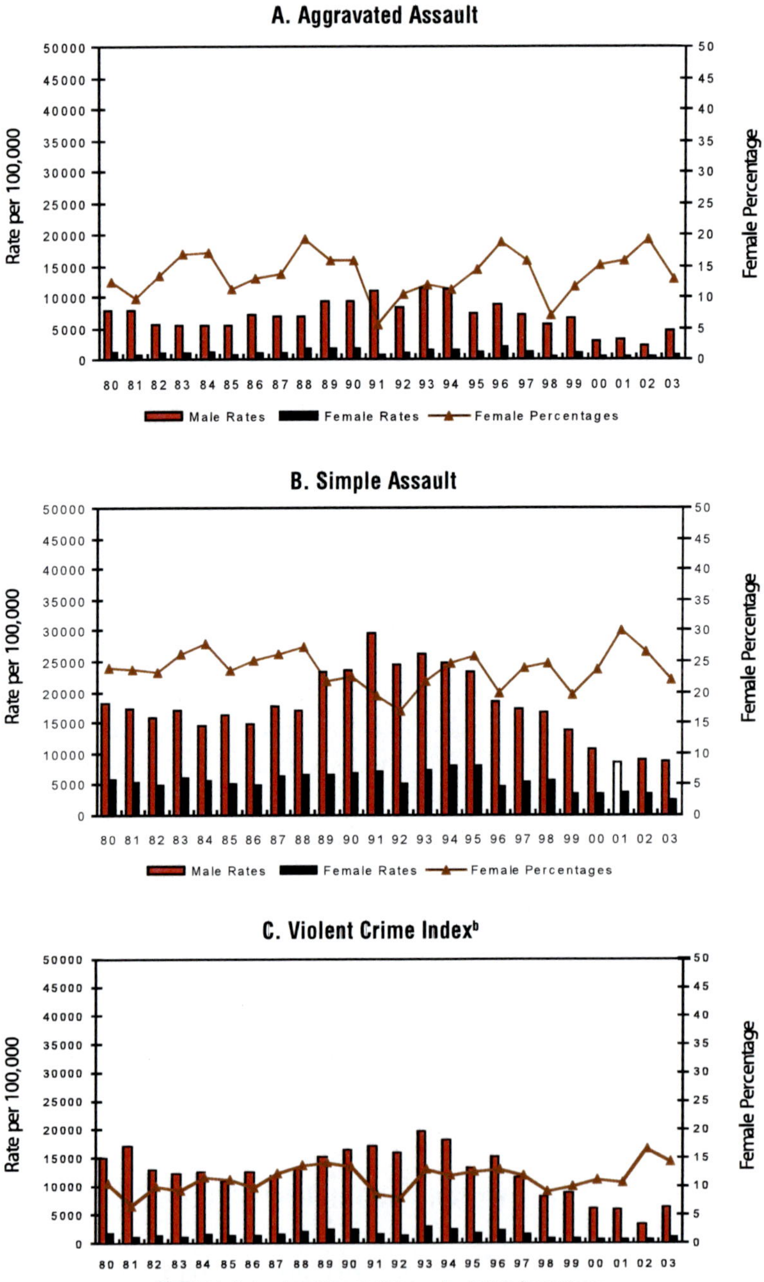

a Data are adjusted to take into account effects of the survey redesign in 1992. The multiplier is offense and sex specific and is calculated based only on juvenile data. The formula is: Multiplier = (n92 + n93 + n94)/(n90 + n91 + n92).

b The Violent Crime Index includes aggravated assault, rape, and robbery.

Source: Steffensmeier et al., 2005. Permission was given by the American Society of Criminology to reprint this figure, which was originally published in Criminology (Vol. 43, No. 2).

Figure 4. Trends in Juvenile Female and Male Violence Rates[a] (per 100,000) and Female Percentage of Violent Offending: National Crime Victimization Survey, 1980–2003.

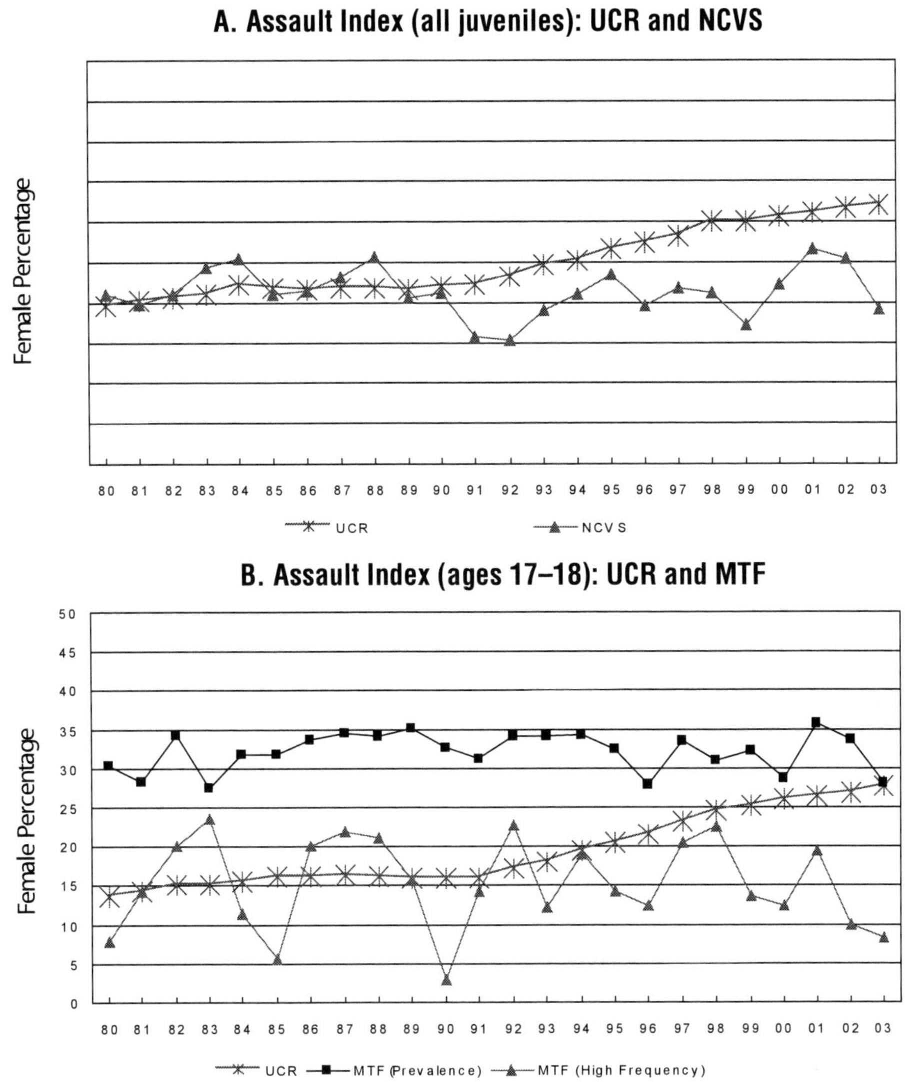

Source: Steffensmeier et al., 2005. Permission was given by the American Society of Criminology to reprint this figure, which was originally published in Criminology (Vol. 43, No. 2.

Figure 5. Summary of Trends in Juvenile Gender Gap for Assault in Arrest Data Compared With Victimization and Self-Report Sources: Uniform Crime Reports, National Crime Victimization Survey, and Monitoring the Future, 1980–2003.

SUMMARY

Figure 5 highlights the differences in trends between official arrest data and self-report (MTF) sources. These graphs clearly show the upward trend in the female percent of arrests for assaults based on UCR arrest data, while the trends based on victimization data and self-reports have been fairly stable over time.

Context of Girls' Violence

In addition to analyzing juvenile violence trends in arrests, victimization, and self-reported behavior togain insight into female offending patterns, the Girls Study Group has explored the context in which girls exhibit violence. In a nationally representative sample, research has found that for both girls and boys, physical aggression is most common among same-sex peers, accounting for about 50 percent of incidents in which adolescents are violent (Franke et al., 2002). For girls who are physi cally assaultive, a family member is the second most common target (20.2 percent of girls' compared with5.7 percent of boys' fights are with family members). The second most common target of boys' assaults is strangers. Consistent with this pat tern, girls' violence more often occurs at home, whereas boys' violence more often occurs away from home. Findings that girls are particularly likely to act violently in certain set tings or under certain conditions affirm the importance of examining the context of violence for insights into why girls are sometimes violent.

What Have We Learned About Trends In Girls' and Boys' Violence?

Across all data sources, the gender difference in trends for minor kinds of violence (e.g., simple assault) is much smaller than the gender difference for more serious violence (e.g., aggravated assault). In contrast to conclusions about rises in girls' violence based on arrest statistics (UCR), the results from other sources (MTF and NCVS) show very little overall change in girls' assault levels or in Violent Crime Index offenses and essentially no change in the gender differences or femaleto-male ratio of violent offending.

Violence Against Peers

Girls and boys are more likely to attack their same-sex peers than any other type of victim (Franke et al., 2002), as noted above. A study by Lockwood (1997) found that, regard less of gender, the most common rea sons youth were violent toward peers was to punish them for something done or said, to get them to back down from offensive actions, and in self-defense. Physical touching, often aggressive, was the most frequent immediate precipitator of a violent incident. The second most common trigger of peer violence was negative verbal exchanges.

Other researchers have examined the relationship between physical violence and relational aggression, which includes trying to damage the social standing or self-esteem of peers by using verbal rejection, gossip, rumor spreading, and social ostracism (Cairns et al., 1989; Galen and Underwood, 1997). In some social and cultural groups, the influences against fighting weaken the connection of relational aggression to physical violence; specifically, Goodwin (1990) found that among middle-class African American youth, episodes of relational aggres sion were followed by nonphysical confrontations and ostracism butnot by physical fighting. Corsaro and Eder (1990) found that relational aggression among economically dis advantaged girls may be more likely to escalate into physical fighting, perhaps due to a need or desire to emphasize one's own toughness and independence. Whether relational aggression leads to physical fighting may be tempered by other factors such as social class and local com munity and peer group norms (on peer group norms, see Crick, Bigbee, and Howe, 1996).

Research indicates that another fac tor in girls' violence against other girls involves the contradictory mes sages girls receive regarding sexuality. For most girls, models and images of healthy sexual desire are rare or nonexistent (Welles, 2005). Rigid imagery about "appropriate" behav ior for girls can emphasize being attractive to and desired by boys and at the same time, send girls messages that they are valued for abstaining from sexual behavior. A great deal of societal emphasis is placed on being thin and looking like a supermodel or a Barbie doll (Schooler, Ward, and Merriwether, 2004; Wolf, 1991; Bordo, 1993; Davis, 1995). Artz (1997) found that the girls at risk for engaging in same-sex peer violence did not have any sense of themselves or other girls as having their own legitimate sexual desires or being valued. They under stood their own sexual value only in relation to how they satisfied males and lived up to idealized standards of femininity. Thus, these girls were quick to strike out at other girls who threatened their view of self or their relationships with valued males.

Violence Against Family Members

After peers, family members are the second most common target of girls' violence. Data from the FBI's National Incident-Based Reporting System for 2001 (FBI, 2003), analyzing reports of assaults by juvenile males and females by type of victim, clearly show that girls are more likely to be involved in both aggravated and simple assaults against adult family members than are their male peers, as shown in table 2 (p. 12).

When a girl uses violence against a family member, a parent—usually the mother—is the most common target.[8]

Prior victimization (in the home, in the community, or at school) appears to be a significant precursor to vio lent behavior for girls (Song, Singer, and Anglin, 1998; Molnar et al., 2005). Violence against a family member may also be a result of social learn ing that takes place when girls watch family and others who are constantly assaulting them and each other (Miller, 2001). Although girls are more likely than boys to internalize negative emotions when victimized (e.g., become depressed or anxious), they do sometimes exhibit external izing behavior, using violence in self- defense, to prevent further attack, or because they are angry.

Research indicates that in cultures that are very patriarchal and/or that devalue females, girls may be more at risk for abuse, neglect, and sexual assault (Jiwani, Janovicek, and Cam eron, 2002). However, no research adequately examines whether this greater abuse or control of girls in some cultural groups translates into the girls' greater use of violence, either inside or outside the family. It is plausible that in very patriarchal families, gender-related restrictions on girls severely limit girls' use of violence and their expression of anger. A study by Heimer and DeCoster (1999) using self-report survey data showed that girls who have traditional views of gender, and, therefore, traditional views of female behavior, are less likely to engage in violence.

CONTEXT DEFINED

Context includes targets (e.g., peers, family members); specific settings (e.g., schools, neighborhoods, peer groups); and the precursors (e.g., prior victimization, relational aggression) leading up to an act of violence.

Table 2. Type of Victim in Aggravated and Simple Assaults by Boys and Girls

	Simple Assault		Aggravated Assault	
Type of Victim	Boys	Girls	Boys	Girls
Juvenile family	5%	5%	4%	7%
Juvenile acquaintance	54	49	45	40
Juvenile stranger	5	3	6	2
Adult family	17	23	12	21
Adult acquaintance	16	17	21	24
Adult stranger	4	3	12	6

Source: Information for this table was provided by Howard Snyder (Director of Systems Research at the National Center for Juvenile Justice), using data from the FBI's National Incident-Based Reporting System for 2001 (FBI, 2003).

VIOLENCE IN SCHOOLS

Although school-related deaths, violent victimizations in school, and overall school crime declined dur ing the 1990s (Kaufman et al., 2001), public concern about school safety increased, especially in the wake

of several highly publicized school shootings between 1992 and 1999(Anderson et al., 2001). The Youth Risk Behavior Surveillance surveys (YRBSS), conducted biannually in schools in 32 States and certain localities by the Centers for Disease Control and Prevention, provide statistics regarding violent behavior by students. The 2003 survey shows that fighting is common among high school students: 33 percent of students (40.5 percent of males and 25.1 percent of females) surveyed had been in a physical fight in the last year (Grunbaum et al., 2004). Research has also shown that girls' violent delinquency is greater in middle schools than in high schools, independent of a girl's age. (Payne and Gottfredson, 2005). Further more, in 2004, 32 percent of all seri ous, violent crimes (including rape, sexual assault, robbery, or aggravated assault) against youth ages 12–18 occurred during school or on the way to and from school (Dinkes et al., 2006).

Bullying in schools appears to differ by gender. Boys are more likely to be the perpetrators and victims of direct bullying, either with physical actions or with words or gestures. Girls, in ontrast, are more likely to be the perpetrators and victims of indirect bullying, or relational aggression, such as spreading rumors. In addi tion, boys are more often the perpe trators in bullying incidents in which girls were the victims (Olweus, 1993; Isernhagen Harris, 2003).

Although girls are not frequently violent in schools, when they behave violently they may do so to protect themselves. Some studies have found that girls intensify their fighting to stop their own victimization (includ ing sexual harassment) and when they feel this victimization is ignored by school officials (Brown, 1998; Belknap, Dunn, and Holsinger, 1997).

Some teachers communicate a very restrictive standard for what is con sidered "appropriate" behavior for boys as compared with girls. When teachers hold girls and boys to dif ferent standards, they can create an atmosphere that indirectly encourag es girls to use violence. Research on a school with a socially diverse student body found that teachers sometimes created a hostile environment that fed antagonisms among groups of youth (Rosenbloom and Way, 2004). In another study, some girls who perceived themselves as negatively "marked" by minority racial and socioeconomic identity maintained their status in school by not backing down when they were threatened by peers and/or when they were angry with teachers. Some also reported saving face or earning status through their prowess in fighting (Leitz, 2003).

Girls may also fight out of a sense of hopelessness. A recent ethnographic study of low-income girls in Philadel phia found that the girls thought their futures were bleak regardless of what they did at school. They felt alienated from legitimate institutions, including schools, and felt that entanglementwith the law could not make things worse (Ness, 2004).

Poverty and Disorganized Communities

Poverty concentrates mothers and their children in neighborhoods characterized by few legitimate opportunities to earn money, a prevalence of illegitimate opportuni ties, and limited and strained public health, mental health, educational, and recreational resources. Several studies have found a link between exposure to violence in disorganized communities and youth's use of vio lence (DuRant et al., 1994; Burman, 2003; Fitzpatrick, 1997). A recent lon gitudinal study (Molnar et al., 2005) of adolescent girls in Chicago found that girls were more likely to perpe trate violence if they had previously been victimized and if they lived in neighborhoods with a high concen tration of poverty or with high homi cide rates.

A girl living in a disorganized neigh borhood may be more likely to use violence for a number of reasons (Leventhal and Brooks-Gunn, 2000). In communities that lack informal institutions for monitoring and supervising youth's behavior, risk of victimization is high, and girls may be violent to prevent or stop attacks on themselves (Leitz, 2003). Parents who are themselves coping with structurally disadvantaged neigh borhoods and poverty may lack the capacity to buffer the negative envi ronment for their daughters by, for example, providing close monitor ing or safe places for recreation and socializing. In such communities, schools and recreational activities often do not provide safe places for youth, leaving girls to their own devices to establish status among peers and to prevent and counteract violence against them selves. As discussed earlier, willing ness to fight and prowess in fighting are two of the few ways that youth feel they can gain status in com munities with few opportunities to develop talents or succeed in school. Status may be enhanced for girls who are willing to fight, because these girls are valuable to friends who might need protection and also because they can protect themselves (Jones, 2004; Ness, 2004).

A girl's physical maturity may place her at special risk in disorganized neighborhoods. Girls with early-onset puberty who live in neighborhoods of highly concentrated disadvantage are at significantly greater risk for violent behaviors when compared to early-maturing girls who live in less dis advantaged neighborhoods (Obeidallah et al., 2004). This finding has several possible explanations. Early-maturing girls who live in dis advantaged neighborhoods may be particularly prone to affiliate with delinquent peers (Ge et al., 2002). These girls might become involved with older boys who are attracted to them, and the older boys might model and encourage girls' use of violence (Ge et al., 2002). Some studies suggest that girls with boyfriends who live in disorganized or poor communities may be more likely to engage in fighting to keep the boyfriend, who may provide important material or financial support (Ness, 2004). Finally, early-maturing girls may become involved with gangs and other negative peers in reaction to parental efforts to protect them by keeping them at home (Haynie, 2003).

Girls and Gangs

A very specific aspect of the context in which girls may exhibit violence is their involvement in gangs. Because research relevant to understanding girls' involvement in gangs is diverse, this section offers an overview in three parts: membership, delinquency, and risk factors.

Membership

Researchers have derived estimates of girls' membership in gangs from official data sources and self-report surveys. In addition to estimating the prevalence of girls' membership, research has also examined the gender composition of gangs.

Data from official sources sometimes underestimate the extent of girls' gang membership, especially when contrasted with self-report data. For instance, Curry, Ball, and Fox (1994) found that in some jurisdictions, law enforcement policies officially exclude females from counts of gang members. Controlling for data from these cities, the researchers still found that girls represented only 5.7 percent of gang members known to law enforcement agencies.

Underestimation of girls' gang involvement based on official reports may also be partly attributable to male gang members' greater likeli hood of being involved in serious crime, as well as to differences in average age of males and females in gangs (Bjerregaard and Smith, 1993; Fagan, 1990). Boys are more likely than girls to remain gang involved into young adulthood; for girls, gang membership is much more likely to be limited to the adolescent years (Hunt, Joe-Laidler, and MacKenzie, 2005; Miller, 2001; Moore and Hage dorn, 1996). These gender-related variations may increase the likeli hood that male gang members will come to the attention of police more often than female gang members (Curry, 1999; Esbensen and Winfree, 1998).

On the other hand, results from youth surveys indicate that girls' gang involvement is only slightly below that of boys, particularly in early adolescence. For instance, find ings from the Rochester Youth Devel opment Study, based on a stratified sample of youth in high-risk, high- crime neighborhoods, found that approximately the same percentage of girls (29.4 percent) and boys (32.4 percent) claimed gang membership when self-definition[9] was used as a measure (Thornberry et al., 2000).

Evidence from this longitudinal study also suggests that girls' gang involve ment tends to be of a shorter dura tion than boys', with girls' peak gang involvement around eighth and ninth grades.

In research based on youth surveys, estimates of girls' share of total gang membership range from 20 percent to 46 percent (Esbensen and Huizinga, 1993; Esbensen and Winfree, 1998; Fagan, 1990; Moore, 1991; Winfree et al., 1992), with wide variations from gang to gang. When female gang members in Columbus, OH, and St. Louis, MO, were asked what percentage of their gang's members were girls, answers ranged from 7 percent to 75 percent; the vast major ity were in predominantly male gangs (Miller, 2001). In a survey of 366 gang members (Peterson, Miller, and Esbensen, 2001), 84 percent of malesand 93 percent of females said their gangs had both male and female members. Approximately 45 percent of the male gang members and 30 percent of the females described their gangs as having a majority of male members, and 38 percent of males and 64 percent of females said their gangs had "fairly equal" numbers of males and females. Several studies suggest that the gender com position of gangs has a significant impact on the nature of gang mem bers' activities, including their involvement in delinquency (JoeLaidler and Hunt, 1997; Peterson, Miller, and Esbensen, 2001; Miller, 2001).

Delinquent Activity

Girls' gang-related delinquency appears to be strongly associated with the gender organization of their groups. Fleisher and Krienert (2004) suggest that having a sizable propor tion of males in their social networks increases young women's participa tion in delinquency and violence (see also Miller and Brunson, 2000).

Peterson, Miller, and Esbensen (2001), examining delinquent activity among members of gangs classified by gender composition, found that delinquency, particularly of a serious nature, was less characteristic of primarily female gangs than of primarily male, all- male, or gender-balanced gangs. Thesame researchers, however, found significant *within-gender* differences in delinquency rates for both girls and boys across the gang gender- composi tion categories (e.g., girls in primarily female gangs had the lowest rates of delinquency, but girls in majority- male gangs had higher rates of delin quency than boys in all-male gangs).

Gang-involved girls tend to partici pate in different types of activities than gang-involved boys. One study (Miller, 2001) found that most gang- involved young women did not participate routinely in the most serious forms of gang crime, in part because male members excluded them from these activities, but also because many of the young women chose not to be involved in activi ties they considered dangerous or morally troubling. Other researchers attribute differences in the delinquent activities of gang-involved girls and gang-involved boys to gender differences in norms supportive of violence and delinquency (Joe and Chesney-Lind, 1995; see also Camp bell, 1993).

RISK FACTORS

Researchers often have focused on the extent to which community disorganization may have contrib uted to the growth of gangs in many cities.[10] These researchers suggest that inner-city youth join gangs as a way of adapting to oppressive living conditions imposed by their environ ments (see Hagedorn, 1998; Huff, 1989; Klein, 1995). A few studies have linked these conditions specifically to female gang involvement. For example, findings from the Rochester Youth Development Study suggest that growing up in disorganized, vio lent neighborhoods is a risk factor for gang involvement among young women (Thornberry, 1997). Gangs may help young women survive inthese neighborhoods by teaching them how to protect themselves (Fishman, 1995) and by offering pro tection and retaliation (Miller, 2001).

Several studies have explored the relationship between gang involve ment and the family. In a study of gangs in Kansas City, MO, Fleisher (1998) documents intergenerational patterns of abuse and neglect, exac erbated by poverty and abject neigh borhood conditions, which Fleisher suggests are at the heart of the gang problem (see also Campbell, 1984; Fleisher and Krienert, 2004). Moore (1991) also documents a myriad of family problems that contribute to the likelihood of gang involve ment and concludes that young female gang members are especially likely to come from deeply troubled families. Female gang members are significantly more likely than male gang members (Moore, 1991) and at-risk nongang girls (Miller, 2001) to say they have experienced multiple family problems.

The ways in which family problems influence girls' gang involvement are varied, but they share a common thread: because of difficulties and dangers at home, girls began spend ing time away from home and meet ing their social and emotional needs elsewhere. Researchers studying both male and female gang members have suggested the idea of the gang as a surrogate family for adolescents who do not see their own families as meeting their needs for belonging, nurturance, and acceptance (Huff, 1993; see also Campbell, 1990, and Joe and Chesney-Lind, 1995). In a gang, girls may find a network of friends who serve as a support sys tem for coping with life problems (Fleisher and Krienert, 2004; Joe and Chesney-Lind, 1995).

Qualitative studies of risk factors for girls' involvement in gangs have focused on the influence of com munity conditions and family problems. Some survey-based stud ies, however, note various school- related attitudes and individual behaviors as risk factors or corre lates for girls' involvement in gangs. School-related attitudes include low expectations for completing school (Bjerregaard and Smith, 1993; Bowker and Klein, 1983; Thornberry, 1997), lack of school commitment (Esbensen and Deschenes, 1998), and negative attitudes toward school (Thornberry, 1997). Individual char acteristics/behaviors include com mitment to negative peers (Esbensen and Deschenes, 1998); delinquency, drug use, and positive values about drugs (Thornberry, 1997); and delin quent peers and early onset of sexual activity (Bjerregaard and Smith, 1993).

Girls and Gangs

Most research on girls and gangs focuses on amounts of gang involvement (over time and relative to boys) or the factors associated with gang involvement. Very little research has examined girls' violence within gangs. The research that has been done shows that boys in gangs are more violent than girls in gangs. Still, girls in gangs are more likely to be delinquent and violent than girls who are not in gangs. Peers, families, and neighborhoods have intersecting influences when girls become involved with gangs.

Conclusions

What We Know about Girls and Violence

Trends

Available evidence based on arrest, victimization, and self-report data suggests that although girls are cur rently arrested more for simple assaults than previously, the actual incidence of their being seriously vio lent has not changed much over the last two decades. This suggests that increases in arrests may be attribut able more to changes in enforcement policies than to changes in girls' behavior. Juvenile female involve ment in violence has not increased relative to juvenile male violence. There is no burgeoning national crisis of increasing serious violence among adolescent girls.

Context

Although more information is need ed, current literature suggests that girls' violence occurs in the following situations, for the following reasons:

- Peer violence. Girls fight with peers to gain status, to defend their sexual reputation, and in self-defense against sexual harassment.
- Family violence. Girls fight more frequently at home with parents than do boys, who engage more frequently in violence outside the household. Girls' violence against parents is multidimensional: for some, it represents striking back against what they view as an overly controlling structure; for others, it is a defense against or an expres sion of anger stemming from being sexually and or physically abused by members of the house hold.
- Violence within schools. When girls fight in schools, they may do so as a result of teacher labeling, in self-defense, or out of a general sense of hopelessness.
- Violence within disadvantaged neighborhoods. Girls in disad vantaged neighborhoods are more likely to perpetrate vio lence against others because of the increased risk of victimiza tion (and the resulting violent self-defense against that vic timization), parental inability to counteract negative community influences, and lack of opportuni ties for success.

- Girls in gangs. Survey research has shown a number of factors associated with girls' involvement in gangs (e.g., attitudes toward school, peers, delinquency, drug use, and early sexual activity); qualitative research points to the role of disadvantaged neighbor hoods and families with multiple problems (violence, drug and alcohol abuse, neglect). Girls associated with primarily male gangs exhibit more violence than those in all-female gangs. Girls in gangs are more violent than other girls but less violent than boys in gangs.

What We Need To Know

Available evidence strongly sug gests that girls are, over time, being arrested more frequently for simple assaults, despite evidence from longitudinal self-report and victim ization surveys that they are not actually more violent. The reasons for increasing arrests, however, are not well established. Studies of police and court practices—particu larly with regard to girls—are sorely needed. Evaluations of domestic violence laws and zero-tolerance school policies and enforcement practices are also crucial.

It is also important to develop a better understanding of the con sequences for girls of increased involvement in the juvenile justice system. Longitudinal studies of girls who are arrested for assaul tive behavior would help us better understand the pathways to and consequences of arrests for violent behavior among girls.

Although there does not appear to be a large increase in physical violence committed by girls, some girls do engage in violent behavior, and it is important to understand the context in which such violence occurs and how these situations differ for girls and boys. Although peers and family members are the most common tar gets of violence by girls, not all family or peer conflicts result in physical assault. Understanding which ones do, and why, remains vital for both prevention and intervention efforts.

Endnotes

[1] The MTF study is funded by the National Institute on Drug Abuse. Findings are available online at www.monitoringthefuture.org.

[2] Note that UCR data count the number of arrests, not the number of individuals arrested. An unknown number of individu als are arrested more than once during a year.

[3] The Violent Crime Index includes homicide, forcible rape, robbery, and aggravated assaults.

[4] The Property Crime Index includes burglary, larceny-theft, motor vehicle theft, and arson.

[5] Nonindex offenses are simple assault, weapons offenses, drug and liquor law violations, driv ing under the influence, disor derly conduct, vandalism, and other categories not included in the FBI's Crime Indexes. Status offenses are acts that are offenses only when committed by juve niles (e.g., running away).

[6] Aggravated assault is defined as "an unlawful attack by one person upon another for the purpose of inflicting severe or aggravated bodily injury. This type of assault usually is

accom panied by the use of a weapon or by means likely to produce death or great bodily harm" (FBI, 2004,p. 23). Simple assault is defined as including "all assaults which do not involve the use of a fire arm, knife, cutting instrument, or other dangerous weapon and in which the victim did not sustain serious or aggravated injuries. Agencies must classify as simple assault such offenses as assault and battery, injury caused by culpable negligence, intimida tion, coercion, and all attempts to commit these offenses" (FBI, 2004, p. 26).

[7] The 12th graders were asked how often during the past 12 months they had: (1) "hit an instructor or supervisor," (2) "gotten into a serious fight at school or at work," and (3) "hurt someone badly enough to need bandages or a doctor."

[8] Some research indicates that parents are more likely to be violent toward adolescents than adolescents are toward their parents (Browne and Hamilton, 1998; Straus and Gelles, 1990). In a survey of college students (Browne and Hamilton, 1998), 80 percent of the youth who were violent toward parents said their parents were violent toward them, whereas only 59 percent of mothers' violence and 71 percentof fathers' violence was met with or precipitated by violence from the youth.

[9] A number of scholars now use self-definition as a measure of gang membership, either alone or in conjunction with more restric tive guidelines. Some researchers suggest that only youth who are members of groups involved in illegal activities should be clas sified as gang members (see Esbensen, Huizinga, and Weihen, 1993; Esbensen and Huizinga, 1993). However, Winfree et al. (1992: 34–35) found that the "self reported definition of gang mem bership proved to be a better predictor of gang-related crime than the more restrictive definition," which they speculate may be a result of fringe or "wannabe" members' efforts to demonstrate gang membership. Additional evidence supporting the utility of self-definition as a measure of gang membership comes from studies that have found large and stable differences between self-identified gang members and nongang youth with regard to rates of involvement in delin quency and serious crime (see Fagan, 1990).

[10] Larger cities and suburban coun ties consistently account for the largest proportion (around 85 percent) of reported gang mem bers (Egley and Major, 2004). Because research has focused on urban gangs, less is known about the social processes that explain gang formation—and girls' gang involvement—in rural and subur ban areas, although some schol ars have hypothesized possible cultural diffusion processes (see Klein, 1995; Miller, 2001).

Acknowledgments

The Girls Study Group is a group of multidisciplinary experts who have been convened to assess current knowledge about the patterns and causes of female delinquency and to design appropriate intervention programs based on this information.

This Bulletin was compiled by Margaret A. Zahn (Principal Investigator of the Girls Study Group project) and Susan Brumbaugh, with the assistance of Tara Williams, and is based on excerpts from manuscripts written for the Girls Study Group by the following authors:

- Barry Feld* and Darrell Steffensmeier*: trends (permission to use previously published material from Darrell Steffensmeier is granted by Criminology).
- Merry Morash* and Meda Chesney-Lind*: context.
- Allison Ann Payne, Denise Gottfredson, Candace Kruttschnitt*: violence within schools.
- Jody Miller*: girls in gangs.

Additional analyses on peers were contributed by Howard Snyder, Director of Systems Research at the National Center for Juvenile Justice.
* Girls Study Group member.

References

Anderson, M., Kaufman, J., Simon, T., Barrios, L., Paulozzi, L., Ryan, G., Hammond, R., Modzeleski, W.,

Feucht, T., Potter, L., and the School- Associated Violent Deaths Study Group. 2001. School-associated violent deaths in the United States, 1994–1999. Journal of the American Medical Association 286:2695–2702.

Artz, S. 1997. On becoming an object. Journal of Child and Youth Care 11(2):17–37.

Belknap, J., Dunn, M., and Holsinger, K. 1997. Moving Toward Juvenile Justice and Youth-Serving Systems That Address the Distinct Experience of the Adolescent Female. Gender Specific Work Group Report to the Governor. Columbus, OH: Office of Criminal Justice Services.

Benson, M.L., Fox, G.L., DeMaris, A., and Van Wyk, J. 2003. Neighborhood disadvantage, individual economic distress and violence against women in intimate relationships. Journal of Quantitative Criminology 19:207–235.

Bjerregaard, B., and Smith, C. 1993. Gender differences in gang participa tion, delinquency, and substance use. Journal of Quantitative Criminology 4:329–355.

Bloom, B., Owne, B., Deschenes, E., and Rosenbaum, J. 2002. Improving juvenile justice for females: A state wide assessment in California. Crime & Delinquency 4:526–552.

Bordo, S. 1993. Unbearable Weight: Feminism, Western Culture and the Body. Berkeley, CA: University of California Press.

Bowker, L.H., and Klein, M.W. 1983. The etiology of female juvenile delinquency and gang membership: A test of psychological and social structural explanations. Adolescence 18: 739–751.

Brown, L.M. 1998. Raising Their Voices: The Politics of Girls' Anger. Cambridge, MA: Harvard University Press.

Browne, K.D., and Hamilton, C.E. 1998. Physical violence between young adults and their parents: Asso ciations with a history of child mal treatment. Journal of Family Violence 13(1):59–79.

Burman, M. 2003. Challenging con ceptions of violence: A view from the girls. Sociology Review 13(4):2–6.

Cairns, R.B., Cairns, B.D., Neckerman, H.J., Ferguson, L.L., and Gariépy, J.L. 1989. Growth and aggression: Child hood to early adolescence. Developmental Psychology 25:320–330.

Campbell, A. 1984. The Girls in the Gang. New York, NY: Basil Blackwell.

Campbell, A. 1990. Female partici pation in gangs. In Gangs in America, edited by C. Ronald Huff. Newbury Park, CA: Sage Publications, pp. 163–182.

Campbell, A. 1993. Men, Women and Aggression. New York, NY: Basic Books.

Chesney-Lind, M. 1988. Girls and status offenses: Is juvenile justice still sexist? Criminal Justice Abstracts 20:144–165.

Chesney-Lind, M., and Sheldon, R. 2004. Girls, Delinquency, and Juvenile Justice. 2d ed. Belmont, CA: Thompson/Wadsworth.

Corsaro, W.A., and Eder, D. 1990. Children's peer cultures. Annual Review of Sociology 16:197–220.

Crick, N.R., Bigbee, M.A., and Howe, C. 1996. Gender differences in children's normative beliefs about aggression: How do I hurt thee? Let me count the ways. Child Development 67:1003–1014.

Curry, G.D. 1999. Race, ethnicity and gender issues in gangs: Reconciling police data. In Problem-Oriented Policing: Crime-Specific Issues and Making POP Work, Volume II, edited by C.S. Brito and T. Allan, Washing ton, DC: Police Executive Research Forum, pp. 63–89.

Curry, G.D., Ball, R.A., and Fox, R.J. 1994. Gang Crime and Law Enforcement Recordkeeping. Research in Brief. Washington, DC: U.S. Depart ment of Justice, Office of Justice Pro grams, National Institute of Justice.

Davis, K. 1995. Reshaping the Female Body: The Dilemma of Cosmetic Surgery. New York, NY: Routledge.

Devoe, J.F., Peter, K., Kaufman, P., Ruddy, S.A., Miller, A.K., Planty, M., Snyder, T.D., and Rand, M.R. 2003. Indicators of School Crime and Safety: 2003. (NCJ 201257). Washington, DC: U.S. Departments of Education and Justice, National Center for Educa tion Statistics and Bureau of Justice Statistics.

Dinkes, R., Cataldi, E.F., Kena G., and Baum, K., 2006. Indicators of School Crime and Safety 2006. Washington, DC: U.S. Departments of Education and Justice, National Center for Edu cation Statistics and Bureau of Justice Statistics.

DuRant, R., Cadenhead, C., Pendergrast, R.A., Slavens, G., and Wand Linder, C. 1994. Factors associ ated with the use of violence among urban black adolescents. American Journal of Public Health 84:612–617

Egley, A., Jr., and Major, A.K. 2004. Highlights of the 2002 National Youth Gang Survey. Fact Sheet. Washing

ton DC: U.S. Department of Justice, Office of Justice Programs, Office of Juvenile Justice and Delinquency Prevention.

Esbensen, F.A., and Deschenes, E.P. 1998. A multi-site examination of gang membership: Does gender matter? Criminology 36:799–828.

Esbensen, F.A., and Huizinga, D. 1993. Gangs, drugs, and delinquency in a survey of urban youth. Criminology 3 1:565–589.

Esbensen, F.A., Huizinga, D., and Weiher, A.W. 1993. Gang and non- gang youth: Differences in explana tory factors. Journal of Contemporary Criminal Justice 9:94–116.

Esbensen, F.A., and Winfree, L.T. 1998. Race and gender differences between gang and nongang youth: Results from a multisite survey. Justice Quarterly 15:505–525.

Fagan, J. 1990. Social processes of delinquency and drug use among urban gangs. In Gangs in America, edited by C.R. Huff. Newbury Park, CA: Sage Publications, pp. 183–219.

Federal Bureau of Investigation. 2003. National Incident-Based Report-

ing System Master File for the year 2001 [machine-readable data files]. Washington, DC: U.S. Department of Justice, FBI.

Federal Bureau of Investigation. 2004. Uniform Crime Reporting Handbook. Washington, DC: U.S. Department of Justice, FBI.

Federal Bureau of Investigation. 2006. Crime in the United States, 2005: Uniform Crime Reports. Washington, DC: U.S. Department of Justice, FBI.

Fishman, L.T. 1995. The vice queens: An ethnographic study of black female gang behavior. In The Modern Gang Reader, edited by M.W. Klein, C.L. Maxson, and J. Miller. Los Angeles, CA: Roxbury Publishing Co., pp. 83–92.

Fitzpatrick, K.M. 1997. Aggression and environmental risk among low- income African-American youth. Journal of Adolescent Health 21:172–178.

Fleisher, M.S. 1998. Dead End Kids: Gang Girls and the Boys They Know. Madison, WI: University of Wisconsin Press.

Fleisher, M.S., and Krienert, J.L. 2004. Life-course events, social net works, and the emergence of vio lence among female gang members. Journal of Community Psychology 32:607–622.

Franke, T.M., Huynh-Hohnbaum, A.L.T., and Chung, Y. 2002. Ado lescent violence: With whom they fight and where. Journal of Ethnic & Cultural Diversity in Social Work 11 (3–4):133–158.

Gaarder, E., Rodriguez, N., and Zatz, M.S. 2004. Criers, liars, and manipu lators: Probation officers' views of girls. Justice Quarterly 21:547–578.

Galen, B.R., and Underwood, M.K., 1997. A developmental investiga tion of social aggression among children. Developmental Psychology 33:589–600.

Ge, X., Brody, G.H., Conger, R.D., Simons, R.L., and Murray, V.M. 2002. Contextual amplification of pubertal transition effects on deviant peer affiliation and externalizing behavior among African American children. Developmental Psychology 3 8:42–54

Girls Inc. 1996. Prevention and Parity: Girls in Juvenile Justice. Indianapolis, IN: Girls Incorporated.

Goodwin, M.H. 1990. He-Said-SheSaid: Talk as Social Organization Among Black Children. Bloomington, IN: Indiana University Press.

Gottfredson, G.D., and Gottfredson, D.C. 1985. Victimization in Schools. New York, NY: Plenum.

Grunbaum, J.A., Kann, L., Kinchen, S., Ross, J., Hawkins, J., Lowry, R., Harris, W.A., McManus, T., Chyen, D., and Collins, J. 2004. Youth risk behav ior surveillance—United States, 2003. In Surveillance Summaries, May

21. Morbidity and Mortality Weekly Report 53:SS–2, pp. 1–96.

Hagedorn, J.M. 1998. People and Folks: Gangs, Crime and the Underclass in a Rustbelt City. 2d ed. Chicago, IL: Lakeview Press.

Haynie, D. 2003. Contexts of risk? Explaining the link between girls' pubertal development and their delinquency involvement. Social Forces 82(1):355–397.

Heimer, K., and DeCoster, S. 1999. The gendering of violent delinquen cy. Criminology 37:277–317.
Huff, C.R. 1989. Youth gangs and public policy. Crime and Delinquency 35:524–537.
Huff, C.R. 1993. Gangs in the United States. In The Gang Intervention Handbook, edited by A.P. Goldstein and C.R. Huff. Champaign, IL: Research Press, pp. 3–20.
Hunt, G., Joe-Laidler, K., and MacKenzie, K. 2005. Moving into motherhood: Gang girls and controlled risk. Youth & Society 36:333–373.
Isernhagen, J., and Harris, S. 2003. A comparison of ninth- and tenth-grade boys' and girls' bullying behav ior in two states. Journal of School Violence. 2(2):67–80.
Jiwani, Y., Janovicek, N., and Camer on, A. 2002. Erased realities: The vio lence of racism in the lives of immi grant and refugee girls of colour. In In the Best Interests of the Girl Child, Phase II Report, edited by H. Berman and Y. Jiwani. Ottawa, Canada: Alli ance of Five Research Centres on Vio lence, Status of Women in Canada, pp. 45–88.
Joe, K.A., and Chesney-Lind, M. 1995. "Just Every Mother's Angel": An anal ysis of gender and ethnic variations in youth gang membership. Gender & Society 9:408–430.
Joe-Laidler, K., and Hunt, G. 1997. Violence and social organization in female gangs. Social Justice 24:148–169.
Jones, N. 2004. "It's not where you live, it's how you live": How young women negotiate conflict and vio lence in the inner city. Annals of the Academy of Political and Social Science 595:49–62.
Kaufman, P., Xianglei, C., Choy, S., Peter, K., Ruddy, S., Miller, A., Fleury, J., Chandler, K., Planty, M., and Rand, M. 2001. Indicators of School Crime and Safety: 2001. Washington, DC: U.S. Departments of Education and Justice, National Center for Educa tion Statistics and Bureau of Justice Statistics
Klein, M.W. 1995. The American Street Gang: Its Nature, Prevalence and Control. New York, NY: Oxford University Press.
Krause, W., and McShane, M. 1994. A deinstitutionalization retrospective: Relabeling the status offender. Journal of Crime and Justice 17:45–67.
Leitz, L. 2003. Girl fights: Exploring females' resistance to educational structures. International Journal of Sociology and Social Policy 23(11): 15–43.
Leventhal, T., and Brooks-Gunn, J. 2000. The neighborhoods they live in: The effects of neighborhood residence on child and adolescent outcomes. Psychological Bulletin 126(2):309–337.
Lockwood, D. 1997. Violence Among Middle School and High School Students: Analysis and Implications for Prevention. Research in Brief. Washington, DC: U.S. Department of Justice, Office of Justice Programs, National Institute of Justice.
Mahoney, A.R., and Fenster, C. 1982. Female delinquents in a suburban court. In Judge, Lawyer, Victim and Thief: Women, Gender Roles and Criminal Justice, edited by N.H. Rafter and E.A. Stanko. Boston, MA: Northeastern University Press.
Miller, J. 2001. One of the Guys: Girls, Gangs and Gender. New York, NY: Oxford University Press.
Miller, J., and Brunson, R.K. 2000. Gender dynamics in youth gangs: A comparison of male and female accounts. Justice Quarterly 17(3):801–830.
Molnar, B.E., Browne, A., Cerda, M., and Buka, S.L. 2005. Violent behavior by girls reporting violent victimiza tion. Archives of Pediatric and Adolescent Medicine 159:731–39.

Moore, J. 1991. Going Down to the Barrio: Homeboys and Homegirls in Change. Philadelphia, PA: Temple University Press.

Moore, J., and Hagedorn, J. 1996. What happens to girls in the gang? In Gangs in America, 2d ed., edited by C.R. Huff. Thousand Oaks, CA: Sage Publications, pp. 205–218.

Ness, C.D. 2004. Why girls fight: Female youth violence in the inner city. Annals of the American Academy of Political and Social Science 595:32–48.

Obeidallah, D., Brennan, R.T., Brooks- Gunn, J., and Earls, F. 2004. Links between pubertal timing and neigh borhood contexts: Implications for girls' violent behavior. Journal of the American Academy of Child and Adolescent Psychiatry 43(12):1460–1468.

Olweus, D. 1993. Bullying at School: What We Know and What We Can Do. Oxford, England: Blackwell.

Payne, A.A., and Gottfredson, D.C. 2005. Gender- and race-based out comes in the effect of school-related factors on delinquency and victim ization. Unpublished manuscript.

Peterson, D., Miller, J., and Esbensen, F.A. 2001. The impact of sex compo sition on gangs and gang member delinquency. Criminology 39(2):411–439.

Rosenbloom, S.R., and Way, N. 2004. Experiences of discrimination among African American, Asian Ameri can, and Latino adolescents in an urban high school. Youth & Society 35(4):420–451.

Scelfo, J. 2005. Bad girls go wild. Newsweek (June 13). [Available online at http://www.msnbc.msn.com/ id/8101517/site/newsweek/page/2/.]

Schneider, A.L. 1984. Divesting sta tus offenses from juvenile court jurisdiction. Crime and Delinquency 30:347–370.

Schooler, D., Ward, L.M., and Merriwether, A. 2004. Who's that girl: Television's role in the body image development of young white and black women. Psychology of Women Quarterly 28:38–47.

Snyder, H. forthcoming. Juvenile Arrests 2005. Bulletin. Washington, DC: U.S. Department of Justice, Office of Justice Programs, Office of Juvenile Justice and Delinquency Prevention.

Snyder, H., and Sickmund, M. 2000. Challenging the Myths. Bulletin. Washington, DC: U.S. Department of Justice, Office of Justice Programs, Office of Juvenile Justice and Delin quency Prevention.

Song, L., Singer, M.I., and Anglin, T.M. 1998. Violence exposure and emotional trauma as contributors to adolescents' violent behaviors. Archives of Pediatric and Adolescent Medicine 152:531–536.

Steffensmeier, D., Schwartz, J., Zhong, S.H., and Ackerman, J. 2005. An assessment of recent trends in girls' violence using diverse longitu dinal sources: Is the gender gap closing? Criminology 43(2):355–406.

Straus, M.A., and Gelles, R.J. 1990. How violent are American families?: Estimates from the National Family Violence Resurvey and other stud ies. In Physical Violence in American Families: Risk Factors and Adaptations to Violence in 8,145 Families, edited by M.A. Straus and R.J. Gelles. New Brunswick, NJ: Transaction Books, pp. 95–112.

Thornberry, T.P. 1997. Membership in youth gangs and involvement in seri ous and violent offending. In Serious and Violent Juvenile Offenders: Risk Factors and Successful Interventions, edited by R. Loeber and D.P. Far rington. Thousand Oaks, CA: Sage Publications, pp. 147–166.

Thornberry, T.P., Krohn, M.P., Lizotte, A.J., Smith, C.A., and Tobin, K. 2000. Gangs in Developmental Perspective: The Origins and Consequences of

Gang Membership. Washington, DC: U.S. Department of Justice, Office of Juvenile Justice and Delinquency Prevention.

Welles, C.E. 2005. Breaking the silence surrounding female ado lescent sexual desire. Women and Therapy 28:31–45.

Winfree, L.T., Jr., Fuller, K., Vigil, T., and Mays, G.L. 1992. The definition and measurement of "gang status": Policy implications for juvenile jus tice. Juvenile and Family Court Journal 43:29–37.

Wolf, N. 1991. The Beauty Myth: How Images of Beauty Are Used Against Women. New York, NY: Anchor Books.

Worcel, S.D., Shields, S.A., and Pat erson, C.A. 1999. "She looked at me crazy": Escalation of conflict through telegraphed emotion. Adolescence 34: 689–697.

Zimring, F.E. 1998. American Youth Violence. New York, NY: Oxford University Press.

Zimring, F.E., and Hawkins, G. 1997. Crime Is Not the Problem: Lethal Violence in America. New York, NY: Oxford University Press.

In: Gangs: Violence, Crime and Antigang Initiatives
Editor: Jay T. Soordhas ISBN 978-1-60692-286-6

Chapter 3

YOUTH GANGS: BACKGROUND, LEGISLATION, AND ISSUES*

Celinda Franco

ABSTRACT

Gang activity and related violence threaten public order in a diverse range of communities in the United States today. Congress has long recognized that this problem affects a number of issues of federal concern, and federal legislation has been introduced in the 110th Congress to address some aspects of the issue.

Youth gangs have been an endemic feature of American urban life. They are well attested as early as the 18th century and have been a recurrent subject of concern since then. Contemporary views of the problem have been formed against the background of a significant adverse secular trend in gang activity during the last four decades. In particular, the rapid growth of gang membership, geographical dispersion, and criminal involvement during the violent crime epidemic — associated with the emergence of the crack cocaine market during the mid-1980s to the early 1990s — have intensified current concerns. The experience of those years continues to mark both patterns of gang activity and public policy responses toward them. Reports about the increased activity and recent migration of a violent California- based gang, the Mara Salvatrucha (MS-13), have heightened concerns about gangs in certain areas of the country.

Policy development and implementation in this area are bedeviled by discrepant uses of the term "gang" and the absence of uniform standards of statistical reporting. There are reasons for special care in the use of data on gangs and their activity. Without a standardized definition of what is meant by "gang," such as the age group or activities engaged in by its members, or standardized reporting among the state, local, tribal, and federal levels of government, it is difficult to target anti-gang initiatives and evaluate their effectiveness. According to a national gang survey, the most recent estimate indicates that there were about 760,000 gang members in 24,000 gangs in the United States in 2004.

In the 110th Congress, several bills have been introduced that would address various aspects of the gang problem. Some of the bills would address the problem through comprehensive gang prevention initiatives, such as H.R. 3846. Other bills address the

* This is an edited, excerpted and augmented edition of a CRS Report RL33400, dated January 25, 2008.

gang problem through combinations of criminal penalty enhancements, targeted prosecutorial efforts and anti-gang task forces, and gang prevention provisions. These anti-gang proposals include H.R. 880, H.R. 1582, H.R. 3547, H.R. 3922, S. 456, S. 990, and S. 2237.

This chapter provides background information on the issue of youth gangs, including data on gangs and gang crime. It reviews existing anti-gang initiatives at the federal, state, and local levels, and describes some of the legislation proposed during the 110th Congress to address the gang problem, as well as some of the issues raised by those bills.

INTRODUCTION

Organized youth gangs[1] and the criminal activity they engage in have long been a concern to policy makers. National attention on gangs reached a high point in the mid-1980s and early 1990s as the violent crime rate reached unprecedented numbers. Although concerns about gangs and gang-related violence during these years were essentially isolated to inner-city urban areas, today the concern has shifted to include violent gang activities that have more recently proliferated into rural and suburban areas. Growing concerns about the number and geographic migration of certain violent Latino gangs into new areas, both rural and suburban, brought the issue before Congress. In addition, concerns about the potential threat gangs pose to domestic security, along with longstanding concerns about the prevalence of gangs in urban areas and the proliferation of gangs in rural areas, continue to fuel congressional interest.

For the most part, gangs and gang crime have been a state and local law enforcement issue. Until recently, the federal role in stemming illegal gang activity was largely limited to grant programs to state and local law enforcement and community-based agencies. As gangs became more sophisticated and expanded the types of illegal activities they engaged in (i.e., money laundering, drug enterprise, etc.), Congress and the Administration began to take note. Although federal laws already existed for prosecuting the types of crimes committed by gang members at the federal level, Congress began to specifically address the gang problem and gang- related violence linked to the "crack" cocaine epidemic of the late 1 980s through the Anti-Drug Abuse Acts of 1986 and 1988 (P.L. 99-570 and P.L. 100-690).[2] Further congressional action on gangs did not occur until 1 994, when Congress passed legislation designed to address the gang problem through more comprehensive approaches.[3]

This chapter provides background information on the issue of youth gangs, including data on gangs and gang crime. It reviews existing anti-gang initiatives at the federal, state, and local levels and describes proposed federal legislation designed to address the problem, as well as some of the issues raised by these proposals. The chapter then briefly discusses policy options for dealing with the gang problem.

BACKGROUND

Gang activity in the United States has been traced back to the late 18th century, in the years following the end of the American Revolution.[4] The earliest identifiable gangs were recorded living in the slums of New York City in 1783.[5] It has been estimated that in 1855,

New York City alone had more than 30,000 gang members.[6] The emergence of youth gangs in the U.S. is thought by some to be connected to immigration patterns, forming as a collective response to urban conditions in many of the large cities populated by recent immigrants as they struggled to make economic, social, and cultural adjustments. One of the earliest researchers on youth gangs, Frederic M. Thrasher, wrote in 1927 that the gangs he studied in Chicago may have emerged from "play groups" in immigrant neighborhoods.[7]

Early in American history, gangs were made up of specific ethnic groups, such as Irish, Italian, Jewish, Slavic, and other ethnic groups who immigrated to the United States and were drawn to the first large cities of New York, Boston, and Philadelphia. Most gang researchers agree that waves of immigration played a major role in the formation and spread of gangs in the United States. For many immigrant groups, gangs have historically provided a way of developing economic or social advantages in a strange country. In more recent history, the past 35 years have brought waves of immigrant groups of Asians (Cambodians, Filipinos, Koreans, Samoans, Thais, and others) and Latin Americans (Colombians, Cubans, Dominicans, Ecuadorians, Mexicans, Panamanians, Puerto Ricans, and many others) into urban areas across the country where many of the same language and cultural barriers have led to the formation of gangs among these groups.[8]

Most of the research on youth gangs has traditionally been based on sociological, ethnographic, and psychological methods. Using the methodological constructs of these disciplines, the majority of the research focuses on how the socioeconomic and environmental factors work to foster youth gangs. Poverty, poor educational opportunities, joblessness, and unstable family structures are among the social structures identified that can influence at-risk youth to join and to remain in gangs. Gangs are found in urban and suburban neighborhoods or rural areas where disaffected youths or migrant populations face poverty, poor schools, and joblessness. Researchers have also identified many factors that contribute to heighten a juvenile's risk of joining a gang, including familial and individual problems, such as juveniles growing up with little or no parental involvement (no parents, single parents, or both parents working) or juveniles with behavioral problems (see Table 1). According to gang researchers, such at-risk juveniles would be more likely to look to gangs to find acceptance, stability, companionship, and a sense of identity, particularly when their communities or the larger society is not perceived to provide opportunities for integration and acceptance.

Table 1. Selected Risk Factors For Youth Gang Membership

Community	Poverty, social disorganization
	Gangs in the neighborhood
	Availability of firearms
	Availability of drugs
	High crime
Family	Broken home, parental drug/alcohol use
	Lack of parental role models

Table 1. (Continued)

Individual	Low socioeconomic status Family violence Prior delinquency Deviant attitudes Aggression Behavioral problems Victimization

Source: Phelan A. Wyrick and James C. Howell, "Strategic Risk-Based Response to Youth Gangs," Juvenile Justice Journal, vol. IX, no. 1 (September 2004).

Gang membership is also influenced by socioeconomic and class distinctions that often stem from prejudice, racism, and alienation from many of society's institutions. Gangs provide affiliation with others who have certain characteristics in common to one another but who may be considered as outsiders in the larger society, often providing income to those with few prospects of finding a job or making a living. Gang membership has not always been associated with serious criminal activity, although research indicates that joining a gang does increase an individual's risk of involvement in crime. Gangs often fight other rival gangs over turf issues and often are involved in petty crimes and misdemeanors. More highly organized gangs are often involved in more serious crimes such as drug trafficking, violence, and illegal possession of firearms.

Definition of a Youth Gang

Academics and other experts on gangs continue to debate the formal definition of the term "gang" and the types of individuals included in gangs. Does a gang consist of members of certain ages? Are gangs always involved in crime? Do gangs vary in composition and organization from community to community, or do they all have some common elements in their organization, activities, and cultures? Despite decades and mountains of research there is still not a common definition of "gang" that is accepted by police, schools, academics, and communities across the nation.

Generally, there is agreement that gangs usually have a name and some sense of identity that can sometimes be indicated by symbols such as clothing, graffiti, and hand signs that are unique to the gang. Typically, gangs tend to have some degree of permanence and organization and are generally, to some degree, involved in delinquent or criminal activity. The criminal activities of gangs can range widely from graffiti, vandalism, petty theft, robbery, and assaults, to more serious criminal activities such as drug trafficking, drug smuggling, money laundering, alien smuggling, extortion, home invasion, murder, and other violent felonies. Some of the characteristics that are used to identify gang membership, often in combination with self-identification, are symbols or symbolic behavior, the association with known gang members, participation in certain criminal behavior, the individual's location or residence, identification by a police informant, or direct observation of certain symbols or symbolic behavior by law enforcement officers.[9]

Gang definitions vary widely and have changed over time. Early in the twentieth century, gangs could be seen by some as benign groups of friends from the same neighborhood providing social support and a sense of community, sometimes bound by kinship, and not established to commit delinquent acts. Gang members could be perceived as providing a protective function for their communities by attacking or driving out unwanted interlopers. However, today gangs are most often seen as juvenile delinquents and criminals who are more likely to be a threat to communities and public order, frequently as drug traffickers and violent criminals. Although this may not be true of all gang members, it is certainly clear that popular images in the media often portray gang members as criminals, and they are widely perceived as such by many.

The Department of Justice (DOJ) Office of Juvenile Justice and Delinquency Prevention (OJJDP), relying on several definitions offered by "leading theorists and researchers," defines a youth gang as a group that is involved in a pattern of criminal acts, typically composed only of juveniles, but may include young adults in their membership. Prison gangs, ideological gangs, hate groups, motorcycle gangs, and gangs whose membership is restricted to adults and that do not have the characteristics of youth gangs are excluded. The DOJ National Criminal Justice Reference Service (NCJRS), while acknowledging that gangs are defined in many ways, provides a common definition of a gang as a group of three or more individuals who engage in criminal activity and identify themselves with a common name or sign.

Gangs are also defined in current federal law. The U.S. Criminal Code defines a "criminal street gang" as:

- an ongoing group, club, organization, or association of 5 or more persons — (A) that has as 1 of its primary purposes the commission of 1 or more of the criminal offenses described in subsection (c); (B) the members of which engage, or have engaged within the past 5 years, in a continuing series of offenses described in subsection (c); and (C) the activities of which affect interstate or foreign commerce.[10]

The criminal offenses ascribed to a criminal street gang in subsection (c) include certain federal felonies that involve a controlled substance with a maximum penalty of five or more years of imprisonment; a federal felony that involves violence, or attempted violence, against another person; or, a conspiracy to commit either of these types of federal felonies.[11]

Several of the broad anti-gang bills introduced in the 1 10th Congress would modify the federal criminal code definition[12] of a criminal street gang as groups, associations, organizations, etc., consisting of three or more (instead of five or more) persons. In addition, most of these anti-gang bills would increase the penalties applied to criminal street gang crime and specified a number of violent crimes that would be punishable under the bills. Introduced in the 1 10th Congress, S. 456, H.R. 1582, H.R. 880, S. 990, and H.R. 1692 contain some version of this type of provision (see discussion below).

For most of the history of the research on gangs, the definition of gang membership relied on most by researchers has been self-identification by gang members themselves. Law enforcement officers, too, most often rely on a suspect's willingness to self-identify or "claim" gang membership for police identification and reporting purposes. For policy makers, how the term "gang" is defined and who is a gang member are important concepts for gauging the extent and nature of the problem, as well as for developing appropriate policy and program responses. The continued absence of a standard definition limits the utility of data collection for research purposes and for criminal reporting. It also limits the ability to quantify and understand the extent of the gang problem and complicates any national public policy response.

Prevalence of the Problem

To establish a framework for considering federal gang policy, it is important to consider the data sources that indicate the pervasiveness of the gang problem. National estimates of gangs and gang members are provided through an annual survey administered by the National Youth Gang Center and funded through grants from the Office of Justice Programs (OJP). The 2004 NYGC survey is discussed below along with a brief look at data trends since the survey began in 1995. In addition, this section will provide an overview of the latest blended-year analysis from the NYGC of the 2002-2003 surveys, which elicited responses to slightly different questions than are included in the standard annual survey. These two surveys provide the only national estimates of how widespread the gang problem is and the extent of gang involvement in certain types of criminal victimization.

National Youth Gang Survey

Since 1995, the National Youth Gang Center (NYGC) has conducted an annual survey of a selected sample of law enforcement agencies on the characteristics of youth gangs. The NYGC survey is federally initiated by the Office of Juvenile Justice and Delinquency Prevention (OJJDP) and administered by the Institute for Intergovernmental Research. The NYGC survey provides the only national estimates of gang membership and activity. The survey is based on responses of a nationally representative sample of law enforcement agencies taken from the U.S. Census Bureau and the Federal Bureau of Investigation (FBI) data. The information reported in the survey concerns solely youth gangs, defined for purposes of the survey as "a group of youths or young adults in your jurisdiction that you or other responsible persons in your agency or community are willing to identify as a 'gang' member." The survey specifically excludes motorcycle gangs, hate or ideology groups, prison gangs,[13] and exclusively adult gangs.

The 2004 Nygc Survey

The 2004 NYGC survey, released April 2006, examined the prevalence of gangs and their illegal activities.[14] According to the survey results, youth gangs were active in more than 2,900 jurisdictions that city and county law enforcement agencies served in 2004. The survey also estimated that approximately 760,000 gang members and 24,000 gangs were active in the United States in 2004. The estimated number of gang members between 1996 and 2002 increased 14%. As Figure 1 indicates, in the larger cities the number of respondents reporting a gang problem dropped slightly for the period 1999-2001 and began to rise slightly for the 2002-2004 period, whereas in rural counties there has been a decline between 1996 and 2004.

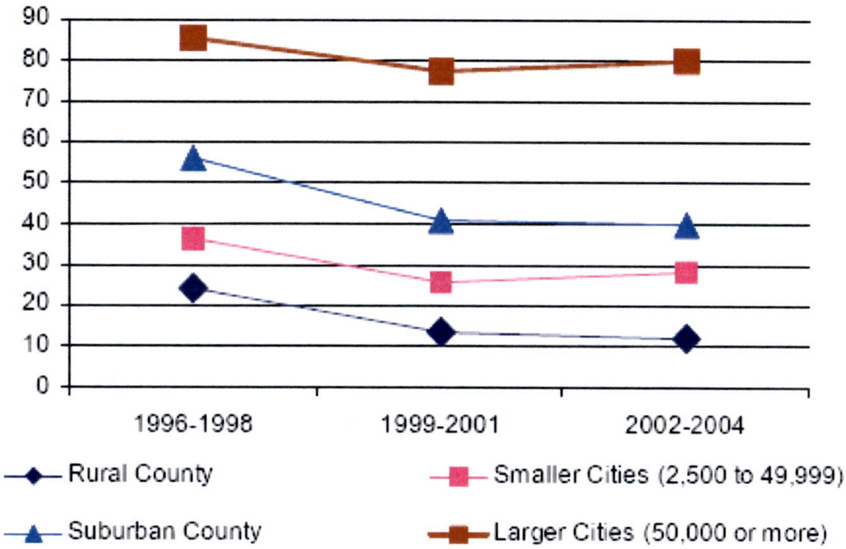

Source: NYGC Survey, 1997-2004.

Figure 1. Respondents Reporting Youth Gang Problems by Size of Jurisdiction, 1996-2004(in averaged percentages).

Of the 2,554 survey recipients, 2,296, or 90%, responded to the 2004 survey.[15] The 2004 survey summary reported that youth gang problems were reported by all large-city[16] law enforcement agencies that responded to the survey for the years 1996- 2004. The majority of larger cities[17] law enforcement agencies that responded to the NYGC survey (82%) also reported youth gang problems. Forty-two percent of responding agencies serving suburban counties, 27% of agencies serving smaller cities with populations below 50,000 reported youth gang problems, as did 14% of responding rural-county law enforcement agencies.

Table 2 provides national estimates of gangs, gang members, and jurisdictions reporting gang problems reported by the NYGC from the annual surveys of law enforcement agencies for 1995-2004. As Table 2 indicates, the national estimates of the number of youth gangs have been declining since 1996, whereas the estimated number of gang members has fluctuated over the years and seems to be rising since 2001. The most notable trend has been the decline in the total number of surveyed jurisdictions reporting gang problems, which decreased 52% between 1996 and 2004 (as shown in the table). The drop in respondents reporting such problems raises questions about how reliably the survey results indicate whether or not the gang problem is or is not growing.

Table 2. NYGC Estimated Youth Gang Problem in the United States, 1995-2004

	1995	1996	1997	1998	1999	2000	2001	2002	2004a
Gangs (000)	23	31	30.5	28.7	26	24.5	N/A	21.5	24
Gang members (000)	664.9	846	816	780	840.5	772.5	693.5	731.5	760.0
Jurisdictions reporting gang problems	N/A	4,824	4,712	4,464	3,911	3,330	3,000	2,850	2,296

Source: U.S. Department of Justice, OJJDP, Highlights of the 2004 National Youth Gang Survey, #01, April 2006; and Highlights of the National Youth Gang Survey, 1995-2002.

a. The OJJDP Highlights of the 2002-2003 National Youth Gangs Surveys June 2005, did not include estimates of gangs, gang members or jurisdictions (described separately below).

N/A = Not available.

A recent detailed reanalysis of the NYGC survey data from 1996 to 2001 provides some clues as to what may underlie these disparate survey responses and declining respondent numbers. According to NYGC reanalysis respondents from all the largest cities (populations greater than 250,000) and the vast majority of large cities (populations greater than 100,0000) reported gang problems in all survey years. Law enforcement agencies in small cities (populations above 2,500 and below 50,000) reported 16% fewer gang problems over the 1996-2001 survey period. In addition, rural and suburban counties reported significantly fewer gang problems over the same period. In the first two survey years, nearly 60% of suburban counties reported gang problems; however, the number of respondents declined steadily, and by the 2001 survey, suburban county respondents had dropped to just over one-third. Similarly, one-fourth of rural counties reported gang problems in the first two survey years; however, the response rate of these jurisdictions also declined, so that by 2001 the response rate of rural counties was just over 1 in 10.[18]

There are many possible explanations for the decline in survey responses among small town and rural jurisdictions that could affect the gang estimates. One possible explanation could be that gang activity varies and may be more entrenched and constant in some areas, whereas in other areas, particularly in areas of low population density, gang activity could be a more episodic, fluctuating problem. In other areas, gangs could be a relatively new problem that perhaps has not yet firmly established itself in a community or area. As a result, the reported experience of gang problems reflected in the NYGC survey for larger cities remained fairly constant over the survey period. In smaller cities and rural and suburban counties, the decline in reported gang problems could reflect the variability of gang problems in these jurisdictions while simultaneously and disproportionately driving down the number of jurisdictions responding to the NYGC survey. Another explanation might be connected to the fact that responding to the survey is voluntary and not linked to any programmatic requirement or receipt of federal funding, which could help explain why law enforcement agencies, particularly in low-population jurisdictions with limited staff, might not consider completion of the NYGC survey to be the most important expenditure of staff time. Finally, the decline in survey respondents and gangs or gang membership might not reflect the experiences of all jurisdictions for reasons related to methodological issues inherent in surveys and population sampling, including sample size and weighting of responses, which are beyond the scope of this chapter.

Although the NYGC survey may indicate that the reported youth gang problem could be receding in some areas, respondents to the survey reported that gang-related violence has been increasing in larger cities and some rural areas. The 2004 NYGC survey indicated that among larger cities (population of 100,000 or more), 173 cities reported both a gang problem and gang homicide data in 2004 (homicides involving a gang member). Of the 171 larger cities, approximately one-fourth of all homicides were considered gang related. In the two remaining large cities, Chicago and Los Angeles, more than half of all homicides were considered gang related. The combined gang related homicides in Chicago and Los Angeles accounted for nearly half of the total number of homicides (nearly 1,000 homicides) reported in the NYGC 2004 survey.[19]

In addition to the survey responses on gang homicides, the NYGC survey reports responses regarding the respondent's perception of whether the gang problem in their jurisdiction was improving or worsening. Of respondents to the 2004 NYGC survey, 52% of law enforcement officers indicated that they thought their youth gang problem was "getting worse," while 48% reported that there was "a decrease or no significant change" in their gang problem. According to the NYGC survey, since2001, law enforcement officers have been reporting that the gang problem in their area is worsening: 27% in 2001, rising to 42% in 2002, and to 52% in 2004 (see Figure 2).

The 2002-2003 NYGC Survey

In June 2005, OJJDP issued a fact sheet, Highlights of the 2002-2003 National Youth Gang Surveys, reporting that law enforcement agencies serving cities with populations of 250,000 or more all continue to report youth gang problems (95.7% responding).[20] Law enforcement agencies in jurisdictions with the smallest populations continued to be the least likely to report gang problems, and this was especially the case in rural counties (31.7% responding). Of the larger cities, more than one-third of the agencies reported an annual maximum of 10 or more gang-related homicides, whereas relatively few agencies serving rural counties and the smallest cities reported gang-related homicides in the study period. The analysis of the surveys over both years provided evidence that gangs, gang members, and gang-related homicides are predominately concentrated in larger cities.

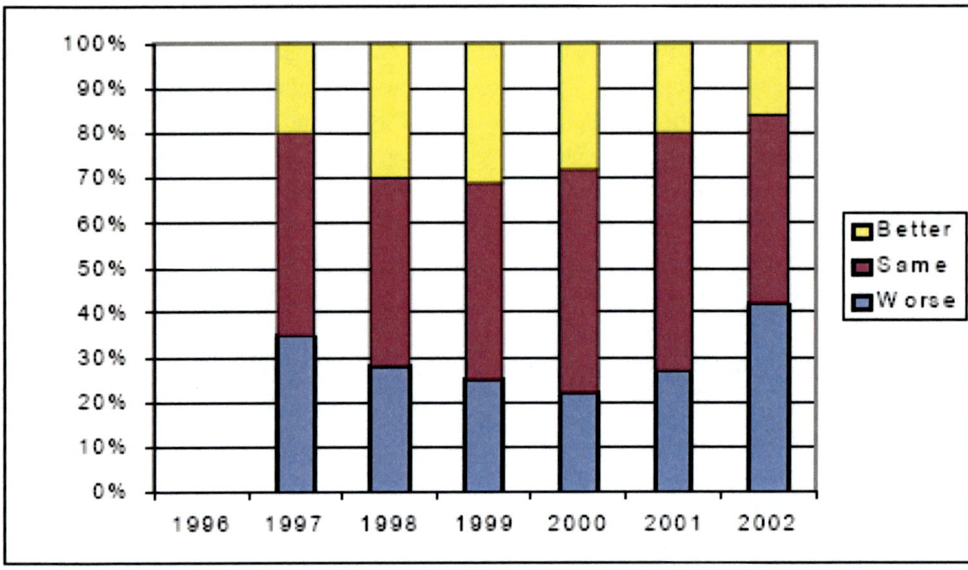

Source: NYGC 2002.

Figure 2. Status of Gang Problem in Jurisdiction of Survey Respondents, 1997-2002.

Although the fact sheet on the analysis of the 2002-2003 survey responses does not provide estimates of the number of gang members for those years, based on unpublished data for 2003, the NYGC survey estimated that the number of gang members was approximately 750,000 nationally.[21] According to the NYGC survey, the increasing number of gang members continues to be a serious policy issue. This trend indicates that there is still much to do at the federal level in the fight against the youth gang problem. Moreover, the migration of gangs into suburban and rural areas, beyond their traditional base of operation in the urban inner-cities, has also raised concerns about the possible spread of gang violence in areas of the country that have not been the types of communities usually besieged by gang activities and violence.

Crime Statistics

Crime statistics are often used as one measure of gauging the impact of gangs on communities. Much of the recent concern about gangs is attributed to the violent crimes that are often linked to gang activities. One would assume that if violent gang activity is increasing, this would result in a similar movement in violent crime statistics; however, as discussed below, this has not always been the case. Two crime data sources administered by the U.S. Department of Justice, the Uniform Crime Report (UCR) and the National Crime Victimization Survey (NCVS), are often used to frame a discussion of trends in gang criminal activity.

The FBI's UCR program compiles monthly crime reports from over 17,000 city, county, and state law enforcement agencies across the country. The UCR provides data on violent crimes, including homicide and nonnegligent manslaughter, forcible rape, robbery, and aggravated assault. Property crimes of burglary, larceny- theft, motor vehicle theft, and arson are also included in the UCR.

According to the most recent UCR, the number of violent crimes decreased 1.7% between 2003 and 2004.[22] The most significant decline was in cities with populations of one million and over, where the violent crime rate dropped an average of 5.4%. The declining trend in violent crime is not a new phenomenon. Since peaking in 1990 at a rate of 729.6 per 100,000 inhabitants, the crime rate dropped to a rate of 475 per 100,000 inhabitants in 2003, a decline of more than 34% over the period.[23] However, by 2004, the murder and nonnegligent manslaughter rates were beginning to inch upward.

JUVENILE GANG HOMICIDE

Much of the concern about the youth gang problem stems from the attendant violence associated with gangs and gang crime. Research indicates that the longer a gang member remains in a gang, the higher the risk they will become involved in crime, generally, and of particular concern, in violent crime. A CRS analysis of data from the FBI's Supplementary Homicide Reports (SHR), provided below, offers some insight into the commonly held view that gangs and youth gangs, particularly older juveniles, are more likely to be involved in violent crime. A similar analysis by the Justice Policy Institute of gang-related violent crime, as reported in the FBI's SHR from 1994 to 2003, concluded that over that period gang-related violent crime declined by 73%.[24]

Some critics have claimed that the FBI data on gangland and juvenile gang homicides may inadvertently give the impression that these homicides are primarily committed by juvenile offenders. Yet juveniles are responsible for a smaller proportion of all homicides included in this crime category than are young adults and adults who are included in the counts of these gang-related killings.[25] The SHR count of gang-related homicides includes offenders of all ages. According to the FBI data, a large majority of offenders of known age in gangland and juvenile gang killings are not juveniles.[26] The 2003 SHR includes records for 1,111 offenders in such killings; age data were reported for 52.8% (n=5 87) of the 1,111. Among offenders of known age, only 18.9% (n=1 11) were under 18 years of age, or juveniles (see Figure 3).

Because no age data are reported for 47.2% (n=524) of offenders reportedly committing juvenile gang homicides, the exact proportion of all 1,111 offenders who are juveniles under 18 years of age is unknown. However, to hypothesize about the likelihood that those of unknown age are under or over 18 years of age, upper and lower bounds for those of unknown age can be established to determine the percentage of all 1,111 offenders who are juveniles. If the age-distribution of the offenders of unknown age were the same as that of offenders of known age, then 18.9% (n=2 10) of all offenders reported in 2003 would be under 18 because that is the proportion of offenders of known age reported in the SHR. Alternatively, if all offenders of unknown age were under 18, then 57.2% of all offenders would be under 18 (n = 111 + 524). Conversely, if all offenders of unknown age were 18 or older (n = 476 + 524), then 10.0% of all offenders would be under 18. Unless 85% or more of offenders of unknown age were under 18 (n = 445), a level that is 4.5 times this age group's share of offenders of known age, then it could be assumed that only a minority of the total number of offenders reported in the FBI's SHR as gangland and juvenile gang killings were in fact committed by juveniles. As a result, data on gang homicides must be considered with care if they are used in isolation as an indication of violent crime rates among juvenile gang members.

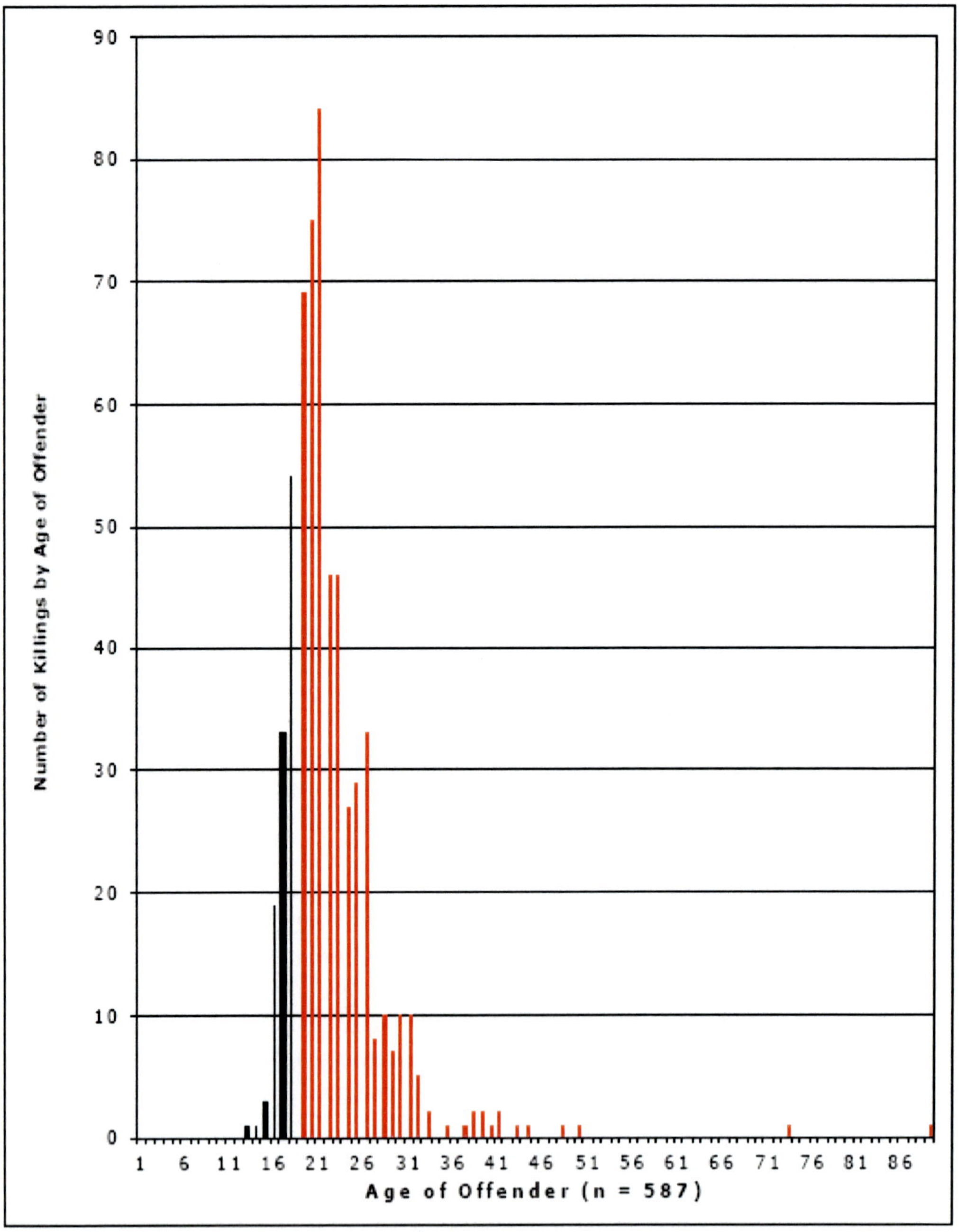

Source. CRS Analysis of FBI, Uniform Crime Reports, Supplementary Homicide Reports, 2003.

Figure 3. Gangland and Juvenile Gang Homicides by Age of Offender, 2003.

Despite the uncertainty about whether or not juvenile homicide rates reported in the SHR are actually perpetrated by juveniles or adults, most gang experts agree that gang members have higher offending patterns while they are actively participating in a gang compared with before they join and after they leave the gang. [27] The historical trend in total juvenile gang murders provided by Figure 4 indicates that juvenile gang homicides, as reported in the SHR, have decreased slightly since 2002. Overall, the rate of juvenile gang homicide in recent years continues to remain below peak levels last reached in 1995.

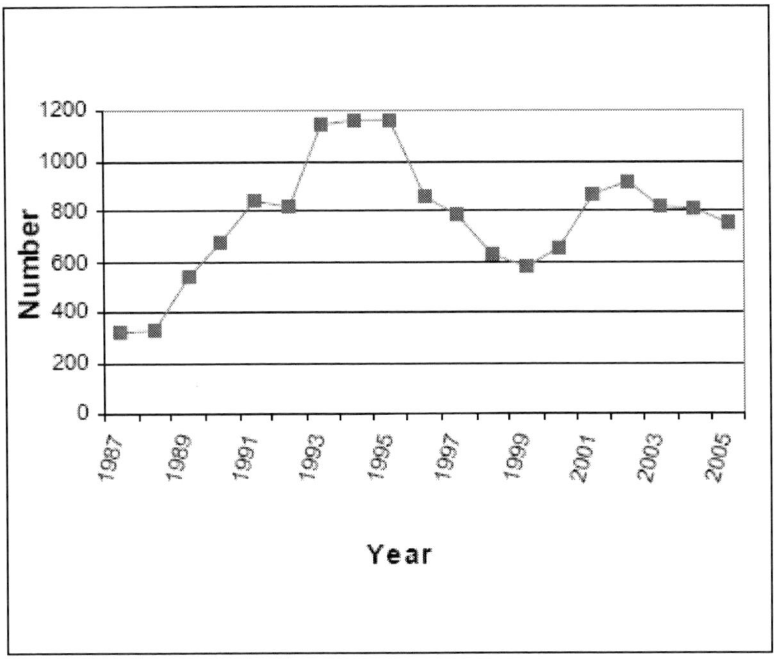

Source: FBI, Uniform Crime Reports, Supplementary Homicide Reports, 2005.

Figure 4. Juvenile Gang Homicides, 1987-2005.

National Crime Victimization Survey

The Bureau of Justice Statistics (BJS) administers the National Crime Victimization Survey (NCVS). Started in 1972, the NCVS is one of two DOJ measures of crime in the United States and is the primary source of information on criminal victimization. The NCVS data are obtained each year from a nationally representative sample of 42,000 households comprising nearly 76,000 persons that are surveyed on the frequency, characteristics, and consequences of criminal victimization. BJS statisticians then use the survey data to estimate the likelihood of victimization by various crimes, including rape, sexual assault, robbery, assault, and theft for the total population and for certain segments of the population such as women or the elderly. The NCVS provides the largest national forum for victims to describe the impact of crime and characteristics of violent offenders.

According to the survey, victims perceived perpetrators to be gang members in about 6% of violent victimizations between 1998 and 2003.[28] As a result, the NCVS estimates that gang members committed, on average for each year, approximately 5.7% (373,000) of the total 6.6 million violent victimizations over this period, including such nonfatal acts as rape/sexual assault, robbery, aggravated assault, and simple assault. In addition, the NCVS reports that, between 1994 and 2003, the rate of reported violent victimizations by perceived gang members declined by 73% over the period, from 5.2 per 1,000 to 1.4 per 1,000, after having peaked at 10% of all violent crime in 1996.[29]

Questions can be raised about the validity of the NCVS survey. Some have argued that the perceptions of crime victims are not an objective measure of anything more than an individual's recollection of a traumatic event, and that data collected through the survey cannot be deemed a reliable and objective source of criminal data. However, the NCVS has been systematically field tested and the methodology has been continually reviewed by an advisory panel of criminal justice policymakers, social scientists, victim advocates, and statisticians working in conjunction with a consortium of criminologists and social and survey scientists.[30]

National Gang Threat Assessment

The U.S. DOJ's Bureau of Justice Assistance (BJA), issued a report, 2005 National Gang Threat Assessment,[31] that provides a national perspective on the threat posed by gangs. The report was produced in collaboration with members of the National Alliance of Gang Investigators Associations (NAGIA), including the FBI, the National Drug Intelligence Center (NDIC), and the Bureau of Alcohol, Tobacco, Firearms and Explosives (ATF). According to the report, gangs were pervasive throughout society and more sophisticated and flagrant in their use of violence and intimidation tactics. The report also found that when today's gangs migrate across the country, they bring drugs, weapons, and criminal activity with them. However, the report was not backed by hard data or crime statistics, and instead was based on a survey of law enforcement agencies and anecdotal accounts and experiences.

Law enforcement respondents to the 2005 assessment's questionnaire identified a number of trends across the country. Gangs were identified as the primary distributors of drugs throughout the U.S., sometimes associating with organized crime entities such as Mexican drug organizations and Russian organized crime groups, and engaged in low-level criminal activities such as protecting territories and facilitating drug-trafficking activities. Gang members were reportedly becoming more sophisticated in their use of computers and technologies for improved communications, facilitating criminal activity and avoiding detection by law enforcement.

Respondents identified the migration of California-style gang culture, along with growing Hispanic gang membership, as a particular threat as these gangs spread into new areas and promote the gang subculture. Although outside of the scope of this report, the expansion of outlaw motorcycle gangs into new territories and the formation of new gangs were also identified as a threat to communities as these types of gangs battled over territories with increasing violence. In addition, 31% of survey respondents indicated that their communities refused to acknowledge the gang problem, and in some cases only began to address gang issues when a high-profile gang-related incident occurred.

The 2005 assessment identified a number of regional trends in gang activity affecting communities in the following areas:

Northeast Region. In the Northeast, neighborhood or homegrown gangs are increasingly visible and the growth of gangs within Hispanic immigrant communities has brought increased violence and crime to many communities. The region is identified as being particularly vulnerable to drug distribution by gangs because of the compact nature of the region and the well-developed transportation system throughout the region. Gangs are most frequently reported to be involved in crimes relating to vandalism and graffiti, firearms possession, assault, and homicide.

The South. In the South, the Mara Salvatrucha (MS-13), an Hispanic gang originally formed in Los Angeles, California, by immigrants from El Salvador, is reportedly one of the newest threats to the region, especially in Washington, DC, Virginia, and surrounding areas. Gangs in the South are reportedly most likely to be involved in the distribution and sale of marijuana and cocaine.

The Midwest. In the Midwest, gang activity has increased around schools and college campuses, and gangs are concealing their affiliations and colors to hide from law enforcement. Gangs are increasingly cooperating with one another to facilitate crime and drug trafficking. Gang and drug activity in Indian Country has increased, and according to the assessment's respondents, Hispanic street gangs are using Native Americans to transport narcotics onto reservations.

The West. In the West, gangs are reportedly using increasingly sophisticated, well planned and executed criminal acts, especially against law enforcement officers. Street gangs are frequently involved in the distribution of both marijuana and methamphetamine, and the number of cases of identity and credit card theft by gang members has increased. In addition, respondents from the West reported that gang members were increasingly using firearms.

CHARACTERISTICS OF GANGS AND GANG MEMBERS YOUTH GANG DEMOGRAPHICS

Historically, gangs have been most prevalent in the central cities of large urban areas and members were primarily young adult males from homogeneous low- income, inner-city, ghetto or barrio neighborhoods. Research indicates that most gang members join a gang as juveniles, some only participate sporadically, and a significant number leave, or 'age-out,' of gangs before they reach adulthood.[32] Typically, gangs have been racially/ethnically segregated and actively involved in a variety of criminal activities. However, there is evidence that some gangs have evolved into hybrid gangs that are mixed ethnically, racially, and by gender.

Based on data from an in-depth analysis of survey data from the 1996-2000 NYCG surveys published in 2002 (see discussion above), law enforcement agency respondents reported that 94% of gang members were male and 6% were female. The analysis also indicated that 39% of youth gangs had some female members. According to the analysis, gangs formed since 1985 were reportedly more likely to have proliferated into less traditional areas such as small cities, towns, suburbs, and rural communities.

Data on age and race/ethnicity were also collected from the NYGC surveys for the years 1996, 1998, and 1999. In 1996, respondents reported that half of gang members were juveniles below the age of 18 and half were adults 18 years of age and older. By 1999, the age balance had shifted toward older gang members and, according to survey respondents, 37% were under the age of 18. In 1999, respondents reported that 47% of gang members were Hispanic, 31% African American, 13% Caucasian/white, 7% Asian, and 2% other. During the three-year period, the reported distribution of race/ethnicity remained relatively constant (see Table 3).

Table 3. Estimated Demographic Characteristics of Gangs

(in percent)

	1996	1998	1999
Age			
Under 15	16	11	11
15-17	34	29	26
18-24	37	46	50
Over 24	13	14	13
Race/Ethnicity			
White	14	12	13
Black	35	34	31
Hispanic	44	46	47
Asian	5	6	7
Other	2	2	2

Source: NYGC (most recent detailed information available).

More recent demographic information on race and ethnicity from the 2001 NYGC survey show slight changes in gang composition (see Figure 5).[33] As Figure 5 indicates, the 2001 demographic data show increases among Hispanic (49%) and African American (34%) gang members, declines among Caucasian/white (10%), and Other (1%), and the percentage of Asian gangs remained the same (6%).

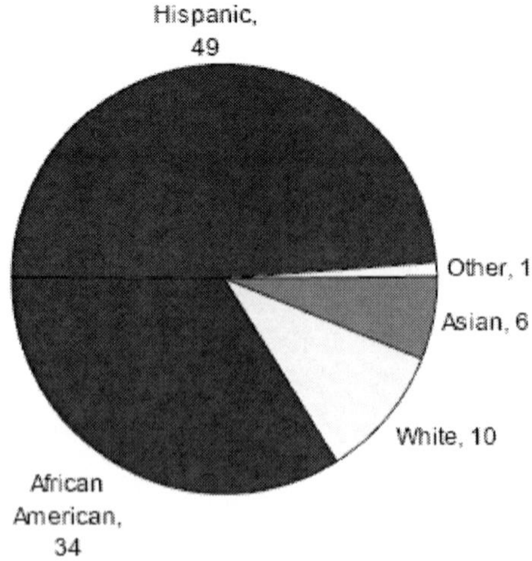

Source: CRS Presentation of NYGC data (most recent detailed information available).

Figure 5. Youth Gang Demographics (2001) (in percent)

RURAL GANGS [34]

Small towns and rural areas across the country report gang problems. In small towns and rural areas the gang problem is not typically chronic and perpetual, but instead is episodic and not likely to persist as it is in larger urban areas where gang problems typically are chronic.[35] In part, this is due to the fact that these areas do not have the population base from which gangs can recruit new members. The small size of most rural or small town gangs makes them more vulnerable to disruptions such as arrest or members dropping out of the gang, and although all gangs are characterized by movement among members in and out of the gang over the course of a year, this dynamic has a more disruptive effect on the permanence of a rural, small-town gang.

A recent analysis of small town and rural county respondents to the NYGC's annual gang survey of state and local law enforcement agencies looked at responses from agencies representing populations between 2,500 and 25,000.36 NYGC's analysis revealed that few of these agencies reported persistent gang problems. Of 27 rural counties responding to the survey, only 4% (1.08 counties) reported persistent gang problems. Similarly, of the [36] small town respondents, only 10% of small towns (3.6 small towns) reported persistent gang problems.[37]

The analysis of small town and rural county agencies found that agencies reporting persistent gang problems had a higher proportion of adult-aged gang members. In addition, jurisdictions reporting persistent gang problems were more likely to have also had gang-related homicides in their jurisdiction than jurisdictions reporting variable gang problems. Thus, the analysis found that the reporting of a sudden gang problem in a particular community might not always signal the beginning of a protracted or persistent gang problem or one which would be likely to develop into a serious problem like that seen in some larger cities.

NYGC's analysis identified population shifts and changing demographics in some small towns and rural areas as potential factors contributing to the emergence or escalation of gang problems. As in larger cities, language barriers and exclusion of newly immigrating youths were identified as factors which could contribute to the formation of groups that could coalesce into a gang. Examples of such possible situations included the rapid growth of Latinos in North Carolina and Salvadorans in northern Virginia, both situations which could potentially contribute to development of local gang problems for these areas. However, no data were presented indicating that these areas were experiencing such gang problems, and the analysis cautioned that the majority of youth gangs are "homegrown" with memberships composed of long-time residents in the particular area. Moreover, the analysis concluded that the formation of gangs was more likely to be the result of failed social institutions even in small towns and rural communities.[38] Broader applicability of the NYGC analysis to other similar areas across the country is, however, limited by the small sample size and small number of survey respondents, among other factors, which make it difficult to infer that the data are representative of all such jurisdictions across the nation.

GANG PRESENCE IN SCHOOLS

The threat of gang crime and violence exists in many schools across the nation. According to an OJJDP report, youth gangs are linked with serious crime problems in elementary and secondary schools in the United States.[39] The OJJDP study indicated that the incidence of several factors, including household income and drug availability, were positively related to the reported presence of gangs in schools.[40] The analysis also found a high correlation between gangs and the incidence of student victimization in schools. However, the authors concluded that although the presence of gangs in a school is correlated with criminal activity, it was not clear that gangs were a direct cause of criminal victimization at schools.[41]

The School Crime Supplement to the National Crime Victims Survey periodically surveys youth in school about the presence of gangs in their schools (see Table 4). From the available data provided in Table 4, survey respondents reported a gang presence in schools that increased dramatically between 1989 and 1995, an increase of 92%. As Table 4 indicates, the percentage of students reporting a gang presence dropped precipitously between 1995 and 1999, a 41% decline; the percentage again rose and remained fairly constant at just over 20% in 2001 and 2003.

Table 4. Percentage of Students Reporting Gang Presence in Schools

Year	1989	1995	1999	2001	2003
	15.3	29.0	17.0	20.1	20.9

Source: U.S. DOJ, BJS, School Crime Supplement to the National Crime Victims Survey, for the most recent years available.

Of the students surveyed, students in urban schools were significantly more likely to report the presence of street gangs at their schools than were students in either suburban or non-metro schools (see Table 5). In every residence category, whether student respondents lived in an urban, suburban, or non-metro area, the percentage of students reporting a gang presence increased significantly between 1989 and 1995. Although the percentage of students surveyed dropped between 1995 and 2003, the reported gang presence remained significantly higher in 2003 than it had been in 1989. The proportional increase between 1989 and 2003 was greatest in non-metro areas (57.7% increase).

Table 5. Percentage of Students Reporting GangPresence By Residence

Year	Central City	Suburban	Non-Metro
1989	24.8	14.0	7.8
1995	40.7	26.3	19.9
2003	30.9	18.4	12.3

Source: School Crime Supplement to the National Crime Victims Survey, for the most recent years available.

Hispanic and black students were more likely than white students to report that there was a gang presence in their schools in 2003 (see Table 6). Among students aged 12-18, Hispanic students in every residence category, except rural, reported the highest percentage of gang presence in their schools. Black students reported the highest percentage of gang presence in rural schools.

Table 6. Percentage of Students, Aged 12-18, Who Reported Gangs Were Present at School During the Previous Six Months, 2003

Race/Ethnicity	Total	Urban	Suburban	Rural
White	14	20	14	11
Black	29	33	28	22
Hispanic	37	43	35	13
Other	22	31	18	11

Source: School Crime and Safety: 2004, November 2004.

Students in public schools were more likely to report the presence of gangs than students in private schools; 35% of urban public schools surveyed reported the presence of gangs compared to only 6% in surveyed urban private schools. Similarly, in suburban public schools students reported 20%, whereas only 2% in suburban private schools reported a gang presence at school. In rural public schools the rate of reported gang presence was 12% compared to 4% in rural private schools.[42]

Gangs remain a serious concern for school safety and many advocate that particular attention should be given to signs of gang activity in schools. Gang-related fights and assaults are of a different nature and tend to escalate to other related, and occasionally larger, conflicts that can spill over into the neighborhood.[43] Some have argued that school-based, gang-related activity is often not reported, perhaps in part because of the negative attention that acknowledging a gang problem may bring to the school, parents, and surrounding community.[44]

Schools play a critical role in the socialization and development of children, and this is especially the case for at-risk children from strained families.[45] According to researchers, schools typically respond to gang problems by suppression methods that include getting rid of the "problem" by separating gang members from the other students. Some researchers have concluded that this type of tactic can further marginalize at-risk youth, bond them more completely to gangs, and reinforce their loyalty to gangs.[46] These and other studies have led some researchers to conclude that a more balanced use of prevention, intervention, and suppression strategies starting in elementary school could help to reduce gang violence in schools.[47]

Latino Gangs: Ms-13, A Case Study

In recent years, there has been growing attention in the press and among policy- makers on gang violence that is linked to gangs in Central America. Much of the concern about such gang members can be linked to the recent spread of certain Latino gangs from their origins in Los Angeles, California, into major urban and rural communities throughout the United States. Connections between gangs in the United States and gangs in other countries including Mexico, El Salvador, Guatemala, and Honduras have heightened concerns among U.S. policymakers about the threat these gangs pose to domestic security.[48]

The Mara Salvatrucha (MS-13) gang was originally formed in Los Angeles, California, by refugees and immigrants from El Salvador who saw the formation of their own gang as a way to neutralize the gang threat to their community posed by the 18th Street Gang and others. MS-13 is reportedly one of the newest threats to the Washington, DC, metropolitan area, including the suburbs of Northern Virginia, Baltimore, MD, and other areas along the East Coast. According to testimony at a recent congressional hearing, the MS-13 gang is "estimated to have some 8,000 to 10,000 hardcore members [in the United States]."[49]

Although the estimated number of MS-13 gang members is a small fraction of the total number of U.S. gang members, they are reputed to be more violent. The MS- 13 gang has followed the migratory pattern of Salvadoran immigrants, fanning out across the United States, and up and down the East Coast, in an effort to establish itself as a "national" gang organization. It is, by most estimates, the largest and most well organized of the Latino gangs, although other Latino gangs of concern across the country include the 18th Street Gang of West Los Angeles, the Latin Kings, and the Surenos 13. Many of these gangs that originated in California have also proliferated across the country, to some extent, but not to the extent of MS- 13.

The FBI, other federal agencies, and local law enforcement agencies view the MS- 13 gang as a national and international threat that must be addressed on several fronts. The Immigration and Customs Enforcement (ICE) bureau of the Department of Homeland Security (DHS) launched an operation focused on helping state and local law enforcement with the gang problem. ICE officials began an effort, Operation Community Shield, to use their immigration authority to detain and deport gang members of MS-13 from the United States.[50] The ICE effort focused on the cities of Los Angeles, Miami, Baltimore, Newark, and Washington, DC, and involved intelligence from state and local law enforcement, as well as the FBI, the Drug Enforcement Agency (DEA), the U.S. Marshals Service (USMS), and ATF.

On August 26, 2005, the ATF led a raid on MS-13 gang members in which 19 individuals were arrested and charged with conspiracy to intimidate the communities of Silver Spring, Langley Park, and Hyattsville, MD, through murders, attempted murders, and kidnappings. These MS-13 suspects were named in a federal indictment alleging that the gang's activities violated federal criminal racketeering laws.[51] These Racketeering Influenced and Corrupt Organizations (RICO) statutes were originally designed to prosecute and convict organized crime groups like La Cosa Nostra under the premise that the violent operations of the Mafia were organized, structured, had leadership, and involved high-level, serious criminal activities. Hence, the organization and hierarchical structure of the MS- 13 gang, rather than their violent criminal activities, will be what determines whether prosecution of MS-13 gang members under RICO statutes will be successful.

Conviction under the federal RICO statutes carries a maximum sentence of life imprisonment without parole.

GANGS AND THE "TRANSNATIONAL THREAT"

The prominence of gangs composed of recent immigrants from Central America, some of whose members are in the United States illegally, raises concerns about the ability of gang members to cross the southern border of the United States undetected. The porous southern U.S. border is often the method by which illegal goods and immigrants are smuggled into the country.[52] The continuing international connections between such Central American gangs raise the possibility that illegal entrants could pay gangs to smuggle them into the United States, and as such terrorists could also be illegally smuggled across the U.S. border by gangs.

The decision of DHS to crack down on MS-13 (discussed above) further indicates the significance of the transnational threat posed by gangs. The involvement of gangs in smuggling weapons, humans, and drugs has long been established. However, following the 9/11 terrorist attacks, there are heightened concerns that gang smuggling interests may be shared by terrorists groups interested in crossing the U.S. border illegally and undetected. Concern about the convergence of these smuggling interests may have been the impetus behind the sharpened focus of DHS on transnational gangs and their illegal activities, and particularly on Latino gangs, as a threat to domestic security.[53]

Despite the specter of transnational Latino gangs undermining domestic security, no evidence has been found linking U.S. gangs, regardless of their members' immigration status, with the smuggling of terrorists into the country. The 2005 National Gang Threat Assessment concluded that despite their vigilance in looking for associations between gangs and international terrorist groups, few investigators identified any associations, and those who did described "the connections in terms of speculation [that was] supported by little evidence."[54] Furthermore, ICE recently reported that of the 1,057 gang members and associates arrested since February 2005 as a part of its recent crackdown on gang members crossing the southern U.S. border, none were found to have any terrorist ties.[55]

FEDERAL ANTI-GANG PROGRAMS AND INITIATIVES

For most of the history of gangs, the crimes they committed were generally the responsibility of state and local law enforcement. Gangs pose a significant threat to public safety, and as gangs have spread across the country the interest in finding adequate solutions to the problem has included all levels of government. In the mid- to late-1980s and early 1990s, Congress passed legislation federalizing certain gang- related crimes and providing additional penalties for individuals convicted under these laws. In addition, the federal government has taken an active role in helping state and local jurisdictions develop anti-gang responses through support for research on gangs, and through grant programs to help jurisdictions develop effective gang prevention and intervention strategies.

Developing an effective response to gangs, however, is complicated by the range of gang criminal activities (from juvenile delinquency to serious violent crimes by criminal organizations). Moreover, gang activities vary from community to community, making it difficult to establish national programs or provide uniform assistance. Strategies developed by the Congress to address the gang problem have included (1) prevention, aimed at preventing youths from joining gangs and engaging in gang behavior, by educating children and teens about the dangers of joining gangs; (2) intervention, aimed at diverting at-risk youth from crime, by providing alternatives such as after-school programs, counseling, work-study, conflict- resolution, etc.; (3) suppression, law enforcement tactics that usually involve arrest, prosecution, and incarceration; or (4) a comprehensive approach which would combine some or all of the strategies to address the spectrum of the gang problem.

SELECTED CONGRESSIONAL ACTION

The federal focus on gangs began in the late 1980s when the OJJDP funded a research project dealing with drug use and delinquency among dropouts and gang members in New York City.[56] In 1987, OJJDP, in cooperation with the University of Chicago's School of Social Service Administration, initiated a major research and development program to address the gang problem. The project, the National Youth Gang Suppression and Intervention Program, was a four-stage process that included an assessment of the gang problem, the development of a model program for preventing youth gangs, a review of the literature on gangs, and a national survey of youth gang problems and programs.[57]

The federal response to youth gangs in the late 1980s was inextricably linked to drug trafficking and violence associated with what is often referred to as the "crack cocaine epidemic." The Anti-Drug Abuse Act of 1 988 (P.L. 1 00-690) addressed the gang problem by establishing grant programs within OJP[58] and OJJDP designed to address a number of gang-related issues, including the prevention and treatment related to juvenile gangs, drug use, and drug trafficking. Further congressional action specifically on gangs did not occur until 1994, when legislation was enacted that took a more comprehensive approach to addressing crime and the youth gang problem.

The Violent Crime Control and Law Enforcement Act of 1994 (P.L. 103-322) contained several anti-gang-related initiatives, including new or enhanced penalties for certain crimes that were often associated with gangs. The act provided new or enhanced penalties for gang-related crimes by (1) imposing an additional term of imprisonment of up to 10 years for involvement in a serious federal drug offense or federal violent felony affecting interstate or foreign commerce, (2) permitting the prosecution of youths 13 years of age and above if the juvenile possessed a firearm during a crime of violence, and (3) tripling the penalty for employing children to distribute drugs near schools and playgrounds. The law also authorized funding for a new grant program, the Gang Resistance Education and Training grants (G.R.E.A.T.) to state and local law enforcement and prevention organizations to be used for gang-prevention activities in schools. It also permitted existing grant programs, the Local Law Enforcement Block Grant and the Edward Byrne Memorial Grant programs,[59] to be used for various purposes, including multi-jurisdictional gang task forces. The act also directed the AG, in consultation with the Secretary of the Treasury, to develop a national strategy to coordinate gang-related investigations by federal law enforcement agencies.

In addition, P.L. 103-322 authorized the Community Oriented Policing Services (COPS) program, which was designed to put more police officers on the streets and make communities safer. The COPS program was generally designed to provide grants to state and local law enforcement agencies to fight crime at the local level through the strategy of having a larger police presence in high crime areas. Thus, COPS, by providing grants that could be used in preventing street crime, was indirectly providing assistance for fighting gangs and gang-related crime.

During the 107th Congress, anti-gang provisions were included in the 21st Century Department of Justice Appropriations Authorization Act (P.L. 107-273). The law included a new Juvenile Accountability Block Grant (JABG) program that provides grants to states for strengthening the juvenile justice system. The grants can be used to fund projects designed to prevent and reduce the rate of participation of juveniles in gangs that commit crimes (particularly violent crimes), including the unlawful use of firearms and other weapons, or that unlawfully traffic in drugs.

JABG funds can also be used to assist prosecutors to address drug, gang, and youth violence problems more effectively, and for acquiring technology, equipment, and training designed to help prosecutors with identifying and expeditiously prosecuting violent juvenile offenders.

More recently, the FY2005 Consolidated Appropriations Act (P.L. 108-447) earmarked $10 million to establish a National Gang Intelligence Center at the FBI. The center is to be a clearing house of information from the FBI, ATF, and other federal law enforcement agencies on gang intelligence on a national and international level. The act also appropriated funding for hiring additional FBI agents, analysts, and support staff to address the most violent gangs throughout the country.

Selected Proposals and Initiatives

Research on youth gangs indicates that each gang and each community is unique, so it is difficult to generalize and develop a "one-size-fits-all" strategy to address the issue. Over the last two decades, there have been many anti-gang projects and initiatives that have been developed and implemented in communities across the country. Federal, state, and local governments have actively developed approaches designed to prevent or stop gang involvement in violence, drug trafficking, firearms offenses, and other related activities of concern.

Research and experimentation on what might effectively end the gang problem has been a busy area of juvenile delinquency research. Currently, a mixture of approaches is being tried across the nation, but most programs attempt to integrate some component of prevention, intervention, and suppression strategies. Even municipalities have passed legislation and/or city ordinances targeting gangs. This section of the chapter will highlight a few of the most recent programs and strategies that have been and are being used to prevent youths from joining gangs and reduce gang membership and gang violence. The section will summarize some of the current federal programs and initiatives, followed by a generalized summary of state and local anti-gang initiatives.

Because gangs are involved in various types of criminal behavior, including juvenile delinquency, crimes of violence, property crime, firearms violations, and drug trafficking, various DOJ agencies are involved in fighting gang activities directly and indirectly. For example, through efforts to stop drug trafficking and crime, generally, the Drug Enforcement Agency (DEA) is working to address part of the gang problem to the extent that gangs are involved in drug trafficking. The U.S. Attorney's Office works to prosecute federal gang cases that are investigated by the FBI, or that involve the ATF, and as such are involved in battling gang criminal activity as it relates to, or involves, firearms violations and falls into their purview.

In addition, several federal agencies outside of DOJ administer programs that indirectly address some aspects of the gang problem. These efforts take varied approaches to countering gang activities. For example, the Department of Education administers grant programs designed to prevent juvenile delinquency and promote safe schools, which can have anti-gang components.

Compassion Capital Fund

In his January 2005 State of the Union address, President Bush proposed an initiative to provide $150 million over three years to community and faith-based groups to help troubled youth avoid gangs and prison. The initiative was proposed as a part of the Compassion Capital Fund (CCF) to help with building "service capacity and knowledge among faith- and community-based organizations and encourage replication of effective approaches to better meet the needs of low-income persons and families."[60]

FBI Efforts: The Safe Streets and Violent Crimes Initiative (SSVCI)

In January 1992, the FBI announced the SSVCI, an initiative designed to allow the Special Agent in Charge of each FBI field division to establish long-term, proactive task forces focused on reducing violent crime.[61] The task forces placed specific emphasis on the identification of major violent street gangs and/or drug enterprises of national scope by applying the same methods used to successfully wage war on traditional organized crime. According to FBI testimony before the Senate Judiciary Committee, one of the first gangs to be targeted by the gang task force was the MS- 13 gang. Moreover, the work of the task force enabled the U.S. Attorney for the Central District of California, Debra Yang, to successfully use statutes to prosecute the leaders of the 1 8th Street Gang and the Mexican Mafia, a prison gang.[62] The need for intelligence sharing forced uniformity and facilitated the FBI's development of an integrated information sharing system for tracking criminal gang activit y through a national system capable of sharing information by computers in "real time."

According to the FBI, the task force concept increases the effectiveness and productivity of limited personnel and logistical resources, avoids duplication of investigations, and expands the cooperation and communication among law enforcement agencies. In response to the threat from gangs, the FBI established the Safe Streets Violent Gang Task Forces

(SSVGTF) to coordinate the efforts of law enforcement at all levels of government and use the same statutes, intelligence, and investigative techniques against violent gangs that are used to fight organized crime. Between FY2001 and FY2006, the SSVGTF accomplished the following:

- 25,792 arrests
- 13,521 information/indictments
- 11,502 convictions
- 1,714 disruptions
- 301 dismantlements
- 344 RICO indictments
- 510 other racketeering statute indictments.[63]

For FY2006, Congress appropriated $5 million for SSVGTFs. The Revised Continuing Appropriations Resolution, 2007 (P.L. 110-5) and the Consolidated Appropriations Act, 2008 (P.L. 110-161) did not specify funding for SSVGTFs.

FBI National Gang Strategy (NGS). The FBI's NGS is designed to incorporate the investigative and prosecutorial practices that had been successful in the Organized Crime/Drug Program National Strategy.[64] The NGS promotes the sharing of information among federal, state, and local law enforcement agencies, which in turn helps the FBI identify violent gangs with coordinated investigations that support prosecutions. The Strategy is a component of DOJ's overall Anti- Violence Crime Initiative, which is designed to promote the development of cooperative strategies among corrections, parole and probation, and law enforcement to work together and share information on gang-involved offenders.

FBI National Gang Intelligence Center (NGIC). Pursuant to P.L. 108- 447, the FBI is in the process of establishing an NGIC. According to testimony at a congressional hearing, the NGIC "will enable the FBI and its local, state, and federal partners to centralize and coordinate the national collection of intelligence on gangs in the United States and then analyze, share, and disseminate" the information to the law enforcement community.[65] The NGIC, maintained and operated by the FBI, received appropriations of $4.7 million for FY2006. For FY2007, P.L. 110-5 did not specify funding for the NGIC. For FY2008, P.L. 110-161 similarly did not specify funding for the NGIC.

FBI's Criminal Investigations of Gangs. In September 2005, the DOJ Office of the Inspector General (OIG) released a report on how terrorism and the September 11, 2001, terrorist attacks transformed the FBI's investigative priorities.[66] Among the FBI's traditional criminal investigations, the OIG reported that the FBI did not reduce the number of agents involved in combating violent gangs between FY2000 and FY2004.[67] Despite the "reprioritization" of the FBI's operations to focus on stopping terrorist attacks, the number of FBI Field Agents used for investigating violent gangs increased from 266 in FY2000, to 315 in FY2004.[68] The number of violent gang cases opened by the FBI increased from 495 in FY2000, to 784 in FY2004, an increase of 58% during a period when the number of all other criminal enterprise cases declined.[69]

For most of the FBI's traditional criminal investigations in FY2004, fewer field agents were available as counterterrorism became the bureau's priority. In FY2004, there were 2,200 fewer field agents investigating criminal matters and the FBI opened 45% fewer criminal cases. However, the bureau's focus on fighting violent gang crime remained a priority.[70]

Organized Crime Drug Enforcement Task Force (OCDETF)

The OIG's report also included data on other criminal enterprise programs. OCDETF, a congressionally funded program administered by the Criminal Division of DOJ that focuses on the disruption and dismantling of major drug trafficking organizations, includes a gangs component. FBI agents participate in OCDETF efforts to combat drug traffickers and violent gangs. Although the number of agents utilized for all OCDETF matters dropped from 1,062 in FY2000 to 540 in FY2004 (49% decrease), the number of agents used on gang-related matters only dropped from 171 in FY2000 to 120 in FY2004 (30% decrease).[71] For FY2006, Congress appropriated $489.4 million for OCDETF. The Revised Continuing Appropriations Resolution, 2007 (P.L. 110-5) specified FY2007 of $494.8 million for OCDETF activities. For FY2008, P.L. 110-161 included $497.9 million for the task force.

The Gang Resistance Education and Training (G.R.E.A.T.) Program

The G.R.E.A.T. program, administered by OJP, is designed to prevent children and young adolescents from joining gangs through a school-based curriculum presented by a law enforcement officer. The G.R.E.A.T program differs from other gang prevention programs because it is not directed at active gang members or at-risk youth, but instead is a broader program for all youths. The curriculum includes the following learning components: (1) crimes, their victims, and the impact of crime on the school and the neighborhood; (2) cultural sensitivity and prejudice and how these factors affect the school and neighborhood; (3) conflict resolution techniques to create an atmosphere of understanding that will help address interpersonal problems and solutions; (4) how to satisfy at-risk youth's basic social needs without joining a gang; (5) the diverse responsibilities of people in an at-risk youth's school and neighborhood; and (6) the need for personal goal setting and ways to establish short- and long-term goals.

The outcomes of the program are determined by followup surveys conducted between 12 and 18 months after completion of the program. The surveys indicate that students report lower levels of gang affiliation and delinquency, including drug use, minor offenses, property crimes, and crimes against other persons. When compared to the control group of students, those who had participated in the G.R.E.A.T. program reported fewer delinquent friends, more positive attitudes towards police, more negative attitudes about gangs, higher self-esteem, more commitment to success at school, higher levels of attachment to both mothers and fathers, and less likelihood of acting impulsively.

From October 1994 through December 2001, the National Institute of Justice (NIJ) funded a national evaluation of the G.R.E.A.T. program.[72] The evaluation had two purposes: (1) to find out if the program's components were being executed as designed, and (2) to observe the actual delivery of the program by law enforcement officers in the classrooms. The evaluation included both a cross-sectional and a longitudinal survey of middle school youths in selected locations.

The evaluation used a control group of students and a group of students that had participated in the G.R.E.A.T. program. The cross-sectional survey obtained information from 5,935 eighth graders in 315 classrooms at 42 different schools located within 11 diverse law enforcement jurisdictions across the country. The cross-sectional survey found that self-reported gang membership was significantly related to self-reported juvenile delinquency. The survey also revealed higher than expected levels of female and white youth gang members (38% female, 25% white).[73] The results of the cross-sectional survey supported the effectiveness of the program. These results were similar to previous evaluations of the program that had yielded modestly positive results.[74]

In addition to evaluating the G.R.E.A.T. program, a longitudinal study was conducted in six cities consisting of 3,500 students in 22 classrooms in 22 schools.[75] One year after participating in the G.R.E.A.T. program, the differences between the students who had participated in the program and those who had not were small. The longitudinal evaluation did not find significant differences in the groups of student participants until three or four years after program exposure.[76] Overall, the evaluation found that the program's outcomes measures were greater "than would be expected by chance."[77]

The evaluation of the G.R.E.A.T program concluded that significant reductions in gang membership or future reductions in delinquent behavior could not be credited to the program's nine-hour curriculum. However, the report credited the program with producing educational benefits and improved police relations with students and their communities. Advocates of the program maintain that G.R.E.A.T. can contribute to anti-gang goals as part of a broader program of prevention and intervention.

Under Title V - Incentive Grants of the Juvenile Justice Programs, Congress included appropriations of $25 million for FY2006 for the G.R.E.A.T. program (P.L. 109-108). The Revised Continuing Appropriations Resolution (P.L. 110-5) did not specify funding for the G.R.E.A.T. program. For FY2008, P.L. 110-161 provided $18.8 million for the program.

Project Safe Neighborhoods (PSN)

Project Safe Neighborhoods is an initiative designed to reduce gun violence. Although not specifically focused on youth gangs, the PSN program is an important part of reducing gun violence among the youth and reducing the use of guns in other criminal acts. The program includes five elements considered essential for a successful gun crime reduction strategy. The program is organized through the U.S. Attorney's Offices in 94 federal judicial districts across the county. The program has received funding of more than one million dollars since its inception in 2001. Funds can be used to hire new federal, state, and local prosecutors; provide training; hire research and community outreach support; and develop and promote effective prevention and deterrence efforts.

Under the PSN program, each U.S. Attorney develops a plan incorporating three national priorities: (1) increased prosecution of violent organizations by aggressively using federal conspiracy, racketeering, narcotics, and all other available laws to attack and punish violent drug traffickers, violent street gangs, and violent robbery rings; (2) strict enforcement of all federal laws against illegal gun traffickers and their suppliers, with an emphasis on those gun traffickers who supply illegal firearms to violent organizations and to juveniles; and (3) aggressive enforcement of federal firearms laws against those persons prohibited from possessing firearms or who use firearms in furtherance of illegal activities, including those persons denied under the Brady Act.[78] The strategic plans are required to reflect the unique features and problems of the particular district, but with the goal of reducing the levels of gun crime.

Training is provided for participants in PSN through the collaborative efforts of several DOJ agencies, including ATF, who conduct the training of prosecutors, agents, and law enforcement officers involved in gun crime cases. U.S. Attorneys are encouraged to design and conduct their own training programs at the local level.

Community outreach, public awareness campaigns, and public service announcements are all methods that can be used to convey the PSN message and get the support of the local community. U.S. Attorneys are encouraged to regularly assess the effectiveness of their plans, noting emerging trends, and they are required to report to DOJ on the status of their PSN strategy.

According to DOJ, the PSN program is responsible for a significant increase in the number of federal firearms prosecutions, which are up 76.2% since the initiative began. DOJ further notes that federal firearms defendants convicted of federal firearms offenses are being sentenced to significant jail time.[79] For FY2007, The Revised Continuing Appropriations Resolution (P.L. 110-5) did not specify funding for PSN. For FY2008, P.L. 110-161 did not include specific funding for the program.

OJJDP Gang Reduction Program

In FY2004, OJJDP initiated the Gang Reduction Program (GRP), a pilot program designed to reduce youth gang crime and violence. GRP is underway in four pilot sites (East Los Angeles, CA; North Miami Beach, FL; Milwaukee, WI; and Richmond, VA) in targeted areas of approximately five square miles. The pilot sites were selected because these communities were characterized as already having significant existing anti-gang program investment, strong indications of citizen involvement in these anti-gang efforts, and high rates of crime and gang activity. The program is designed to integrate state, local, and federal resources to focus on prevention, intervention, and suppression with state-of-the-art, research-based practices. The program is designed to identify the needs at the individual, family, and community level and address those needs with a coordinated, comprehensive response. A three-year evaluation is being conducted by the Urban Institute to assess program implementation, examine outcomes related to reductions in crime and gang-activity, improvements in "prosocial" or positive activities for at- risk youth, and improved protective factors in the lives of high-risk youth.

Selected State and Local Programs and Strategies

States and cities have long been developing local approaches to the gang problem. Some of the areas that these initiatives and programs fall under are prevention, intervention, and suppression of youth gang activity. The following discussion is not intended to be a comprehensive review of the numerous anti-gang programs that have been initiated and developed by state and local governments, but a mere sampling of initiatives that are considered models for programs that may be generally applicable and replicable in other communities.[80]

Prevention programs developed by states and localities include those designed to improve the living conditions of at-risk youth and provide them with opportunities to replace gang activities with safer and more beneficial activities and services. Examples of these types of programs include providing alternative recreation opportunities where at-risk or high-risk youth and others involved in the juvenile justice system can be involved in safe alternatives to being out on the streets late at night. Prevention programs can also include early intervention programs for parents and infants or small children designed to provide parental training and childhood skills development, including preschool for early social and cognitive development. Preventive programs can also include school-based programs, to ensure in-school safety and control, in-school enrichment procedures, with formal links to community-based programs, as well as afterschool activities to keep youths safe and involved in recreational or educational activities such as mentoring programs.

Intervention programs seek to coax youth away from gangs and reduce the criminal activities of gangs, and can include such services as employment counseling, job placement assistance, advocacy assistance with the police and courts, and other social assistance such as health care and other services. Boys & Girls Clubs across the country provide gang intervention programs that provide life-skills development, education, and employment programs. Other programs are designed to provide alternatives to gang life through jobs in the community or through the enterprises developed by the project to provide employment opportunities for participants. One example of a California-based program funds a daycare center, a homeless shelter, an alternative school for gang members, and a tattoo-removal service. Another example of a gang intervention initiative developed by a faith-based organization provides jobs and refurbishes neighborhoods, including removing graffiti and providing landscaping.

Suppression programs are also designed to reduce gang crime by deterring such crimes through the arrest, prosecution, and incarceration of gang members. As early as 1979, Los Angeles, CA, created a prosecutorial gang suppression program through the city's District Attorney's office that targeted serious and violent juvenile gang- related crime. The formation of specialized "gang units" among local police departments improved intelligence gathering, investigation, and suppression of gangs through the use of gang sweeps, targeting gang gathering places or "hotspots," and intensified patrols in communities plagued by gang violence and drug trafficking to bring pressure to bear on gangs. In addition, there has been an emphasis on reducing handgun violence among gang members through various initiatives, often supported through grants from the federal COPS program (previously discussed).

Numerous communities across the country have used combinations of these examples and techniques to develop their anti-gang strategies. Community policing has been one strategy used to respond to gang activity, whereas other communities have approached the problem with strategies that combine local law enforcement with federal and state agencies. Many of these multiagency initiatives have been developed in Los Angeles, and other cities of southern California, where the gang problem is endemic. However, an influential multiagency project was developed in Boston, Massachusetts. Known as the Boston Gun Project, or Operation Ceasefire, the program is considered a "model" multiagency gang suppression initiative.[81] Under the program, gang violence is tracked to the neighborhoods where it occurs, there is an explicit communication campaign to let the community and gang members know that there will be zero tolerance of all gang violence, and that those offenders who violate these conditions will receive long prison sentences.

California's Street Terrorism Enforcement and Prevention Act

California has long had an endemic gang problem and, as a result, has been at the forefront of innovative approaches to respond to gang activity. The Street Terrorism Enforcement and Prevention (STEP) Act enacted on September 23, 1988,[82] combines prevention, intervention, and suppression approaches to the gang problem. The STEP defines what constitutes a "criminal street gang," what offenses are "gang offenses," and imposes penalty enhancements for gang-related crimes. Once an individual has been convicted under the STEP Act, the law requires the offender to register with the local law enforcement agency on release from prison, and failure to register is a misdemeanor offense, which if ignored can lead to further imprisonment.

Under the STEP Act, targeted gang members are notified that they can be prosecuted under this law and subjected to its penalties. The police and/or prosecutors then gather evidence on targeted gang members that fit the act's definition, and the information is presented to the court for a judicial order. Once a judicial order has been issued, convicted targeted gang members will have their imprisonment penalties enhanced.[83]

Several states have followed California's example and have enacted, or have considered enacting, gang-specific laws.[84] The California STEP Act has raised many constitutional questions involving freedom of association, vagueness, and overreaching, but has withstood the scrutiny of California's appellate court.

Gang Civil Injunctions

Gangs are often cited as major contributors to various types of crime, including violent crime. One response that is being taken by cities and jurisdictions across the country has been to use civil injunctions or nuisance ordinances to curtail the activities of gang members. Los Angeles, a city with one of the worst gang problems in the country, pioneered this response in 1987 in neighborhoods around the city particularly hard-hit by gang violence and crime.

Civil injunctions are legal actions that prohibit specifically named individuals from engaging in particular activities within a specified area. A civil gang injunction (CGI) can restrict or prohibit both legal and illegal gang activities.[85] For example, a CGI could be used to ban a gang from using public parks or wearing certain articles of clothing or publicly associating with known gang members. CGIs could also be used to make it a violation of the injunction to possess graffiti tools (spray paint) or to carry a pager or cell phone because these items could be used for illegal activities. CGIs have been applied to specifically named gang members who have been prohibited from engaging in certain activities within a specified area, in an attempt to create a "safety zone" within a high-crime neighborhood. If permitted by courts, CGIs have also included curfews, although generally these types of restrictions are typically only imposed on juvenile gang members named in an injunction. Violations of a CGI generally carry a fine or incarceration that varies depending on whether the case is brought in civil or criminal court. Typically, CGIs go into effect as soon the named gang members are served with a copy of the injunction order.[86]

Since Los Angeles first issued an injunction against a gang in 1987, the use of this type of local ordinance has spread throughout southern California communities and into other states. The rationale for CGIs is based on the finding that much of gang-related crime is perpetuated by a small proportion of gang members who are repeat offenders that can be identified and targeted. Proponents of CGIs report that a drop in crime in the target areas after a CGI is imposed provides communities some "gang-free" time to organize and develop constructive ways of limiting a gang's effect on their community. If a CGI worked as intended, communities that impose such measures would expect gang-related crime rates to drop, and this experience has been reported by communities employing CGIs, at least in the short-run. However, CGI critics argue that the use of injunctions infringes on the rights of targeted gang members, violating their constitutional right to freely associate and assemble peacefully. Several of the CGIs have been litigated; however, generally the courts have upheld their use.

A recent study of the use of CGIs in five neighborhoods in San Bernardino, CA, provides evidence supporting the use of CGIs as a strategic method of gang suppression.[87] The study found that CGIs were "relatively flexible tools" for fighting gang violence because they could be customized to address the particular needs of a community.[88] The study found that CGIs may also have an important psychological effect on gang members deterring them from criminal activities simply because of their concern about added police scrutiny resulting from a CGI.[89]

Surveys of residents in the CGI-covered communities found that the injunctions had an immediate impact on the visibility of gang members, and that the CGI, in turn, actually lowered the fear of gang members among residents.[90] Over time, the study found that the CGIs did have a positive effect on residents' perception of the gang threat even if the effect was temporary. The study concluded that even temporary reductions in gang activity and violence through CGIs have the potential to help communities reduce persistence of gang activity.

Legislative Proposals in the 110th Congress

In the 110th Congress, several bills have been introduced to address various aspects of the gang problem. These proposals comprise some comprehensive bills that include both enhanced criminal penalties for violent gang crime and authorize gang prosecution and prevention grants, while other bills would address the gang problem with more targeted prevention or intervention efforts. The following section briefly discusses some of the major anti-gang provisions under consideration by Congress.[91]

Criminal Street Gang and Associated Crimes and Penalties

Several anti-gang bills have been introduced, and one bill (S. 456) has been passed by the Senate, that would amend Title 18 of the U.S. Code to expand the definition of a criminal street gang and specify additional penalty enhancements for certain violent offenses committed by criminal street gang members. H.R. 880, H.R. 1582, H.R. 3156, H.R. 3547, S. 456, S. 990, and S. 2237 would specify federal gang- related crimes and increase the penalties related to violent criminal street gang activity.

H.R. 880 would provide mandatory minimum sentences for certain violent gang- related crimes, and would permit the imposition of a death sentence in cases where the violent crime resulted in the victim's death. H.R. 1582, H.R. 1692, H.R. 3156, H.R. 3547, H.R. 3922, S. 456, S. 990, S. 1860, and S. 2237 would provide mandatory minimum sentences of no less than 15 years and up to life in prison in cases where the gang offender had three prior convictions for violent or drug- trafficking felonies, the last of which had been committed within 10 years of the current offense. S. 990 and H.R. 1692 would make it unlawful to participate or cause another to participate in specified violent gang criminal activities, and would provide criminal penalties of up to 30 years. Under all of these bills, conviction for certain violent gang-related offenses could carry penalties of up to life imprisonment.

Among other provisions, H.R. 1582, H.R. 1692, H.R. 3547, H.R. 3922, S. 456, S. 990, and S. 2237 would also make it unlawful to knowingly recruit, employ, solicit, induce, or otherwise cause a person to remain as a criminal street gang member, or attempt or conspire to do so, with the intent that the person would participate in a gang crime.

Amendments to the Racketeer Influenced and Corrupt Organizations Statute

H.R. 880, H.R. 1582, H.R. 3150, H.R. 3156, H.R. 3547, S. 456, S. 990, and S. 2237 would increase the penalties for violent crimes committed in aid of racketeering. These bills would also increase the criminal penalties for certain violent offenses committed in the course of interstate and foreign travel or transportation in aid of racketeering.

Transfer of Juveniles for Adult Prosecution

H.R. 880, H.R. 3156, and S. 1860 would amend current law to permit the Attorney General (AG) to transfer juveniles for federal prosecution as adults if the alleged violent felony occurred after the juvenile's 16th birthday. Under these bills, the AG's decision to prosecute a juvenile as an adult would not be subject to judicial review in any court. H.R. 1692 and S. 990 would require a study to determine the costs and benefits of expanding federal authority to prosecute offenders under the age of 18.

GANG TASK FORCES AND PROSECUTORIAL ASSISTANCE

Several bills would address the gang problem with targeted approaches such as establishing gang task forces designed to coordinate the investigation and prosecution of gang-related crime. For example, H.R. 638, H.R. 880, H.R. 1582, H.R. 1692, H.R. 3156, H.R. 3547, H.R. 3922, S. 144, S. 456, S. 990, S. 1296, S. 1860, and S. 2237 would designate High-Intensity Interstate Gang Activity Areas (HIIGAAs) where teams of federal, state, and local law enforcement authorities would coordinate the investigation and prosecution of criminal street gangs. Federal assistance would be provided by various federal agencies, and all necessary funding for the operation of the HIIGAAs would be federally authorized. In addition, these bills would authorize the AG to hire 94 additional Assistant U.S. Attorneys for assignment to the HIIGAAs and would authorize appropriations to fund the HIGAAs. H.R. 638 would authorize appropriations for grants to assist state and local prosecutors to fund technology, equipment, and training for prosecutors and law enforcement to help them identify and prosecute gang members and violent offenders, among other purposes, and it would authorize appropriations for the hiring 94 additional prosecutors to fight violent gang crime through the HIIGAAs.

Similarly, H.R. 1069 and S. 144 would establish comprehensive gang prevention and relief areas, as well as task forces to coordinate federal assistance to provide a comprehensive response to gang problems by focusing on early childhood intervention programs, at-risk youth intervention, literacy, employment, community policing, and comprehensive community anti-gang programs. In addition, the task forces would prioritize the federal funding needs of the areas under a number of federal programs. Among other provisions, H.R. 2466 includes a provision which would authorize the establishment of multi-jurisdictional anti-gang task forces. H.R. 3152 would also authorize multi-jurisdictional anti-gang task forces.

In addition, some bills would establish grant programs designed to assist state and local prosecutors in combating violent crime. H.R. 880, H.R. 1582, H.R. 3156, H.R. 3568, H.R. 3922, S. 1860, and S. 2237 would provide grants to prosecutors and law enforcement to combat violent crime, generally, and to fund technology, equipment, and training in order to increase the accurate identification of gang members and maintain databases of this information to facilitate coordination among law enforcement and prosecutors.

H.R. 3150, H.R. 3474, H.R. 3922, and S. 2237 would expand the FBI's Safe Streets Program to establish a National Gang Activity Database for use in supporting criminal street gang enforcement teams. The bill would require the AG to establish a DOJ-administered database designed to collect and disseminate gang information to law enforcement agencies at all levels of government, as well as provide aggregate statistical information on gangs, subject to appropriate controls. H.R. 3384 would authorize additional appropriations for the PSN program to improve the enforcement of criminal laws against violent gangs.

H.R. 367 would require the Attorney General (AG) to develop and report to Congress on a national strategy to eliminate the illegal operations of the top three international drug gangs whose illegal activities include drug-related offenses with any international terrorist organization or state. S. 456, H.R. 1582, and H.R. 3922 would authorize appropriations to provide the FBI with more resources for the investigation and prosecution of violent criminal street gangs.

Gang Prevention Grants

H.R. 1070 would fund gang prevention programs from the proceeds of the sale of certain specially issued postage stamps. H.R. 1184 would permit the Secretary of Education to make grants to state educational agencies to award sub-grants to alternative schools or programs serving at-risk youth that agree to develop and implement a 100-hour community service requirement for students per school year. In addition, the bill would also require that students receive training and attend conflict resolution classes as a prerequisite to performing community service. H.R. 3168 would establish a grant program designed to help communities provide training, mentoring, and education programs designed to deter and prevent gang and youth violence by helping high-risk young adults become employable.

H.R. 1582, H.R. 3150, H.R. 3384, H.R. 3922, S. 456, and S. 2237 would expand the Project Safe Neighborhoods program, an initiative designed to reduce gun violence, to require each U.S. Attorney to identify, investigate, and prosecute significant criminal street gangs operating within their district. In addition, U.S. Attorneys would be required to coordinate these activities among federal, state, and local law enforcement agencies. The bills would authorize the AG to hire additional staff for carrying out the program.

H.R. 3846 would establish a series of new grants and would provide funding for coordinating entities charged with overseeing the implementation of the grants and creating an infrastructure between local units of government, state and local law enforcement agencies, and the federal government. Under H.R. 3846, evidence- based measures of local and tribal juvenile delinquency and criminal street gang activity prevention and intervention efforts would be used to identify promising prevention and intervention programs.

Other prevention initiatives would be supported by grant programs that would permit the development of a wide range of community-based programs for prevention and intervention alternatives for high-risk youth. H.R. 1582, H.R. 1692, H.R. 3922, and S. 456, S. 990, and S. 2237 would authorize grants for community programs designed to prevent young people from joining gangs. Generally, the grants could be used for a variety of gang prevention activities, including community and school-based projects designed to eliminate gang related crime through employment of security personnel; physical improvements designed to enhance security; measures designed to reduce gang activity in and around public and low-income housing; mentoring, counseling, and other activities to improve educational attainment and employability; as well as intervention initiatives designed to enhance reintegration strategies for offender reentry. Among other provisions, H.R. 1806 would similarly authorize school and community based gang prevention grants.

Selected Issues Raised by Legislative Proposals

Most of the comprehensive anti-gang bills introduced in the 1 10th Congress focus on making changes to federal criminal law that would provide longer prison sentences for gang members convicted of certain violent felonies. These provisions would amend the current law definition of what constitutes a "criminal street gang" by lowering the number of affiliated persons required to trigger additional criminal penalties for serious violent offenses. Some of the bills address the gang problem through other indirect punitive measures, such as increasing the penalties for specified violent crimes, including the use of mandatory minimum sentences. Similarly, a few of the bills would permit the AG to determine whether a juvenile offender should be transferred for prosecution as an adult.

Proponents of these gang-related sentencing enhancements argue that these enhanced federal penalties are needed to address the rising gang crime in many communities. They argue that longer sentences could deter violent gang-related crime. In addition, the threat of a longer time in prison could encourage greater cooperation of gang members with prosecutors, which could lead to the identification, arrest, and prosecution of other gang members in exchange for a shorter sentence. Proponents of the anti-gang legislation argue that such measures are supported by law enforcement officials who contend that they need these tougher sentences to stop gang violence.[92] Similarly, proponents of mandatory minimum sentences argue that this type of sentencing offers greater incentives for criminals to cooperate with law enforcement, providing evidence in exchange for prosecution for a different or lesser charge that does not carry a mandatory minimum or carries a lesser sentence. Proponents of new additional federal criminal penalties for gang crimes argue that tougher penalties and federal mandatory minimum sentences for gang crimes are an essential deterrent to gang crime, particularly violent crimes.

Critics of mandatory minimum sentences argue on several levels against these proposals. On the broadest level, there are critics opposed to the further federalization of laws that have traditionally been under the sole jurisdiction of states and localities. They cite the growing number of new federal crimes, recently estimated at almost 4,000 crimes,[93] and that a federal approach is less desirable and unnecessary when there are already adequate federal, state, and local laws to address gang-related crime. It is also argued that, not only are federal resources strained as they cope with investigating and prosecuting national threats, but it is the state and local law enforcement officers that have the necessary experience and local intelligence sources to investigate and prosecute gang crimes which may vary greatly by state, region, or locality. Opponents of mandatory minimum sentences for gang- related crime also point to the greater expense of imprisonment versus the costs of prevention and rehabilitation efforts. Moreover, it has also been argued that in certain situations, many individuals will break the law nothwithstanding severe criminal penalties,[94] questioning the crime deterrence effect of harsher penalties.

The issue of prosecuting juveniles as adults is a highly contentious issue discussed voluminously in the literature on juvenile delinquency, and is beyond the scope of this report.[95] However, provisions such as the one proposed in H.R. 880 that would permit federal prosecution of juveniles who commit gang-related crimes after their 1 6th birthday could have significant implications. For example, under provisions of this bill, juveniles prosecuted and convicted as adults for serious gang- related violent offenses could be subject to mandatory minimum sentences. Under provisions such as the enhanced criminal penalties for gang-related crimes found in H.R. 880, juvenile gang members transferred for federal prosecution as adults could be eligible to receive a sentence of death for certain violent crimes. Opponents of prosecuting juveniles as adults point to research that shows juveniles who are tried as adults and imprisoned in adult facilities have higher recidivism rates and higher rearrest rates compared to those of juveniles sentenced in juvenile court. Others argue that these measures could disproportionately affect racial and ethnic minority juveniles. In addition, they point to data from the FBI Uniform Crime Reports and the National Crime

Victimization Survey (NCVS) reports (discussed above — Crime Statistics section) that indicate that juvenile gang crime has been declining.

Most of the comprehensive bills would amend the federal organized crime and racketeering statutes (RICO) to include provisions to make racketeering a gang predicate offense and increase penalties the penalties for such crimes. Proponents of such federal RICO amendments argue that these amendments are necessary to prosecute cases where drug trafficking activity has been conducted by gangs onto federal land and Indian reservations to avoid detection and state prosecution. Proponents argue that additional federal gang-specific RICO laws, as provided by some of these bills, would provide an important addition to the federal arsenal for investigating and prosecuting gang-related crime. Opponents argue that the existing federal RICO laws are sufficiently broad to provide for successful prosecution of gang-related crime. RICO prosecutions can present a number of obstacles to prosecuting gang violence and murder using these statutes. For example, one significant obstacle in a gang-related RICO prosecution can be the statutes requirement that a gang being prosecuted must be shown to have a defined structure and hierarchical organization, and that the crimes were committed, or that there was a conspiracy to commit crimes in furtherance of the gang.[96] Despite these and other evidentiary obstacles under existing federal RICO statues, there have been a number of successful RICO prosecutions for gang-related crimes.[97]

A more general criticism of many anti-gang legislation that has been introduced in previous Congresses has been that many of the bills were not sufficiently focused on gang prevention assistance and that there was a lack of innovation or expansion of prevention strategies. Similarly, some have criticized the lack of focus on intervention efforts designed to help keep ex-offender gang members from falling back into the gang life after imprisonment.

Supporters of gang prevention and intervention programs have long argued that these types programs have been subjected to funding cuts in recent years despite research indicating that gang prevention can be an important and effective way of stopping gang growth. Moreover, there are few specifically targeted OJP or OJJDP anti-gang prevention programs and no gang-specific intervention programs. Most of the remaining OJP and OJJDP programs are broad grant programs with numerous programmatic purposes among which anti-gang initiatives are one among many. Opponents of prevention programs raise concerns about the costs of such programs and their effectiveness. They argue that rigorous evaluations are needed to substantiate the cost and the outcomes of initiatives. Critics also argue that grant programs may not sufficiently reduce the gang problems facing communities across the nation. Given that, as some observers conclude, the root causes of gang formation and gang violence stem from poverty, a lack of employment opportunities, and alienation from the larger society, much more than grant programs may be needed to fully address the country's gang problem.

SELECTED OPTIONS FOR CONGRESS

The proliferation of youth gang problems has heightened interest in what can be done about gangs. Gang research indicates that youth gangs vary greatly, within and among communities, as well as across the nation. Gang members also vary by a number of factors including age, race or ethnicity, gender, and educational attainment, among many others.

Research also indicates that there is much about youth gangs that authorities do not know, and may never fully understand because of the inherent complexity of the communities that give rise to gangs. As one researcher put it, "gangs emerge, grow, dissolve, and disappear for reasons that are poorly understood."[98] It is also important to note that gangs are dynamic entities that evolve over time further defying easy or static responses.

Evaluations of youth gang initiatives are complicated by the numerous levels that must be assessed. Often anti-gang strategies must encompass broad contributing factors such as the formation and dissolution of gangs, the diversion of youth from gangs, delinquency, and crime prevention and/or reduction. Anti-gang strategies also involve gang members, their parents, educators, community leaders, community organizations, providers, law enforcement, the police, prison systems, parole and probation officers, and judges. Once again, the lack of a commonly accepted definition of "youth gang" perhaps most fundamentally hampers evaluation measures.

Despite this array of obstacles, numerous evaluations of federal, state, and local anti-gang initiatives have been conducted and model programs have been identified by gang researchers as promising responses to the gang problem. Careful consideration of the outcomes of anti-gang program evaluations could also contribute to the development of federal programs and policies. The following are a small sample of the numerous anti-gang options that could be implemented or expanded at the federal level to address the problem of youth gangs in the United States.

Prevention Programs

- Congress could consider legislation to expand the G.R.E.A.T. program and require that it be provided (1) in all schools for all grades; or (2) in high-risk schools, in every grade; or (3) in all high- risk schools in each grade of middle school and high school.
- Congress could consider legislation to increase funding for grants to help fund after-school programs at schools with students at high-risk for gang participation. Research indicates that a disproportionate amount of juvenile crime occurs between 3-6 PM.

Gang Data Improvements

- Congress could consider legislation that would require the expansion of the National Youth Gang Survey to provide a larger sample of law enforcement agencies so that more data on state and regional gang activity could be available for policy development on gangs.
- Congress could consider legislation that would require greater standardization of crime statistics reporting at all levels of government with an emphasis on reporting gang-related crime. This could result in consistent crime statistics reporting and provide better informed policy development and strategically targeted anti-gang programs.

- Congress could consider enacting an anti-gang task force required to work with all interested parties (researchers, law enforcement, judiciary, policy makers) to reach a consensus on the definition of the term "youth gang" in order to assure a better measurement and response to the gang problem.

Comprehensive Approaches

- Congress could consider enacting a comprehensive, community- wide anti-gang program that would include prevention, intervention, and suppression elements, similar to the on developed by Spergel, et al,[99] for OJJDP as a model program that would include five core strategies: (1) community mobilization; (2) provision of academic, economic, and social opportunities; (3) social intervention; (4) gang suppression; and (5) organizational change and development.[100]
- Congress could consider enacting legislation to fund a program designed to target older gang members (age 17-24), designed to provide services to individuals rather than to the gangs as groups through two coordinated strategies: (1) control of violent or potentially violent youth gang offenders through increased supervision and suppression by probation and police officers, and (2) the provision of a wide range of social services and opportunities that would encourage and provide support to ex-offenders during their transition to legitimate behavior through education, employment, job training, family support, and brief periods of counseling.

Suppression Strategies

- Congress could consider enacting legislation to support the development of programs similar to the Comprehensive Strategy for Serious, Violent, and Chronic Juvenile Offenders, an OJJDP project first implemented in Rochester, NY, which provides for strategic community planning and program development targeting serious violent and chronic juvenile offenders through a framework of prevention, early intervention, and graduated sanctions.
- Congress could consider enacting legislation to support anti-gang programs that would consist of multi-agency initiatives, like the Boston Gun Project, for other cities. The Boston Gun Project is a model suppression program that targeted youth and adult gang members who are repeat offenders in high-crime areas. The community is involved along with the police and probation officers to communicate and enforce a "zero tolerance approach" to gang violence.
- Congress could consider legislation to enact a grant program to assist communities with implementing anti-gang-related city ordinances and civil injunctions. As the experience of localities in California have shown, this type of strategy alone could not solve a community's gang problem, but coupled with some other strategies, it could provide communities with a pause in gang crime that is long enough to put in place more long-term anti-gang programs or initiatives designed to stop gang criminal activity.

- Congress could introduce legislation to provide for foreign policy initiatives to assist Latin American countries in addressing their serious and mounting gang problems like those of El Salvador and Guatemala.

No single program or initiative will work in every community facing a gang problem. Thus, program evaluations and other outcome measures would help to inform the development and evolution of programs and initiatives. Programmatic flexibility permitting adaptive changes to suit local needs also would be an important element of future federal efforts to address the gang problem at a national level.

CONCLUSION

The gang problem in the United States is complex and requires multiple strategies to fully address the problem. The history of gang problems indicates that total elimination of gangs or the social problems that foster their formation and development may always persist as a national concern. The range of gang problems, which span juvenile delinquency to drug trafficking and the serious violent offenses, indicates the complexity of addressing the problem and the need for multiple strategies targeted at different populations. Efforts to address the problem could be significantly improved by greater attention to data collection efforts on gang prevalence, characteristics, and criminal activities, as well as careful program evaluation measures to ensure that efforts to address the problem are functioning at optimal levels.

Law enforcement approaches at all levels of government could benefit from more coordinated efforts to assure that resources are being used in the most effective manner. Information and intelligence sharing between law enforcement at all levels of government could also enhance the development and execution of anti-gang strategies and could foster greater cooperation to address the gang problem.

Gang researchers have long advocated that a balance of strategies in the areas of prevention, intervention, and suppression may begin to effectively address the gang problem. Prevention strategies targeted on keeping juveniles from ever joining gangs, such as the G.R.E.A.T. program or Boys and Girls Clubs, offer some possible prevention approaches. Intervention strategies, such as training and employment assistance, to provide alternatives to the gang life for active members, is also suggested as a mechanism for providing economic alternatives to criminal gang activity. Imprisonment and other punitive measures such as forfeiture and fines are appropriate for serious violent gang perpetrators; however, such measures alone have not proven to be sufficient to stem the growth of gangs.

REFERENCES

[1] The terms "youth gang,""street gang," and "gang" are often used interchangeably in much of the literature on youth gangs, and generally, these terms are used to refer to individuals ranging in age between 12 and 25 years. In contrast, the term "juvenile" generally refers to individuals who are under 18 years of age. When the term "youth

gang" is used, as it is in most of the literature on gangs, it is possible for some to assume incorrectly that a gang member is typically a juvenile although gang memberships also include adults. See Irving A. Spergel and G. David Curry, "Strategies and Perceived Agency Effectiveness in Dealing with the Youth Gang Problem," Gangs in America, 1990, p. 289.

[2] Both acts provided mandatory minimum sentences for drug traffickers who were found to be in possession of certain types of illicit drugs. The illicit drug trade is often associated with more highly organized criminal gangs.

[3] See the Violent Crime Control and Law Enforcement Act of 1994 (P.L. 103-322).

[4] Luc Sante, Low Life: Lures and Snares of Old New York, 1991, pp. 198-199. In the late 1780s, there were at least five known gangs in New York City: the Smith's Vly gang, the Bowery Boys, and the Broadway Boys, who were white, and the Fly Boys and the Long Bridge Boys, who were black. Historically, most gangs have been locally based groups that often took names that indicated the neighborhoods where they lived and carried on their activities. For example, the Fly Boys were from the area around Fly Market, and like the Smith's Vly gang, their name was derived from the Dutch word vly, meaning valley.

[5] James C. Howell, "Youth Gangs: An Overview," American Youth Gangs at the Millennium, by Finn-Aage, p. 17.

[6] Kenneth J. Peak and Timothy Griffin, "Gangs: Origin, Status, Community Responses, and Policy Implications," in Visions for Change Crime and Justice in the Twenty-First Century, Roslyn Muraskin and Albert R. Roberts, eds. (2005), p. 44.

[7] Frederic M. Thrasher, The Gang: A Study of 1,313 Gangs in Chicago (1927), pp. 26-32

[8] U.S. Department of Justice, Office of Juvenile Justice and Delinquency Prevention, The Growth of Youth Gang Problems in the United States 1970-1998 (April 2001).

[9] 9.U.S. Department of Justice, Office of Justice Programs, OJJDP, Youth Gang Programs and Strategies (August 2000), p. 27.

[10] 18 U.S.C. 521.

[11] This definition was added to current law in 1994 by Title XV § 150001 of the Violent Crime Control and Law Enforcement Act of 1994 (P.L. 103-322).

[12] The definition of a criminal street gang in federal statute is used for the purposes of federal prosecutions as sentencing enhancements, but is not a definition that has been used by the larger community of gang experts and researchers.

[13] It is important to note that in much of the literature on gangs, connections exist between street gangs and prison gangs, particularly among certain Latino gangs.

[14] U.S. Department of Justice, Office of Justice Programs, OJJDP Fact Sheet, Highlights of the 2004 National Youth Gang Survey, no. 1, April 2006.

[15] For the 2004 NYGC survey, local agencies in the nationally representative sample included all police departments serving cities with a population of 50,000 or more (n = 625); all suburban county police and sheriff's departments (n = 741); a randomly selected sample of police departments serving cities with a population between 2,500 and 49,999 (n= 696); and a randomly selected sample of rural county police and sheriffs departments (n = 492).

[16] Cities with a population of 250,000 or more.

[17] Cities with a population of 50,000 or more.

[18] Finn-Aage Esbensen, Stephen G. Tibbetts, and Larry Gaines, American Youth Gangs at the Millennium, "Recent Patterns of Gang Problems in the United States," by Arlen Egley, Jr., James C. Howell, and Aline K. Major, p. 96.
[19] According to the NYGC, Chicago and Los Angeles have historically had the highest rates of gang-related homicides of all U.S. cities.
[20] U.S. Department of Justice, Office of Justice Programs, OJJDP, Highlights of the 2002-2003 National Youth Gang Surveys, OJJDP Fact Sheet #01, June 2005.
[21] Personal communication with Arlen Egley, Jr. Ph.D., Senior Research Associate with NYGC, operated for OJJDP by the Institute for Intergovernmental Research, September 7, 2005.
[22] U.S. Federal Bureau of Investigation, Uniform Crime Report (2004).
[23] CRS Report RL32824, Federal Crime Control: Background, Legislation, and Issues, by Lisa Seghetti, Coordinator.
[24] Justice Policy Institute, "Gang Violence Declined 73% from 1994-2003," July 15, 2005, available online at [http://66.24 1.21 6.26/releases/press0507 1 5gang-crime.dwt], accessed on October 2, 2007.
[25] Tom Hayden, Street Wars: Gangs and the Future of Violence (New York: The New Press, 2005), pp. 7-8.
[26] Justice Policy Institute, Ganging Up on Communities?: Putting Gang Crime in Context (Washington, July 15, 2005).
[27] Cheryl L. Maxson, "Gang Homicide A Review and Extension of the Literature,"American Youth Gangs at the Millennium, 2004, p. 275.
[28] U.S. Department of Justice, Office of Justice Programs, Bureau of Justice Statistics, Crime Data Brief, Violence by Gang Members, 1993-2003, NCJ 208875, June 2005.
[29] Ibid.
[30] Information on the NCVS is available at [http://www.ojp.usdoj.gov/bjs/cvict.htm], accessed on May 20, 2007.
[31] U.S. Department of Justice, Bureau of Justice Assistance, 2005 National Gang Threat Assessment, National Alliance of Gang Investigators Associations, available at [http://www.nagia.org/PDFs/2005 _national _gang _threat _assessment.pdf], accessed on May 18, 2007.
[32] T.P. Thornberry, D. Huizinga, and R. Loeber, "The Causes and Correlates Studies: Findings and Policy Implications," Juvenile Justice, vol. 10, no. 1, pp. 3-19, at [http://www.ncjrs.org/pdffiles1/ojjdp/203555.pdf], accessed on October 2, 2007.
[33] National Youth Gang Center, forthcoming, Frequently Asked Questions: What is the racial and ethnic composition of youth gangs?, at [http://www.iir.com/nygc/faq.htm], accessed on October 2, 2007.
[34] The NYGC analysis of small town and rural gangs is based on responses to the annual survey described at the beginning of this report from which national estimates of gangs and gang activities are derived. However, this analysis is a separate and special analysis based on data that are not reported in the annual summary of the NYGC survey.
[35] James C. Howell and Arlen Egley, Jr., "Gangs in Small Towns and Rural Counties," NYGC Bulletin, DOJ, OJJDP, no. 1 (June 2005), p. 1.
[36] NYGC's analysis is based on data collected between 1996-2001. In 2002, the survey began using a new sample of smaller city and rural counties.
[37] Ibid., p. 2.

[38] Ibid., p. 3.
[39] U.S. Department of Justice, Office of Justice Programs, OJJDP, Juvenile Justice Bulletin, "Youth Gangs in Schools," James C. Howell and James P. Lynch (August 2000).
[40] Ibid., pp. 5-6.
[41] Ibid., p. 7.
[42] U.S. DOJ, BJS, School Crime and Safety: 2004, p. 47.
[43] Kenneth S. Trump, "Gangs, Violence, and Safe Schools," Gangs in America III, 3rd Edition, ed. C. Ronald Huff (2002), pp. 12 1-122.
[44] Ibid., p. 124.
[45] James Diego Vigil, "Streets and Schools: How Educators Can Help Chicano Marginalized Gang Youth," Harvard Educational Review, vol. 69, no. 3 (Fall 1999), p. 272.
[46] Ibid., p. 278.
[47] K. Trump, "Gangs, Violence, and Safe Schools," pp. 126-128.
[48] For more information on Latin American gangs, see CRS Report RS22 141, Gangs in Central America, by Clare Ribando.
[49] Testimony of FBI Assistant Director-Criminal Investigative Division Chris Swecker, in U.S. Congress, House of Representatives International Relations Subcommittee on the Western Hemisphere, Gangs and Crime in Latin America, hearings April 20, 2005.
[50] U.S. DHS, ICE, "ICE Launches Operation Community Shield, Arrest 103 MS-13 Gang Members in 6 Major U.S. Cities," News Release, March 14, 2005, available at [http://www.ice.gov/pi/investigations/comshield/index.htm], accessed on October 2, 2007.
[51] For more information on RICO statutes see, CRS Report 96-950, RICO: A Brief Sketch, by Charles Doyle.
[52] For more information on smuggling and related issues on the southwest border, see CRS Report RL33 106, Border Security and the Southwest Border: Background, Legislation, and Issues, by Lisa Seghetti, coordinator.
[53] Testimony of FBI Assistant Director-Criminal Investigative Division Chris Swecker, in U.S. Congress, House of Representatives International Relations Subcommittee on the Western Hemisphere, Gangs and Crime in Latin America, hearings April 20, 2005.
[54] U.S. DOJ Bureau of Justice Assistance, 2005 National Gang Threat Assessment, (February 2005).
[55] Congressional Quarterly, Homeland Security, ICE Sweep Nets Nearly 600 Gangsters — but No Terrorists So Far, by Eileen Sullivan, CQ Staff, (August 1, 2005).
[56] Jeffrey Fagan, Drug Use and Delinquency Among Dropouts and Gang Members, DOJ OJJDP, Grant #87JNCX0012, 1987.
[57] Irving Spergel and Ronald L. Chance, National Youth Gang Suppression and Intervention Program, National Institute of Justice Research in Action, June 1991, pp. 21-22.
[58] The law created the Edward Byrne Memorial Grants, which were recently replaced by the Edward Byrne Memorial Justice Assistance Grant (JAG) program (P.L. 108-447) and provide grants to state and local and tribal law enforcement agencies for a number of purposes that can include anti-gang initiatives.

[59] Funding formerly provided through the Edward Byrne Memorial Formula Block Grant program is now funded through the Edward Byrne Memorial Justice Assistant Grant (JAG) program (P.L. 108-447). For additional information, see CRS Report RS224 16, Edward Byrne Memorial Justice Assistance Grant Program: Legislative and Funding History, by Nathan James.

[60] For additional information on the CCF, see CRS Report RS21844, The Compassion Capital Fund: Brief Facts and Current Developments, by Joe Richardson.

[61] Testimony of FBI Special Agent Grant Ashley, Assistant Director, Criminal Investigative Division, in U.S. Congress, Senate Committee on Judiciary, Combating Gang Violence in America: Examining Effective Federal, State, and Local Law Enforcement Strategies, (September 17, 2003).

[62] Ibid.

[63] FBI, About Us - Our Post 9/11 Transformation - Fighting Gang Violence, available at [http://www.fbi.gov/aboutus/transformation/gangs.htm], accessed on October 2, 2007.

[64] In the Spotlight - Gangs, U.S. Department of Justice, Office of Justice Programs, National Criminal Justice Reference Service, available at [http://www.ncjrs.gov/spotlight/ gangs/summary.html], accessed on May 20, 2007. For more detailed information, see [http://www.fbi.gov/publications/strategicplan /strategicplanfull.pdf], accessed on October 2, 2007.

[65] Testimony of FBI Assistant Director-Criminal Investigative Division Chris Swecker, in U.S. Congress, House of Representatives International Relations Subcommittee on the Western Hemisphere, Gangs and Crime in Latin America, hearings April 20, 2005.

[66] U.S. Department of Justice Office of Inspector General, The External Effects of the Federal Bureau of Investigation's Reprioritization Efforts, Audit Report 05-3 7, September 2005.

[67] Ibid., p. 68.

[68] Ibid., p. 56.

[69] Ibid., p. 57.

[70] Ibid.

[71] Ibid., p. 68

[72] Finn-Aage Esbensen, Adrienne Freng, Terrance J. Taylor, Dana Peterson, D. Wayne Osgood, "Final Evaluation of the Gang Resistance Education and Training (G.R.E.A.T.) Program," Responding to Gangs, Winifred L. Reed, Scott H. Decker, eds., DOJ, OJP, NIJ, NCJ 190351, July 2002, pp. 139-167.

[73] Curry, G. David, Decker, Scott H., Confronting Gangs: Crime and Community (2003), p. 58.

[74] Ibid., p. 369.

[75] The cities participating in the program were: Philadelphia, PA, Portland, OR, Phoenix, AZ, Omaha, NE, Lincoln, NE (non-gang city), and Las Cruces, NM (small border town).

[76] Esbensen, Finn-Aage, Osgood, D. Wayne, Taylor, Terrance J.K., Peterson, Dana, Frang, Adrienne, "How Great is G.R.E.A.T.? Results from a Longitudinal Quasi-Experimental Design," Criminology and Public Policy, vol. 1, no. 1 (November 2001), pp. 108-109.

[77] American Youth Gangs at the Millennium, “Gang Prevention A Case Study of a Primary Prevention Program,” by Finn-Aage Esbensen, Dana Peterson, Terrance J. Taylor, Adrienne Freng, & D. Wayne Osgood (2004), p. 363.

[78] The Brady Act (Brady Handgun Control Act), an amendment to the 1993 amendments of the Gun Control Act of 1968 (P.L. 103-159), requires a waiting period of up to five days for handgun purchases and requires purchasers to undergo a background check (18 U.S.C. 922(s)(1)(C), (D)).

[79] Project Safe Neighborhoods, Executive Summary and other information on the program is available at the PSN website at [http://www.psn.gov/], accessed on May 18, 2007.

[80] For more detailed information on programs and initiatives designed for addressing the gang problem, see U.S. DOJ, OJP, NIJ, Responding to Gangs: Evaluation and Research, July 2002, pp. 329, available at [http://www.ncjrs.gov/pdffiles1/nij/19035 1 .pdf], accessed on October 2, 2007.

[81] Ibid., pp. 265-288.

[82] “Selected 1988 California Legislation,” Pacific Law Journal, Vol. 20 No. 2, 1998. (Cal. Penal Code §§ 186.20-186.33.)

[83] Some law enforcement sources think that these provisions may be responsible for the recent trend among gang members of trying to conceal their membership status.

[84] Arizona, Arkansas, Florida, Georgia, Illinois, Indiana, Iowa, Louisiana, Minnesota, Mississippi, Montana, Nevada, North Dakota, Rhode Island, and South Dakota have enacted STEP laws.

[85] Jeffrey Grogger, “The Effects of Civil Gang Injunctions on Reported Violent Crime: Evidence from Los Angeles,” Journal of Law and Economics, vol. XLV, April 2002, pp. 69- 90.

[86] Ibid., p. 86.

[87] Cheryl L. Maxson, Karen M. Hennigan, David C. Sloane, “‘It’s Getting Crazy Out There’: Can A Civil Gang Injunction Change A Community?,” Journal of Criminology and Public Policy, August 2005, vol. 4, no. 3., pp. 577-606.

[88] Ibid., p. 579.

[89] Ibid., p. 582.

[90] Ibid., p. 591, 596.

[91] This section does not discuss certain issues that are beyond the scope of a discussion of anti-gang legislation. For example, S. 456, H.R. 3547, H.R. 3922, and S. 2237 include provisions pertaining to short-term witness protection that are discussed in CRS Report RL3 3473, Judicial Security: Comparison of Legislation in the 110th Congress, by Nathan James. H.R. 3547 also includes a provision that would authorize the Attorney General to deny the sale, delivery, or transfer of a firearm or the issuance of such a license or permit to a terrorist, which is discussed in detail in CRS Report RL330 11, Terrorist Screening and Brady Background Checks For Firearms, by William J. Krouse.

[92] Supported by the Fraternal Order of Police, the National Sheriffs’ Association, and the National Association of Police Officers, statement by Rep. John Gingery, Congressional Record, May 11, 2005, p. H3120.

[93] Paul Rosenzweig, “The Gang Act Needs Modification,” Heritage Foundation, WebMemo, May 3, 2004, available at [http://www.heritage.org/Research /Crime/wm494.cfm], accessed on October 2, 2007.

[94] Dan M. Kahan, Yale Law School, John M. Olin Center for Studies in Law, Economics, and Public Policy Working Paper Series, The Logic of Reciprocity: Trust, Collective Action, and Law, Paper 281, 2002, p. 23.
[95] For more information on juvenile justice, see CRS Report RL33947, Juvenile Justice: Legislative History and Current Legislative Issues, by Blas Nuñez-Neto.
[96] BNA Criminal Law Reporter, Murdering Members of Rival Street Gang is Not Economic Activity for RICO Purposes, September 22, 2204, Vol. 75, No. 23.
[97] For a recent example of successful prosecution and conviction under existing federal RICO statutes see, "3 MS-13 Leaders Convicted of Killings," by Ruben Castaneda, Washington Post, Saturday, April 28, 2007, p. B02, available at [http://www.washingtonpost.com/wp-dyn/content/article/2007/04/27 /AR2007042702.html], accessed on May 18, 2007
[98] Howell, James C., Youth Gang Programs and Strategies, National Youth Gang Center
[99] Institute for Intergovernmental Research, August 2000, p. 1.
[100] Spergel, I.A., Chance, R., Ehrensaft, K., Regulus, T., Kane, C., Laseter, R., Alexander, A., and Oh, S., Gang Suppression and Intervention: Community Models, U.S. Department of Justice Office of Justice Programs, OJJDP, 1994. (Also known as the NYGC Comprehensive Gang Model.)
[101] Howell, James C., Youth Gang Programs and Strategies, U.S. Department of Justice Office of Justice Programs, OJJDP, August 2000, pp. 34-35.

Index

9

9/11, 119, 141

A

abatement, 33
academic, 136
academics, 102
access, 7, 12, 14, 25, 27, 28, 29, 33, 35
accountability, 4, 35, 37
accounting, 79, 82
accuracy, 68
active site, 54
ad hoc, 49
administration, 12, 25, 35
administrative, 8, 11, 12, 18, 28, 40, 60, 62, 63
administrators, 12
adolescence, 86, 93
adolescents, 67, 79, 82, 88, 91, 93, 96, 124
adult, 9, 27, 47, 83, 104, 113, 115, 130, 133, 136
adulthood, 86, 113
adults, 56, 92, 103, 104, 109, 111, 113, 130, 132, 133, 138
advocacy, 10, 42, 127
African American, 82, 94, 96, 114
African-American, 13, 45, 94
after-school, 120, 135
age, viii, 7, 20, 46, 47, 50, 56, 69, 79, 84, 86, 99, 109, 113, 120, 130, 134, 136, 137
agent, 58
agents, 121, 123, 124, 126
aggression, 82, 84, 93, 94
aging, 28
aid, 16, 87, 130
alcohol, 38, 39, 47, 56, 57, 90, 101
alcohol abuse, 39, 90
alcohol use, 57, 101
alien smuggling, 102
alienation, 102, 134
alternative, 13, 34, 127, 132
alternatives, 120, 127, 132, 137
amendments, 5, 134, 142
American Revolution, 100
American Society of Criminology, 75, 78, 80, 81
analysts, 74, 121
anger, 83, 89
appendix, 6, 8
application, 46, 53, 58
appropriations, 123, 125, 131
Arizona, 50, 142
Arkansas, 142
arrest, 49, 50, 51, 68, 69, 70, 72, 73, 76, 77, 78, 79, 81, 89, 115, 120, 127, 133
arson, 90, 108
Asian, 96, 114
assault, 70, 71, 72, 73, 74, 75, 76, 77, 78, 79, 80, 83, 84, 90, 108, 111, 112, 113
assaults, 70, 72, 73, 74, 77, 79, 81, 82, 83, 89, 90, 91, 102, 117
assessment, 3, 6, 8, 9, 10, 15, 16, 17, 19, 20, 22, 23, 24, 27, 29, 35, 40, 41, 42, 51, 52, 53, 54, 55, 59, 60, 62, 92, 96, 112, 120, 139
assignment, 131
ATF, 118, 121, 122, 126
atmosphere, 85, 124
attachment, 124
attacks, 76, 85, 119, 123
attempted murder, 118
attitudes, 32, 69, 88, 90, 102
Attorney General, 14, 24, 36, 58, 130, 131, 142
authority, 15, 76, 118, 130

availability, 116
avoidance, 46
awareness, 12, 13, 14, 19, 21, 23, 28, 35, 36, 40, 58, 126

B

background information, vii, viii, 100
barriers, 10, 101, 115
base rate, 72
basic needs, 28
basic research, 55
basketball, 21
battery, 91
behavior, vii, 4, 19, 28, 34, 37, 45, 46, 51, 53, 67, 68, 74, 76, 79, 82, 83, 84, 85, 89, 90, 94, 95, 96, 102, 120, 125, 136
behavioral problems, 21, 101
beliefs, 93
bell, 87
benefits, 16, 39, 56, 125, 130
benign, 103
Best Practice, 1, 8
bilingual, 31
black students, 117
black women, 96
bodily injury, 90
body image, 96
bonds, 30
Boston, 95, 101, 127, 136
bounds, 109
boys, vii, 67, 68, 70, 72, 73, 76, 77, 79, 82, 83, 84, 85, 86, 87, 89, 90
broad spectrum, 57
buffer, 85
bullying, 29, 84, 95
Bureau of Alcohol, Tobacco, Firearms and Explosives (ATF), 112
bureaucracy, 54
burglary, 90, 108
business management, 12

C

Cambodians, 101
campaigns, 126
Canada, 95
capacity, 22, 29, 40, 46, 55, 85, 122
career development, 33
caretaker, 76
catalyst, 9, 53
cation, 93
Caucasian, 114
cell, 128
Census, 16, 69, 104
Census Bureau, 69, 104
Centers for Disease Control, 84
Central America, 13, 18, 118, 119, 140
charitable organizations, 1
childhood, 127, 131
children, 2, 7, 43, 76, 85, 94, 117, 120, 124, 127
citizens, vii, 1, 5, 9
classes, 21, 34, 132
classrooms, 124, 125
clients, 12, 14, 20, 23, 25, 26, 27, 28, 31, 32, 33, 34, 35, 36, 37, 38, 39, 40, 42, 48, 53, 54, 55, 56, 57, 59, 60, 64, 65, 66
Co, 94, 141
coalitions, 10, 16
cocaine, vii, viii, 99, 100, 113, 120
coercion, 91
cognitive, 127
cognitive development, 127
collaboration, 2, 16, 18, 23, 36, 47, 51, 58, 65, 112
collaborative process, 4, 30
college campuses, 113
college students, 91
Colorado, 68
colors, 113
commerce, 103, 120
communication, 16, 34, 58, 122, 128, 139
communities, vii, 1, 2, 3, 4, 6, 7, 8, 16, 21, 24, 28, 32, 35, 40, 41, 45, 46, 48, 51, 52, 53, 54, 55, 56, 58, 85, 86, 99, 101, 102, 103, 108, 112, 113, 118, 121, 125, 126, 127, 129, 132, 133, 134, 136
community, vii, 1, 2, 3, 4, 5, 6, 7, 9, 10, 11, 12, 13, 14, 15, 16, 17, 18, 19, 20, 21, 22, 23, 24, 25, 27, 28, 29, 30, 31, 32, 33, 34, 35, 36, 37, 38, 39, 40, 41, 42, 43, 44, 46, 47, 49, 50, 51, 53, 54, 55, 56, 57, 59, 61, 62, 65, 83, 88, 89, 100, 102, 103, 104, 106, 115, 117, 118, 120, 121, 122, 123, 125, 126, 127, 128, 129, 131, 132, 135, 136, 137, 138
Community Oriented Policing Services (COPS), 121, 127
community service, 22, 132
competence, 21
competition, 58
competitive process, 52
complement, 3
complexity, 5, 135, 137
components, 3, 19, 36, 41, 49, 55, 58, 122, 124
composition, 20, 26, 75, 86, 87, 102, 114, 139
Comprehensive Community- Wide Gang Program Model, 4

Comprehensive Gang Model, 1, 2, 3, 4, 5, 6, 8, 9, 13, 14, 15, 18, 21, 25, 29, 32, 35, 42, 43, 44, 46, 47, 49, 50, 51, 59, 60, 143
concentrates, 85
confidentiality, 17, 26
confinement, 7, 33
conflict, 7, 15, 19, 95, 97, 120, 124, 132
conflict resolution, 15, 19, 124, 132
Congress, vii, viii, 2, 99, 100, 103, 119, 120, 121, 123, 124, 125, 129, 131, 132, 134, 135, 136, 137, 140, 141, 142
Congressional Record, 142
consensus, 10, 136
consent, 11, 17, 23, 27
Consolidated Appropriations Act, 121, 123
conspiracy, 103, 118, 125, 134
constraints, 12, 55
contingency, 29
contracts, 11, 17
control, 4, 5, 11, 15, 30, 35, 42, 44, 45, 47, 48, 50, 76, 83, 124, 125, 127, 136
control group, 45, 48, 124, 125
controlled substance, 103
convergence, 119
conviction, 130, 143
correlation, 53, 116
costs, 11, 130, 133, 134
counseling, 19, 22, 29, 30, 31, 33, 34, 44, 47, 48, 120, 127, 132, 136
counterterrorism, 123
courts, 4, 127, 128, 129
coverage, 32, 75
crack, vii, viii, 99, 100, 119, 120
credibility, 11, 12, 14, 28
credit card, 113
crime, vii, viii, 2, 7, 12, 13, 14, 15, 17, 18, 20, 22, 32, 33, 35, 36, 37, 38, 39, 42, 45, 46, 47, 48, 53, 57, 58, 59, 68, 69, 72, 75, 76, 84, 86, 87, 91, 100, 101, 102, 103, 108, 109, 111, 112, 113, 116, 118, 120, 121, 122, 123, 124, 125, 126, 127, 128, 129, 130, 131, 132, 133, 134, 135, 136, 139
crimes, 13, 37, 38, 45, 46, 47, 51, 58, 69, 70, 72, 79, 100, 102, 108, 111, 113, 119, 120, 121, 122, 124, 127, 128, 130, 133, 134
criminal activity, 12, 45, 69, 100, 102, 103, 108, 112, 116, 122, 136
criminal acts, 4, 50, 103, 113, 125
criminal behavior, 103, 122
criminal gangs, 138
criminal justice, 5, 15, 28, 38, 45, 64, 68, 112
criminal justice system, 5, 28, 68
criminals, 103, 133
criminology, 68
crisis intervention, 44, 45
criticism, 134
cross-sectional, 69, 124, 125
culture, 1, 31, 35, 112
curriculum, 13, 124, 125

D

data analysis, 17, 36, 37
data collection, 15, 16, 17, 20, 24, 25, 35, 39, 40, 53, 62, 104, 137
database, 42, 131
death, 91, 130, 133
death sentence, 130
deaths, 84, 92
decision making, 63
decisions, 23, 33
defendants, 126
defense, 82, 83, 89
definition, viii, 87, 91, 97, 99, 102, 103, 128, 130, 132, 135, 136, 138
deinstitutionalization, 95
delinquency, vii, 7, 13, 33, 49, 67, 68, 69, 84, 87, 88, 90, 91, 92, 93, 94, 96, 102, 120, 124, 135
delinquent acts, 49, 103
delinquent behavior, 51, 68, 69, 125
delinquent friends, 124
delinquents, 95, 103
delivery, 31, 33, 43, 47, 50, 124, 142
demographic data, 17, 114
demographic factors, 17
demographics, 20, 115
denial, 20
Department of Education, 122
Department of Homeland Security, 118
Department of Justice (DOJ), 2, 41, 43, 44, 57, 60, 93, 94, 95, 96, 97, 103, 106, 108, 121, 138, 139, 140, 141, 143
depressed, 83
desire, 83, 97
detection, 112, 134
deterrence, 51, 125, 133
diffusion, 91
diffusion process, 91
direct observation, 103
discrimination, 96
dispersion, vii, viii, 99
displacement, 58
disseminate, 69, 123, 131
distress, 28, 92
distribution, 109, 113, 114
divergence, 73
division, 36, 59, 122

domestic violence, 74, 76, 90
dosage, 46
draft, 60
dropouts, 120
drug dealing, 45
Drug Enforcement Agency (DEA), 118, 122
drug offense, 120
drug smuggling, 102
drug trafficking, 102, 113, 120, 121, 122, 124, 127, 134, 137
drug treatment, 29
drug use, 88, 90, 94, 120, 124
drug-related, 46, 47, 51, 131
drugs, 57, 88, 93, 101, 112, 119, 120, 121, 138
duplication, 35, 43, 122
duration, 46, 57
duties, 55

E

ears, 27
education, 25, 29, 52, 93, 95, 120, 122, 124, 132, 141
educational attainment, 132, 134
educational services, 27
educators, 135
El Salvador, 113, 118, 137
elderly, 111
elementary school, 56, 117
emotion, 97
emotional, 15, 21, 88, 96
employability, 132
employees, 49
employment, 5, 25, 27, 33, 34, 45, 56, 127, 131, 132, 134, 136, 137
employment status, 45
empowerment, 21, 33
England, 96
enrollment, 57
enterprise, 100, 123, 124
enthusiasm, 15
entrepreneurship, 36
environment, vii, 1, 7, 85
environmental factors, 101
epidemic, vii, viii, 99, 100, 120
estimating, 86
ethnic groups, 101
ethnic minority, 133
ethnicity, 93, 113, 114, 134
etiology, 92
evidence-based practices, 57
evolution, 137
exclusion, 115
execution, 54, 137
exercise, 15
expertise, 17
exposure, 16, 32, 46, 85, 96, 125
externalizing, 94
externalizing behavior, 94
extortion, 102
extra help, 56
eyes, 27

F

failure, 9, 55, 60, 61, 128
faith, 1, 5, 6, 7, 9, 22, 24, 27, 29, 36, 39, 48, 122, 127
familial, 101
family, 7, 13, 28, 29, 39, 44, 48, 57, 76, 79, 82, 83, 84, 88, 90, 101, 126, 136
family conflict, 28
family members, 76, 82, 83, 90
family structure, 101
family support, 136
fear, 129
Federal Bureau of Investigation (FBI), 67, 68, 69, 72, 83, 84, 91, 94, 104, 109, 110, 111, 112, 118, 121, 122, 123, 124, 131, 133, 139, 140, 141
federal criminal law, 132
federal felonies, 103
federal government, 119, 132
federal law, 100, 103, 121, 125
feedback, 32, 40, 51
felony, 44, 103, 120, 130
females, 50, 51, 68, 71, 72, 78, 83, 84, 86, 87, 92
femininity, 83
field agents, 123
financial crisis, 10
financial problems, 55
financial resources, 7
financial support, 86
fines, 137
fire, 91
firearm, 120, 142
firearms, 101, 102, 113, 121, 122, 125, 126
first responders, 76
first-time, 33
flexibility, 137
fluctuations, 77
focus group, 17, 19, 22
focus groups, 17, 22
focusing, 24, 59, 131
food, 14, 31
foreign policy, 137
foreign travel, 130
forfeiture, 137
freedom, 128

fuel, 100
funding, 2, 5, 14, 19, 22, 24, 25, 30, 36, 40, 41, 44, 53, 54, 58, 65, 106, 120, 121, 123, 125, 126, 131, 132, 134, 135
funds, 1, 2, 11, 12, 15, 16, 25, 39, 41, 53, 54, 58, 121, 127
futures, 85

G

gang crimes, 45, 46, 58, 133
gang members, vii, viii, 4, 7, 12, 13, 17, 19, 20, 22, 26, 27, 28, 31, 33, 34, 35, 36, 37, 38, 39, 44, 45, 46, 48, 50, 51, 66, 86, 87, 88, 91, 92, 93, 94, 95, 99, 100, 101, 102, 103, 104, 105, 106, 107, 108, 110, 111, 112, 113, 114, 115, 117, 118, 119, 120, 121, 124, 125, 127, 128, 129, 130, 131, 132, 133, 134, 135, 136, 138, 142
Gang Reduction Program, vii, 1, 2, 6, 8, 13, 18, 21, 22, 32, 33, 43, 57, 60, 126
Gang-Free Schools, 8, 10, 14, 20, 31, 32, 53, 54, 55, 56, 59, 60
gangs, vii, viii, 1, 2, 3, 4, 7, 9, 10, 13, 16, 17, 20, 24, 31, 32, 35, 37, 42, 44, 45, 47, 48, 49, 50, 51, 57, 86, 87, 88, 90, 91, 92, 93, 94, 95, 96, 99, 100, 101, 102, 103, 104, 105, 106, 107, 108, 109, 112, 113, 114, 115, 116, 117, 118, 119, 120, 121, 122, 123, 124, 125, 127, 131, 132, 134, 135, 136, 137, 138, 139, 140, 141
gel, 8
gender, 67, 68, 69, 72, 73, 75, 76, 77, 78, 79, 82, 83, 84, 86, 87, 93, 94, 95, 96, 113, 134
gender differences, 67, 73, 76, 79, 87, 94
gender gap, 78, 96
Georgia, 142
gestures, 84
gift, 31
girls, vii, 67, 68, 70, 72, 73, 76, 77, 79, 82, 83, 84, 85, 86, 87, 88, 89, 90, 92, 94, 95, 96
goal setting, 124
goals, 4, 6, 7, 16, 18, 20, 24, 26, 28, 33, 36, 42, 46, 124, 125
gossip, 82
governance, 58
government, viii, 9, 10, 22, 43, 58, 59, 62, 99, 119, 121, 123, 127, 131, 132, 135, 137
grades, 20, 37, 87, 135
graffiti, 102, 113, 127, 128
grants, 12, 15, 41, 53, 54, 104, 120, 121, 127, 129, 131, 132, 135, 140
grassroots, 4, 5, 10, 15, 19, 27, 29, 35, 47, 49, 50
groups, 5, 6, 7, 9, 10, 16, 22, 29, 31, 34, 35, 44, 45, 49, 66, 72, 82, 83, 85, 87, 91, 101, 103, 104, 112, 115, 118, 119, 122, 125, 136, 138
growth, vii, viii, 88, 99, 113, 115, 134, 137
Guatemala, 118, 137
guidance, 2, 21, 38, 65
guidelines, 41, 91
guns, 125

H

harm, 24, 29, 91
Harvard, 92, 140
hate, 103, 104
Hawaii, 68
health, 14, 19, 29, 31, 33, 34, 56, 127
Health and Human Services, 2
health care, 33, 127
hearing, 118, 123
heart, 88
high risk, 7, 19, 25, 29, 35, 63
high school, 21, 25, 31, 39, 84, 96, 135
high-frequency, 77
high-level, 25, 118
high-risk, 7, 19, 29, 30, 32, 33, 57, 87, 126, 127, 132, 135
high-risk populations, 30
hip, 24
hiring, 11, 28, 54, 121, 131
Hispanic, 13, 30, 44, 112, 113, 114, 117
Hispanic population, 13, 30
homeland security, 59, 118, 140
homeless, 127
homicide, 72, 74, 75, 90, 107, 108, 111, 113
homicide rates, 111
Honduras, 118
hopelessness, 85, 89
hostile environment, 85
hostility, 30
House, 140, 141
household, 89, 116
household income, 116
households, 69, 111
housing, 38, 132
Housing and Urban Development, 2
human, 7
humans, 119
hybrid, 113
hypothesis, 76, 79

I

ice, 140
id, 35, 49, 53, 63, 87, 96
identification, 6, 22, 57, 102, 103, 122, 131, 133
identity, vii, 1, 85, 101, 102, 113
ideology, 104
Illinois, 142
imagery, 83
images, 83, 103
immigrants, 101, 113, 118, 119
immigration, 101, 118, 119
Immigration and Customs Enforcement (ICE), 118, 119, 140
implementation, viii, 2, 3, 5, 6, 8, 10, 11, 12, 14, 15, 18, 20, 21, 22, 23, 26, 35, 39, 40, 41, 44, 45, 47, 48, 51, 52, 53, 54, 57, 58, 60, 62, 99, 126, 132
imprisonment, 103, 119, 120, 128, 130, 133, 134
incarceration, 38, 120, 127, 129
incentive, 34
incentives, 133
incidence, 89, 116
income, 44, 85, 94, 102, 113, 116, 122, 132
independence, 83
Indian, 113, 134
Indiana, 19, 94, 142
indication, 110
indicators, 46, 73
Indicators of School Crime and Safety, 93, 95
infancy, 13, 19
infant care, 7
infants, 127
inflammatory, 15
information sharing, 12, 26, 27, 30, 34, 36, 37, 122
information systems, 41
infrastructure, 11, 55, 132
initiation, vii, 1
injunction, 128, 129
injuries, 91
injury, 73, 91
inmates, 38, 39
innovation, 134
insight, 79, 82, 109
Inspector General, 123, 141
institutional change, 64
institutionalization, 55
institutions, 9, 25, 46, 85, 102
instruments, 17, 41
integration, 7, 101
integrity, 28
intelligence, 14, 20, 22, 27, 29, 33, 35, 38, 118, 121, 122, 123, 127, 133, 137
intelligence gathering, 22, 127
intensity, 45, 53
intentions, 48
interaction, 38
interactions, 34
intergenerational, 88
interpersonal relations, 29
interpersonal relationships, 29
interpersonal skills, 34, 55
interstate, 103, 120, 130
intervention, 4, 5, 7, 8, 11, 12, 13, 14, 15, 18, 19, 20, 21, 22, 23, 26, 27, 28, 29, 30, 31, 32, 33, 34, 35, 36, 37, 38, 40, 41, 42, 44, 45, 46, 47, 48, 49, 50, 51, 53, 54, 55, 56, 57, 64, 66, 90, 91, 117, 119, 120, 121, 125, 126, 127, 128, 129, 131, 132, 134, 136, 137
intervention strategies, 56, 119
interview, 34, 39, 66
interviews, 51, 61, 69
intimidation, 45, 112
Investigations, 123
investigative, 37, 123
investment, 126
isolation, 110

J

JAG, 141
job performance, 30
job skills, 34
job training, 14, 22, 30, 34, 36, 38, 136
jobs, 27, 28, 46, 127
judges, 135
judiciary, 122, 136, 141
Judiciary Committee, 122
junior high, 47
jurisdiction, 96, 104, 107, 115, 133
jurisdictions, 41, 86, 104, 105, 106, 107, 115, 119, 125, 128
justice, 5, 10, 15, 28, 35, 38, 42, 45, 59, 64, 76, 90, 92, 93, 112, 121, 127, 143
Justice Assistance Grant (JAG), 140, 141
juvenile crime, 69, 135
juvenile delinquency, 57, 92, 120, 121, 122, 125, 132, 133, 137
juvenile delinquents, 103
juvenile justice, 10, 35, 90, 92, 93, 121, 127, 143
Juvenile Justice and Delinquency Prevention Act, 5, 76
juveniles, 56, 70, 73, 101, 103, 109, 111, 113, 121, 125, 130, 133, 137

L

labeling, 89
land, 134
language, 1, 13, 21, 56, 101, 115
language barrier, 115
language skills, 13
large-scale, 2
Latin America, 101, 137, 140, 141
Latin American countries, 137
Latino, 45, 96, 100, 118, 119, 138
Latino gangs, 100, 118, 119, 138
Latinos, 115
laundering, 100, 102
law, 4, 6, 9, 10, 11, 12, 13, 14, 15, 17, 18, 21, 27, 28, 30, 31, 32, 33, 36, 37, 38, 39, 42, 53, 55, 60, 62, 64, 74, 76, 85, 86, 90, 100, 103, 104, 105, 106, 107, 108, 112, 113, 115, 118, 119, 120, 121, 122, 123, 124, 125, 126, 127, 128, 130, 131, 132, 133, 135, 136, 137, 138, 140, 142
law enforcement, 4, 6, 9, 10, 11, 12, 13, 14, 17, 18, 21, 27, 28, 30, 31, 32, 33, 36, 38, 39, 42, 53, 55, 60, 62, 64, 76, 86, 100, 103, 104, 105, 106, 107, 108, 112, 113, 115, 118, 119, 120, 121, 122, 123, 124, 125, 126, 127, 128, 131, 132, 133, 135, 136, 137, 140, 142
laws, 90, 100, 118, 119, 125, 128, 131, 133, 134, 142
lead, 2, 8, 11, 12, 14, 22, 28, 30, 39, 43, 45, 47, 48, 49, 50, 51, 54, 59, 60, 62, 63, 128, 133
leadership, 5, 7, 10, 11, 24, 25, 39, 43, 49, 57, 59, 63, 118
learning, 56, 124
legislation, vii, viii, 99, 100, 119, 120, 121, 133, 134, 135, 136, 137, 142
lending, 10
lien, 102
likelihood, 88, 109, 111, 124
links, 30, 127
liquor, 90
literacy, 21, 32, 131
living conditions, 88, 127
local authorities, 7
local community, 1, 4, 5, 37, 126
local government, 22, 121, 127
location, 11, 38, 47, 69, 103
longitudinal study, 87, 125
long-term, 10, 23, 24, 25, 36, 38, 39, 55, 56, 65, 122, 124, 136
Los Angeles, 2, 6, 8, 11, 14, 15, 18, 19, 22, 24, 25, 30, 32, 34, 41, 43, 54, 57, 58, 94, 107, 113, 118, 126, 127, 128, 129, 139, 142
Louisiana, 142
low-income, 44, 85, 122, 132
low-level, 112
loyalty, 117

M

machine-readable, 94
mainstream, 25
males, 19, 47, 50, 51, 68, 71, 72, 78, 83, 84, 86, 87, 113
management, 9, 11, 12, 13, 18, 19, 21, 22, 30, 33, 34, 39, 41, 42, 45, 47, 48, 49, 57, 64
manslaughter, 108, 109
mapping, 19, 35
Mara Salvatrucha (MS-13), viii, 99, 113, 118, 119, 140, 143
marijuana, 113
market, vii, viii, 99
Massachusetts, 127
maximum penalty, 103
measurement, 97, 136
measures, 4, 35, 58, 77, 111, 125, 129, 132, 133, 135, 137
media, 16, 68, 70, 103
mediation, 29
membership, vii, viii, 9, 10, 13, 19, 48, 86, 87, 91, 92, 93, 95, 99, 102, 103, 104, 107, 112, 121, 125, 142
men, 21
mental health, 27, 85
mentoring, 14, 19, 22, 29, 31, 34, 35, 56, 127, 132
mentoring program, 31, 127
messages, 83
methamphetamine, 113
metropolitan area, 118
Mexican, 44, 59, 112, 122
Mexico, 18, 118
Miami, 2, 6, 8, 11, 14, 21, 22, 31, 32, 34, 36, 38, 39, 41, 43, 54, 57, 58, 60, 68, 118, 126
middle schools, 19, 84
migrant, 101
migrant population, 101
migrant populations, 101
migration, viii, 99, 100, 108, 112
millennium, 138, 139, 142
Minnesota, 68, 142
minority, 85, 109, 133
mirror, 3
Mississippi, 142
Missouri, 68
modeling, 14
models, 21, 28, 56, 83, 101, 127
momentum, 10, 23, 25
money, 2, 11, 25, 54, 85, 100, 102

money laundering, 100, 102
Montana, 142
motherhood, 95
mothers, 10, 19, 33, 85, 124
motor vehicle theft, 90, 108
mountains, 102
movement, 53, 73, 108, 115
multidimensional, 89
multidisciplinary, 13, 14, 19, 20, 22, 24, 25, 33, 91
multimedia, 19, 21
multiplier, 80
murder, 102, 109, 134
mutual respect, 30

N

narcotics, 113, 125
nation, 102, 115, 116, 121, 134
national, viii, 3, 5, 16, 44, 53, 68, 69, 89, 99, 104, 105, 111, 112, 118, 120, 121, 122, 123, 124, 125, 131, 133, 137, 139
National Crime Victimization Survey (NCVS), 69, 76, 78, 79, 80, 81, 108, 111, 112, 134, 139
National Incident-Based Reporting System, 83, 84
National Strategy, 123
National Youth Gang Center, 1, 3, 6, 8, 42, 43, 54, 60, 67, 104, 139, 143
Native American, 113
Native Americans, 113
negative attitudes, 88, 124
negative emotions, 83
neglect, 83, 88, 90
negligence, 91
network, 55, 88
Nevada, 8, 142
New York, 43, 93, 94, 95, 97, 100, 101, 120, 138, 139
non-profit, 58
norms, 37, 83, 87
North Carolina, 8, 67, 115
Northeast, 113
nurturance, 88

O

obedience, 76
obligations, 7
observations, 8, 51, 61
offenders, 7, 38, 39, 42, 45, 50, 109, 121, 123, 128, 129, 130, 136
Office of Justice Programs (OJP), 16, 43, 44, 60, 93, 95, 96, 104, 120, 124, 134, 138, 139, 140, 141, , 142, 143
Office of Juvenile Justice and Delinquency Prevention (OJJDP), vii, 1, 2, 3, 4, 5, 6, 8, 9, 15, 16, 18, 24, 35, 41, 43, 44, 46, 47, 51, 52, 53, 54, 58, 59, 60, 61, 67, 96, 97, 103, 104, 106, 107, 116, 120, 126, 134, 136, 138, 139, 140, 143
Oklahoma, 8
online, 3, 21, 90, 96, 139
on-the-job training, 34, 36
operator, 2
orchestration, 53
organization, 3, 7, 24, 42, 48, 58, 87, 95, 102, 103, 118, 127, 131, 134
organizations, 1, 4, 5, 6, 7, 9, 10, 18, 19, 22, 24, 26, 27, 29, 30, 31, 41, 46, 47, 48, 50, 55, 58, 59, 69, 103, 112, 120, 122, 124, 125, 135
organized crime, 112, 118, 122, 123, 134
orientation, 22, 23, 24
oversight, 7, 10, 14, 22, 49, 55
overtime, 32
ownership, 10, 39

P

Pacific, 142
parental authority, 76
parental involvement, 101
parenting, 21, 34, 39
parents, 17, 19, 29, 76, 89, 91, 92, 101, 117, 127, 135
parole, 9, 27, 37, 38, 48, 50, 119, 123, 135
partnership, 10, 14, 22, 26, 36, 38, 41, 58
partnerships, 14, 16, 26, 42, 58
pathways, 90
peer, 29, 82, 83, 90, 93, 94
peer conflict, 90
peer group, 83
peers, 31, 57, 79, 82, 83, 85, 86, 88, 89, 90, 92
penalties, 103, 119, 120, 128, 129, 130, 132, 133, 134
penalty, viii, 100, 120, 128, 130
Pennsylvania, 68
perception, 31, 107, 129
perceptions, 15, 17, 20, 112
performance, 30
periodic, 24
permit, 29, 130, 132, 133, 142
personal, 1, 23, 27, 38, 46, 124
personal problems, 46
personal relations, 1
personal relationship, 1
personality, 55

Philadelphia, 96, 101, 141
philosophy, 36
Phoenix, 141
phone, 66, 128
physical aggression, 79, 82
pions, 23
planning, 2, 3, 8, 9, 10, 11, 12, 15, 17, 18, 20, 23, 26, 36, 38, 39, 40, 41, 42, 51, 53, 54, 57, 58, 62, 65, 136
play, 24, 26, 37, 64, 101, 117
police, 5, 7, 10, 12, 13, 14, 15, 17, 18, 19, 20, 25, 27, 28, 30, 32, 33, 35, 36, 37, 38, 43, 46, 48, 49, 50, 51, 55, 59, 60, 69, 70, 73, 76, 86, 90, 93, 102, 103, 121, 124, 125, 127, 128, 129, 135, 136, 138
policy makers, 100, 103, 136
policymakers, 68, 112, 118
political leaders, 12, 24
politics, 11, 12, 40
poor, 2, 52, 86, 101
population, 6, 7, 13, 16, 18, 21, 30, 31, 32, 35, 38, 56, 65, 75, 106, 107, 111, 115, 138
population density, 106
porous, 119
positive attitudes, 124
poverty, 85, 88, 101, 134
power, 16
predicate, 134
predictors, 46, 56
prejudice, 102, 124
preschool, 127
President Bush, 122
pressure, 127
prevention, viii, 5, 6, 7, 8, 13, 14, 19, 20, 22, 29, 31, 32, 35, 36, 39, 40, 41, 51, 53, 54, 56, 57, 63, 66, 90, 99, 117, 119, 120, 121, 124, 125, 126, 128, 129, 131, 132, 133, 134, 135, 136, 137
priorities, 5, 24, 58, 123, 125
private, 2, 14, 25, 31, 41, 47, 117
private sector, 2
proactive, 122
probation, 9, 22, 27, 30, 37, 38, 46, 47, 48, 49, 50, 123, 135, 136
probation officers, 46, 47, 48, 49, 50, 135, 136
problem behavior, 7
problem behaviors, 7
problem-solving, 9
productivity, 122
professional development, 28
profit, 22, 58
program, 2, 3, 4, 5, 7, 8, 9, 10, 11, 12, 13, 14, 15, 17, 18, 19, 20, 21, 22, 23, 24, 25, 26, 27, 28, 29, 30, 31, 32, 33, 34, 35, 36, 37, 38, 39, 40, 41, 42, 43, 44, 45, 46, 47, 48, 49, 50, 51, 53, 54, 55, 56, 57, 59, 61, 62, 65, 104, 108, 120, 121, 124, 125, 126, 127, 131, 132, 135, 136, 137, 140, 141, 142
program outcomes, 39
programming, 4, 12, 21, 24, 35, 55
proliferation, 100, 134
promote, 33, 112, 122, 123, 125
property, 2, 14, 45, 47, 69, 122, 124
property crimes, 45, 69, 124
prosecutor, 33
protection, 85, 142
protective factors, 42, 57, 67, 126
protocol, 30
protocols, 17, 22, 27
pubertal development, 94
puberty, 86
public, vii, viii, 2, 9, 14, 15, 19, 24, 25, 32, 34, 47, 68, 70, 84, 85, 95, 99, 103, 104, 117, 119, 126, 128, 132
public awareness, 126
public education, 24
public health, 85
public housing, 2
public policy, vii, viii, 95, 99, 104
public safety, 25, 119
public schools, 117
public service, 126
public support, 9
Puerto Rican, 101
punitive, 132, 137

Q

qualifications, 28
qualitative research, 90
questioning, 133
questionnaire, 112

R

race, 20, 69, 96, 113, 114, 134
racism, 95, 102
racketeering, 118, 123, 125, 130, 13
random, 77
range, vii, 3, 4, 15, 16, 57, 87, 99, 120, 132, 136, 137
rape, 72, 75, 80, 84, 90, 108, 1
real time, 122
reality, 2
rearrest, 133
recidivism, 133
recidivism rate, 133
recollection, 112

recreation, 13, 29, 85, 127
recreational, 21, 27, 85, 127
recruiting, 27
reduction, 7, 45, 46, 47, 48, 51, 58, 125, 135
refugees, 118
regional, 112, 135
regular, 17, 21, 23, 24, 34, 38, 39
rehabilitation, 133
rejection, 82
relationship, 27, 28, 38, 39, 58, 82, 88
relationships, 1, 27, 29, 30, 31, 32, 55, 83, 92
repair, 42
replication, 122
reputation, 9, 39, 89
research, 2, 3, 4, 5, 7, 15, 17, 40, 42, 43, 44, 55, 57, 60, 62, 76, 77, 79, 82, 83, 86, 87, 90, 91, 101, 102, 103, 119, 120, 121, 125, 126, 133, 134
research and development, 3, 4, 44, 120
Research and Development, 3
researchers, 3, 4, 50, 68, 82, 86, 87, 88, 91, 101, 103, 117, 135, 136, 137, 138
residential, 39
resistance, 95
resolution, 15, 19, 120, 124, 132
resources, 2, 5, 6, 7, 16, 17, 18, 21, 24, 25, 29, 31, 35, 39, 40, 42, 43, 54, 57, 60, 65, 85, 122, 126, 131, 133, 137
responsibilities, 7, 11, 16, 23, 24, 27, 34, 55, 62, 124
retaliation, 88
retirement, 21
Rhode Island, 142
RICO, 118, 119, 123, 134, 140, 143
rings, 125
risk, 7, 13, 14, 15, 16, 19, 21, 25, 29, 31, 32, 33, 34, 35, 42, 47, 53, 57, 63, 66, 67, 83, 85, 86, 87, 88, 89, 94, 95, 101, 102, 109, 117, 120, 124, 126, 127, 131, 132, 135
risk [illegible]ctors, 15, 19, 42, 53, 86, 88
risks, [illegible]
robber[illegible] 74
robbery, [illegible]2, 74, 75, 80, 84, 90, 102, 108, 111, 112, 1[illegible]
RTI Intern[illegible]al, 67, 68
rural, 51, 6[illegible] 100, 101, 105, 106, 107, 108, 113, 115, 11[illegible] 138, 139
rural areas, [illegible], 101, 107, 108, 115
rural commu[illegible] 51, 113, 115, 118
Rural Gang In[illegible] 8, 51, 52, 53, 60
Russian, 112

S

safety, vii, 1, 2, 2[illegible] 117, 127, 128
sample, 69, 79, 82, 87, 104, 107, 111, 115, 135, 138, 139
sampling, 107, 127
sanctions, 46, 49, 136
satisfaction, 46
school, 5, 7, 9, 10, 12, 13, 14, 17, 19, 20, 21, 25, 27, 28, 29, 30, 31, 32, 34, 35, 37, 39, 46, 47, 48, 54, 55, 56, 57, 60, 62, 69, 76, 78, 83, 84, 85, 88, 89, 90, 91, 92, 96, 101, 102, 113, 116, 117, 120, 122, 124, 125, 127, 132, 135
scientists, 112
search, 16, 17
searches, 37
secondary school students, 69
secondary schools, 116
Secretary of the Treasury, 121
secular, vii, viii, 99
secular trend, vii, viii, 99
security, 59, 100, 118, 119, 132
seed, 54
selecting, 8, 51, 60
self, 21, 25, 45, 69, 77, 78, 81
self-definition, 87, 91
self-esteem, 82, 124
self-help, 31
self-report, 4, 47, 49, 68, 69, 76, 77, 81, 82, 83, 86, 89, 90, 125
self-report data, 69, 86, 89
self-reports, 49, 81
Senate, 122, 130, 141
sensitive data, 12
sensitivity, 29, 76, 124
sentences, 38, 128, 130, 132, 133, 138
sentencing, 133, 138
September 11, 59, 123
series, 67, 78, 79, 103, 132
service provider, 12, 13, 16, 17, 21, 29, 34, 35, 40, 41, 48
services, 4, 5, 6, 7, 9, 12, 13, 14, 15, 18, 19, 20, 21, 22, 24, 25, 26, 27, 28, 29, 30, 33, 34, 35, 36, 37, 38, 40, 41, 44, 45, 46, 47, 48, 49, 50, 51, 53, 55, 59, 60, 64, 65, 66, 127, 136
sex, 79, 80, 82, 83, 96
sexual activity, 88, 90
sexual assault, 83, 84, 111, 112
sexual behavior, 83
sexual harassment, 85, 89
sexuality, 83
sharing, 12, 14, 16, 18, 26, 27, 30, 33, 34, 36, 37, 122, 123, 137
shelter, 127
short-term, 4, 142
siblings, 35, 76

sign, 103
signs, 33, 102, 117
singular, 37
sites, 3, 6, 8, 16, 17, 22, 46, 51, 52, 53, 54, 57, 58, 126
skills, 13, 14, 15, 21, 22, 28, 33, 34, 55, 62, 127
skills training, 33
slums, 100
smuggling, 102, 119, 140
social assistance, 127
social class, 83
social control, 5, 25, 35, 64
social institutions, 115
social network, 87
social organization, 95
social problems, 137
social services, 9, 15, 24, 25, 29, 46, 47, 50, 52, 136
social standing, 82
social structure, 101
social support, 46, 103
socialization, 117
socioeconomic, 85, 101, 102
socioeconomic status, 102
software, 32
solidarity, 42
solutions, 119, 124
South Dakota, 142
specter, 119
spectrum, 57, 120
speculation, 119
spreading rumors, 84
St. Louis, 48, 68, 87
stability, 77, 101
staffing, 53, 60
stages, 4, 39
stakeholders, 24
standardization, 135
standards, viii, 83, 85, 99
State of the Union address, 122
statistics, 5, 16, 17, 38, 68, 69, 73, 79, 84, 108, 112, 135
statutes, 118, 119, 122, 123, 134, 140, 143
strategic, 3, 10, 18, 19, 20, 22, 42, 57, 58, 126, 129, 136
strategic planning, 3, 10, 18, 42, 57, 58
strategies, vii, 3, 4, 5, 6, 7, 9, 10, 15, 20, 23, 25, 31, 35, 37, 38, 39, 40, 41, 42, 46, 47, 49, 51, 53, 56, 63, 64, 65, 66, 67, 117, 119, 120, 121, 123, 127, 132, 134, 135, 136, 137
strategy use, 127
streams, 2
strength, 10, 16
students, 19, 20, 32, 36, 69, 84, 91, 116, 117, 124, 125, 132, 135
subgroups, 45
substance abuse, 14, 19, 21, 34
substance use, 92
suburban, 91, 95, 100, 101, 105, 106, 108, 116, 117, 138
suburbs, 113, 118
summer, 13, 36
supervision, 5, 18, 25, 35, 38, 48, 136
supervisor, 78, 91
suppliers, 125
supply, 125
support services, 53
support staff, 121
suppression, 4, 5, 8, 15, 18, 19, 20, 22, 32, 33, 35, 37, 38, 39, 40, 42, 44, 45, 46, 48, 49, 51, 54, 55, 57, 58, 59, 64, 66, 117, 120, 121, 126, 127, 128, 129, 136, 137
surgery, 93
surveillance, 44, 47, 48, 94
suspects, 118
suspensions, 37
sustainability, 8, 23, 24, 40, 41, 55, 58
symbolic, 102
symbols, 102
systems, 10, 15, 35, 41, 55, 135

T

tactics, 4, 6, 48, 112, 120
tar, 35, 90
target population, 15, 31, 38, 53
target populations, 15, 53
targets, 7, 20, 33
task force, viii, 9, 100, 120, 122, 124, 131, 136
teachers, 85
teaching, 88
team members, 18, 23, 30, 31, 33, 36, 37, 38, 40
technical assistance, 4, 5, 6, 32, 57
technology, 121, 131
teens, 120
telephone, 38
tenants, 2
terrorism, 123
terrorist, 119, 123, 131, 142
terrorist attack, 119, 123
terrorist groups, 119
terrorist organization, 131
terrorists, 119, 140
testimony, 118, 122, 123
Texas, 49
theft, 2, 70, 90, 102, 108, 111, 113

theory, 5, 43
threat, 100, 103, 112, 116, 118, 119, 122, 129, 133, 139
threatened, 83, 85
threats, 113, 118, 133
threshold, 76
tics, 76
time frame, 16
timing, 96
title, 55
tolerance, 76, 90, 128, 136
toughness, 83
tracking, 18, 32, 51, 122
trade, 138
traditional views, 83
traffic, 121
training, 4, 5, 6, 13, 14, 18, 19, 20, 21, 22, 23, 24, 25, 28, 29, 30, 33, 34, 36, 38, 40, 121, 125, 126, 127, 131, 132, 136, 137
training programs, 126
trans, 1, 83
transfer, 130, 142
transformation, 141
transition, 10, 39, 94, 136
transnational, 119
transport, 113
transportation, 14, 34, 113, 130
trauma, 96
Treasury, 121
trend, vii, viii, 69, 70, 72, 73, 77, 81, 99, 105, 108, 109, 111, 142
tribal, viii, 99, 132, 140
truancy, 7, 38
trust, 28, 29, 30, 34
turnover, 24, 29, 53, 58, 60
tutoring, 13, 29, 35

U

uncertainty, 111
unemployment, 32
uniform, viii, 99, 120
Uniform Crime Reports (UCR), 16, 69, 70, 72, 75, 76, 77, 78, 79, 81, 90, 94, 108, 109, 110, 111, 133
United States, vii, viii, 3, 13, 72, 92, 94, 95, 99, 100, 101, 104, 106, 111, 116, 118, 119, 123, 135, 137, 138, 139
urban areas, 100, 101, 113, 115
Utah, 8

V

validity, 112
values, 29, 69, 88
vandalism, 2, 90, 102, 113
variability, 106
variable, 115
variation, 58
vehicles, 29, 37
victim advocates, 112
victimization, 68, 69, 76, 81, 82, 83, 85, 89, 104, 111, 116
victims, 42, 73, 76, 78, 84, 111, 112, 124
violence, vii, 2, 6, 7, 18, 27, 32, 35, 44, 45, 46, 48, 51, 58, 59, 62, 67, 68, 69, 73, 76, 77, 78, 79, 82, 83, 85, 86, 87, 89, 90, 91, 92, 93, 94, 96, 99, 100, 102, 103, 107, 108, 109, 112, 113, 116, 117, 118, 120, 121, 122, 125, 126, 127, 128, 129, 132, 133, 134, 136
violent, vii, viii, 16, 28, 31, 33, 44, 45, 46, 47, 48, 50, 68, 69, 70, 71, 73, 74, 76, 77, 78, 79, 82, 84, 85, 86, 89, 90, 91, 92, 95, 96, 99, 100, 102, 103, 108, 109, 110, 111, 118, 120, 121, 122, 123, 124, 125, 127, 128, 129, 130, 131, 132, 133, 136, 137
violent arrests, 71
violent behavior, 46, 68, 74, 84, 86, 90, 96
violent crime, vii, viii, 16, 46, 48, 50, 69, 70, 73, 76, 84, 99, 100, 103, 108, 109, 110, 112, 120, 121, 122, 128, 130, 131, 133
Violent Crime Control and Law Enforcement Act, 120, 138
violent crimes, 46, 48, 73, 84, 103, 108, 109, 120, 121, 130, 133
violent offenders, 33, 45, 111, 131
visible, 7, 113
vision, 43
vocational, 19, 29, 34
vocational training, 19, 29, 34
voids, 122
vouchers, 33

W

walking, 38
war, 122
warrants, 27
Washington Post, 143
watches, 10
weapons, 29, 73, 90, 112, 119, 121
Western Hemisphere, 140, 141
White House, 43
Wisconsin, 32, 43, 94

women, 87, 88, 92, 111
workers, 13, 18, 27, 28, 30, 31, 33, 36, 37, 38, 39, 44, 45, 46, 47, 48, 49, 50, 56, 57
workforce, 28
writing, 15, 53
WWW, 16

Y

yield, 56
young adults, 56, 92, 103, 104, 109, 132
young men, 21
young women, 21, 87, 88, 95
youth gangs, vii, viii, 1, 95, 96, 100, 101, 103, 104, 105, 109, 113, 115, 116, 120, 121, 125, 134, 135, 137, 139